Zayd

DIVINATIONS: REREADING LATE ANCIENT RELIGION

SERIES EDITORS

Daniel Boyarin
Virginia Burrus
Derek Krueger

A complete list of books in the series is available from the publisher.

Zayd

David S. Powers

PENN
University of Pennsylvania Press
Philadelphia

Published by
University of Pennsylvania Press
Philadelphia, Pennsylvania 19104-4112
www.upenn.edu/pennpress

Printed in the United States of America on acid-free paper
10 9 8 7 6 5 4 3 2 1

Library of Congress Cataloging-in-Publication Data:

Powers, David Stephan.
Zayd / David S. Powers. — 1st ed.
p. cm. — (Divinations : rereading late ancient religion)
Includes bibliographical references and index.
ISBN 978-0-8122-4617-9 (hardcover : alk. paper)
1. Zayd ibn Harithah, –629 or 630. 2. Usamah ibn Zayd, –673? 3. Muhammad, Prophet, –632—Companions—Biography. 4. Qur'an—Relation to the Bible. 5. Islam—Origin. I. Title. II. Series: Divinations.
BP80.Z27P69 2014
297.6′44—dc23 2014003709

To my mother,

Geraldine (Feigeh) Adelman Powers-Volper (b. 1922)

who has enriched the lives of her loved ones with her wonderful stories, and passed on to me her determination to recover the past and preserve its memory.

Contents

Preface

Many of the believers who formulated the Islamic foundation narrative were converts to Islam or their descendants. Inevitably these men and women were engaging in a conversation with earlier Jewish and Christian traditions, both written and oral. On the following pages, I shall attempt to demonstrate that the Muslims who related and transmitted stories about the subject of the present study—a man named Zayd—drew freely upon biblical and postbiblical texts, characters, themes, and motifs. At each stage of his life, the figure of Zayd—as well as that of his wife Zaynab and his son Usāma—is modeled on that of a different biblical or postbiblical figure. Initially, the audiences in whose presence these stories were related or performed would have been familiar with these biblical models. Over time, however, the interest of Muslims in biblical texts waned, and the textual links between the Islamic narratives and their biblical antecedents weakened and eventually were lost. Similarly, many readers of this book will have only a passing knowledge of these biblical figures. For this reason, I have divided each of the four chapters of this book into three sections: Islamic Narratives, Biblical Models, and Textual Encounters. In the Islamic Narratives section, I rely exclusively on Islamic sources. In the Biblical Models section, I summarize the relevant biblical and postbiblical stories that, in my view, served as literary models for the Islamic figures. Finally, in the Textual Encounters section, I identify the parallels between the Islamic figures and their biblical counterparts. Note well: I do not claim to have identified every relevant biblical model nor do I claim that every episode in the life of Zayd and his family is based on a biblical model.

The Islamic sources upon which the following biography is based have been accessible in the form of manuscripts for a thousand years and in printed editions for more than a century. What distinguishes the present study from earlier scholarship is that I treat the reports about Zayd and his family as literary narratives rather than as "history as it really was." Although Zayd, his son Usāma, and other members of his family may have been real historical personages, the reports that were transmitted about them do not, in my view, bear any relation to real historical events. The challenge for the historian is to identify the literary functions performed by Zayd and his entourage within the larger Islamic foundation narrative. In the Conclusion, I will argue that Zayd and Usāma initially were key players in the bitter contest within the early Muslim community over the issue of legitimate leadership and succession to Muḥammad. In addition, Zayd played a central role in securing the theological doctrine of the finality of prophecy.

Zayd

Introduction

This book is the first scholarly attempt to reconstruct the biography of a man named Zayd who was a Companion of the Prophet Muḥammad. Although Zayd is well known to Muslim audiences, past and present, he has not been viewed as a figure of major importance, and he is virtually unknown in the West. The task of the writer is facilitated by the fact that information about Zayd may be found in a wide range of sources, including the *Sīra* or biography of the Prophet, historical treatises, and biographical dictionaries. It is important to keep in mind, however, that these sources were written 150 years or more after the events about which they report and that their contents, including the narratives about Zayd, were shaped by the interests and worldview of their authors. About Zayd there is only one solid and undisputed "fact," a passing reference to him in a single verse of the Qur'ān. This verse, which would trigger much of the information about Zayd found in later sources, merits close attention.

Verse 37 of *Sūrat al-Aḥzāb* ("The Confederates")

The thirty-third *sūrah* or chapter of the Qur'ān, called *al-Aḥzāb*, takes its name from the Arabic noun *ḥizb* (pl. *aḥzāb*), which signifies "a party," "a company of men," or "troops." The plural noun occurs twice in v. 20 of this chapter, both times with reference to a coalition of pagan and Jewish forces that attacked Medina but was repelled—with divine assistance—at the Battle of the Trench in the year 5/626–27.

In the standard text of the Qur'ān, said to have been compiled during the reign of the third caliph ʿUthmān b. ʿAffān (d. 36/656), *al-Aḥzāb* contains seventy-three verses. But this may not have been its original size: It is related on the authority of Ubayy b. Kaʿb (d. between 19/640 and 35/656) that during the lifetime of the Prophet *Sūrat al-Aḥzāb* had as many verses as, or more than, *Sūrat al-Baqara* (286 verses); on the authority of ʿĀʾisha (d. 58/678) that it originally had two hundred verses; and on the authority of Abū Mūsā al-Ashʿarī (d. 52/672), that it originally was as long as *Sūrat al-Barāʾa* (129 verses). If so, then, for reasons that are not specified, between fifty and two hundred verses were removed from *Sūrat al-Aḥzāb*, leaving the seventy-three verses found in the standard text.[1]

Our immediate concern here is with v. 37, which, with thirty-six verses on either side of it, is located at the center of the chapter. In v. 37, the authorial voice that controls the text speaks directly to an unidentified addressee as follows:

> [Recall] when you said to the one on whom God and you yourself have bestowed favor, "Keep your wife to yourself and fear God," and you hid within yourself what God would reveal, and you feared the people when God had better right to be feared by you. When Zayd had finished with her, We gave her to you in marriage, so that there should be no difficulty for the believers concerning the wives of their adopted sons, when they have finished with them. God's command was fulfilled.

Verse 37 appears to refer to a specific episode in the life of the Prophet Muḥammad. Even if the modern reader is unfamiliar with this episode, it is possible to reconstruct its general outlines based solely on what the Qurʾān says. The authorial voice that controls v. 37 ("We")—generally understood to be that of the Divinity—asks a male addressee ("you"), no doubt the Prophet Muḥammad, to recall an earlier conversation between Muḥammad and a third party ("the one on whom God and you yourself have bestowed favor") regarding the latter's wife. The authorial voice quotes the very words uttered by Muḥammad on this earlier occasion ("Keep your wife to yourself and fear God"), demonstrates knowledge of Muḥammad's state of mind ("you hid within yourself"), and rebukes the Prophet ("you feared the people when God had better right to be feared by you"). In addition to invoking the recent past ("[Recall] when"), the authorial voice anticipates a forthcoming divine pronouncement ("what God would reveal"). The purpose of this pronouncement, which is embedded in the second half of the verse, was to resolve an unspecified anxiety. The authorial voice explains that when a man identified only as Zayd—no doubt the doubly favored man mentioned in the opening clause—was "finished with her" (one wonders what this means), "We"—God—gave "her"—the woman—to "you"—Muḥammad—"in marriage." This was a marriage made in Heaven. The reference to "the wives of their adopted sons" toward the end of the verse suggests that the woman married by the Prophet was the former wife of his adopted son. The marriage itself was facilitated by a legal distinction introduced by the Divinity: Whereas previously it had been forbidden for a believer to marry the former wife of his adopted son, henceforth such a marriage would be permissible ("there should be no difficulty") on the condition that her first husband had, again, "finished" with her. The verse concludes with the announcement that "God's command"—presumably a reference to the divinely ordained marriage—did in fact take place ("was fulfilled").

The preceding gloss on v. 37 of *Sūrat al-Aḥzāb* is faithful to the manner in which this remarkable verse has been understood by Muslim commentators on the Qurʾān.

A Man Named Zayd

The precise circumstances of the revelation of v. 37 would have been well-known to the Prophet's immediate audience, and this knowledge would have been transmitted over time through numerous channels, both oral and written, to subsequent generations of believers. Although we do not have direct access to the initial response to this verse by its immediate audience, we do have access to its reception and understanding by Muslims living one or more generations after the revelations had been gathered into the ʿUthmānic *muṣḥaf* or codex. These were the storytellers, preachers, exegetes, traditionists, and historians who preserved the memory of the events associated with the rise of Islam, shaped the formulation of those events, and produced the Islamic foundation narrative.

Verse 37 invites speculation about the three figures who were involved in the episode to which it refers: First, who was the man named Zayd, what were the circumstances of his adoption by Muḥammad, and how was it that he came to be favored by both God and His Prophet? Second, who was the unnamed woman who married first Zayd and then the Prophet and what were the circumstances of her marriages to these two men? Third, why did Muḥammad instruct Zayd to keep his wife to himself, what was he hiding within himself, why did he fear the people, and why did God rebuke him?

The answers to all of these questions revolve around the man referred to in the opening clause of Q. 33:37 as "the one on whom God and you yourself have bestowed favor." In the middle of the verse, this doubly favored man is identified as Zayd, with no further specification. If Zayd was a believer—and he was—then the mere mention of his name in v. 37 of *Sūrat al-Aḥzāb* is extraordinary. The Prophet himself is mentioned by name ("Muḥammad") only four times in the Qurʾān (Q. 3:144, 33:40, 47:2, and 48:29; see also 61:6, where the mention of "Aḥmad" is widely understood as a reference to Muḥammad). Apart from Muḥammad, Zayd is the *only* believer whose name is mentioned in the Qurʾān. That he is not further identified as the son of so-and-so or the father of so-and-so or of such-and-such a tribe suggests that he was well-known to the community of believers and a person of some standing. One would like to know more about this doubly favored man named Zayd.

Zayd in the *Sīra* of Ibn Isḥāq/Ibn Hishām

Information about Zayd may be found in commentaries on the Qurʾān, *ḥadīth* collections, the *Sīra* or *Biography* of the Prophet Muḥammad, biographical dictionaries, and historical chronicles.

For the moment, we are concerned only with the *Sīra* of Ibn Isḥāq (d. 150/767) composed for the ʿAbbasid caliph al-Manṣūr (r. 136–158/754–775). This text is said to have consisted of three volumes: *al-Mubtadaʾ* ("In the beginning") treated the creation of the world, the prophets from Adam to Jesus, and the Arabs prior to the emergence of Islam; *al-Baʿth* ("The Mission") treated the life of Muḥammad up to the hijra or emigration; and *al-Maghāzī* ("The Military Expeditions") treated the Prophet's career in Medina. Alas, Ibn Isḥāq's *Sīra* is no longer extant, although we do possess a redacted version of his text undertaken by Ibn Hishām (d. ca. 218/833), who omitted the first volume and also removed from the remaining text passages that he found offensive. Even without the first volume, Ibn Hishām's edition of the *Sīra* is a substantial text that covers the life and career of Muḥammad from his birth until his death.[2]

Let us perform a thought experiment by assuming, for the sake of argument, that Ibn Hishām's edition of the *Sīra* is our *only* source of information about the man named Zayd who is mentioned in v. 37 of *Sūrat al-Aḥzāb*. If so, then what would a Muslim living in Baghdad in the middle of the third/ninth century have known about the man identified as Zayd in v. 37?

The first reference to Zayd in the *Sīra* occurs in connection with the birth hour of Islam. Shortly after Muḥammad received his first revelation in 610 C.E., four people are said to have become believers, in the following order: (1) Khadīja bt. Khuwaylid, the wife of Muḥammad; (2) ʿAlī b. Abī Ṭālib, Muḥammad's ten-year-old cousin and future son-in-law; (3) Zayd the *mawlā* of the Messenger of God, shortly thereafter identified as Zayd b. Ḥāritha; and (4) Abū Bakr b. Abī Quḥāfa, a merchant who would soon become the Prophet's father-in-law.

Zayd is identified at first mention as Muḥammad's *mawlā*, a noun derived from the verb *waliya*, which signifies *inter alia* "to follow," "to befriend," "to be close to, or connected with, someone or something." In the Qurʾān the singular form *mawlā* occurs eighteen times and the plural form *mawālī* occurs three times.[3] Used with reference to God, *mawlā* signifies "master" or "protector" (e.g., Q. 22:78). Used with references to human beings, it signifies "ally," "friend," "ward," or "protégé" (e.g., Q. 33:5, 44:41) or "heir" (Q. 4:33). Thus, the identification of Zayd as the *mawlā* of the Messenger of God signals a close relationship between the two men. And the timing of his conversion—immediately preceding that of Abū Bakr and following that of ʿAlī—marks Zayd as a charter member of the new community while at the same time raising questions about his relationship with the men who would become the first and fourth caliphs, respectively.[4]

The next reference to Zayd in the *Sīra* occurs in connection with the Prophet's *Miʿrāj* or Ascension, which is said to have taken place circa 621 C.E., a year or so before the hijra. It is related on the authority of the Companion Abū Saʿīd al-Khudrī (d. 64/684) that after passing through the gates of Heaven, Muḥammad encountered a series of earlier prophets: Adam, Jesus, John the Baptist, Joseph, Idris, Aaron, Moses, and, finally, his "father" Abraham. It was Abraham who took Muḥammad by the hand and led him into Paradise itself. No sooner did Muḥammad enter Paradise than he caught sight of an attractive slave girl (*jāriya*) with dark red lips. After describing his reaction to the woman ("she pleased me much when I saw her"), Muḥammad enquired, "To whom do you belong?" "To Zayd b. Ḥāritha," she responded.

Upon his return to Mecca, the Prophet gave Zayd the "good news" about the beautiful woman waiting for him in Paradise.[5]

The prominence of Zayd b. Ḥāritha in the Ascension narrative is striking. On this momentous occasion, after encountering eight prophets and entering the precincts of Paradise, Muḥammad's eyes just happen to fall upon an attractive slave girl with dark red lips, perhaps a houri, one of the virgins of Paradise who are promised as a reward for God-fearing believers. Muḥammad engages the woman in conversation, and she informs him that she "belongs" to Zayd b. Ḥāritha. The narrative points to—one might say that it foreshadows—Zayd's death under circumstances as yet unknown to our imaginary reader of the *Sīra*. Ironically, the foreshadowing of Zayd's death is "good news," a guarantee of entry to Paradise. Upon his return to Mecca, Muḥammad conveys this good news to Zayd. Again, the narrative signals a close connection between the two men.

According to the *Sīra*, Zayd married shortly after the Prophet received his first revelation. His wife bore him a son named Usāma.[6] Otherwise, the *Sīra* is silent about Zayd's activities during the thirteen years between the beginning of revelation and the hijra.

In 622 C.E. Muḥammad instructed his Companions to leave Mecca and travel to Yathrib, located approximately two hundred miles to the north, where they would receive food and shelter from inhabitants of the town who were believers (the latter are known as the *anṣār* or Helpers). The *muhājirūn* or Emigrants traveled in small groups. The first to depart were ʿĀmir b. Rabīʿa and his wife Layla bt. Ḥathma.[7] This couple was followed by ʿAbdallāh b. Jaḥsh and his family, including his two sisters, Zaynab and Umm Ḥabīb (we will learn more about ʿAbdallāh and Zaynab in Chapter 2). The next group included ʿUmar b. al-Khaṭṭāb and ʿAyyāsh b. Abī Rabīʿa. Later waves of Emigrants included the Prophet's uncle Ḥamza b. ʿAbd al-Muṭṭalib ("the lion of God and the lion of the Apostle"), and Zayd b. Ḥāritha—presumably accompanied by his wife and son.[8] Apparently, none of these Emigrants experienced any hardship or difficulty during the long journey from Mecca to Yathrib.

The last three believers to depart from Mecca were the Prophet, Abū Bakr, and ʿAlī. Although their experience is not directly related to Zayd, it nevertheless merits attention, as we will return to it in the Conclusion. When the tribe of Quraysh learned that the inhabitants of Yathrib had forged an alliance with the believers of Mecca, they realized that the balance of power was shifting in favor of Muḥammad's new community. In response to this threat, representatives of each clan within the tribe gathered to decide how to deal with the situation (the devil himself, disguised as a handsome old man wearing a mantle, is said to have been present at the gathering). After listening to several proposals, Abū Jahl (literally, "father of ignorance") suggested that several strong young warriors representing different clans should thrust a sharp sword into the body of the Prophet at precisely the same moment, thereby distributing responsibility for blood money across many clans. When Abū Jahl's proposal received the endorsement of the handsome old man, the clans set their plan into motion. By nightfall, a large group of strong young men had gathered outside the Prophet's house, waiting for him to fall asleep so that they might kill him the next morning when he awoke and emerged from his house.[9]

The devil's machinations were countered by the Angel Gabriel, who now appeared to the Prophet and ordered him not to sleep in his bed that night. From the safety of his house, Muḥammad could see the would-be assassins outside. The situation was perilous. The only two Companions who remained in Mecca were Abū Bakr and ʿAlī. The Prophet now made a difficult decision: He ordered ʿAlī to wrap himself in his—that is to say, the Prophet's—green mantle and to take his place in his bed. If the plot succeeded, it would be ʿAlī, not Muḥammad, who would die. The Prophet now emerged from his house and boldly walked past the would-be assassins, who had been temporarily blinded by God so that they could not see Muḥammad. After sprinkling dust on the head of each man—a sign of his presence—the Prophet escaped. When the men recovered their eyesight, they entered the house and saw a man in the bed wearing a green mantle. "By God, it is Muḥammad sleeping in his mantle," they whispered. When the sun rose the next morning, however, it was ʿAlī who rose from the bed and emerged from the house. The assassination plot had been foiled, at least temporarily.[10]

The other believer remaining in Mecca was Abū Bakr, who repeatedly had asked the Prophet for permission to migrate, only to be told that he must wait until God would give him a "companion." Hoping that this "companion" would be Muḥammad himself, Abū Bakr purchased two camels, one for himself and one for the Prophet, and he kept the animals tethered next to his house, ready to depart at a moment's notice. On the day after the failed assassination attempt, God finally gave the Prophet permission to migrate. At noon, Muḥammad appeared unexpectedly at Abū Bakr's house to let him know that God had given him—that is to say, the Prophet—permission to depart for Yathrib. "Together with me?" Abū Bakr asked. "Yes," he responded.

Abū Bakr wept for joy. The situation remained perilous, however, as the would-be assassins were still searching for Muḥammad. To avoid capture, the two men exited Abū Bakr's house through a back window and then made their way to a cave located on Mount Thawr, south of Mecca. When the Qurashīs learned that Muḥammad had left town, they offered one hundred camels to anyone who would capture him and bring him back. Abū Bakr and Muḥammad remained in hiding in the cave for three days. Their safety was insured by three people: Under cover of darkness, Abū Bakr's daughter Asmāʾ brought the men food and his son ʿAbdallāh brought them news about the situation in Mecca; and during the day, Abū Bakr's *mawlā* ʿĀmir b. Fuhayra drove his sheep back and forth between Mecca and the cave to cover the tracks left by the two siblings.[11] On the evening of their third day in hiding, the two "companions," Abū Bakr and Muḥammad, accompanied by a servant and a guide, departed for Yathrib, riding the camels that had been purchased by Abū Bakr. They arrived in Yathrib on Monday 12 Rabīʿ I at high noon.[12]

With the arrival of Muḥammad, Yathrib came to be known as *madīnat al-nabī* ("the city of the Prophet") or, simply, *al-madīna* ("the city")—hence, Medina. In Medina, the Emigrants received food and shelter from different Helpers. Initially, Muḥammad, Ḥamza, ʿAlī, and Zayd b. Ḥāritha all stayed with Kulthūm b. Hidm in the area known as al-Qubāʿ.[13] Shortly after his arrival in Yathrib, the Prophet created brotherhood pacts between pairs of Emigrants and Helpers. Exceptionally Muḥammad took ʿAlī as his "brother" and he paired Ḥamza b. ʿAbd al-Muṭṭalib with "Zayd b. Ḥāritha the *mawlā* of the apostle" (all four were Emigrants).[14]

In 2 AH, the first of three major military encounters between the Meccans and the community of believers took place at the wells of Badr. Zayd participated in the battle, together with his "brother" Ḥamza—the two men reportedly shared a single camel.[15] Prior to the battle, the Prophet instructed Zayd's son Usāma, who would have been approximately twelve years old at the time, to remain in Medina, together with ʿUthmān b. ʿAffān, in order to attend to a sick believer, the Prophet's daughter Ruqayya, ʿUthmān's wife. Following the Muslim victory, the Prophet charged Zayd with the task of bringing the good news to the people of lower Medina (a second messenger, ʿAbdallāh b. Rawāḥa, was sent to the upper part of the town; on him see further below). Once again the good news was bittersweet. The military victory coincided with the premature death of one of the Prophet's daughters. Indeed, Ruqayya's body had already been placed in the ground when Zayd arrived in lower Medina. He made his way to the mosque, where, surrounded by a large crowd, some of whom were believers (including Usāma) and some not, he announced the names of eight polytheists who had been killed at Badr. Upon hearing their names, a Jew by the name of Kaʿb al-Ashraf was incredulous: "Is this true? Did Muḥammad actually kill those mentioned by Zayd?" Usāma too was incredulous. "Is this true, my father?" he asked. "Yes, by God it is, my son," Zayd replied.[16]

At the same time that Muḥammad was mourning the death of one daughter, Ruqayya, he was also concerned about the fate of another, Zaynab. Some fifteen years earlier, before receiving his first revelation, Muḥammad had arranged for Zaynab to marry Abū al-ʿĀṣ b. al-Rabīʿ, a wealthy merchant who was the nephew of Muḥammad's wife Khadīja. At that time Khadīja was sonless, and she is said to have treated Abū al-ʿĀṣ as if he were her son (the *Sīra* is silent about Muḥammad's attitude toward his son-in-law). In 610 C.E., when Muḥammad received his first revelation, Zaynab bt. Muḥammad became a believer, but Abū al-ʿĀṣ remained a polytheist. Despite the difference of religion, the marriage remained in force. Twelve years later, following the hijra, the Prophet's daughter found herself in Mecca with her pagan husband, a predicament that surely was troubling to Muḥammad. What a stroke of good fortune that Abū al-ʿĀṣ should have been captured at Badr and taken to Medina. The capture of this Meccan polytheist provided the Prophet with an opportunity to recover his daughter, who was stranded in Mecca living among pagans and polytheists. The Prophet made an agreement with Abū al-ʿĀṣ: In return for his release and repatriation, Abū al-ʿĀṣ would send Zaynab to her father in Medina. The exchange is said to have taken place approximately one month after the Battle of Badr. Following his return to Mecca, Abū al-ʿĀṣ gave his wife permission to leave the town so that she could rejoin her father in Medina. In light of recent hostilities, it would have been dangerous for a woman to make such a trip on her own. For this reason, the Prophet dispatched "Zayd b. Ḥāritha" (and one other man) to ensure the safe return of his daughter. The two men traveled to the valley of al-Ya'jaj, eight miles from Mecca, where, after a rendezvous with Zaynab, they escorted the Prophet's daughter to Medina. Mission accomplished.[17]

In 3 A.H. another major military encounter between the polytheists of Quraysh and the community of believers took place at Uḥud. Once again the two "brothers," Ḥamza and Zayd, rode together. Before the battle was engaged, Ḥamza—who had been singled out as a target by the Quraysh—entrusted Zayd with his last will and testament (about which the *Sīra* is otherwise silent).[18] Ḥamza did in fact fall as a martyr that day, killed by Waḥshī, an Abyssinian slave who belonged to Jubayr b. Muṭʿim. His corpse was mutilated, and, in an act of vengeance, Hind bt. ʿUtba, the wife of Abū Sufyān, is said to have removed the dead man's liver from his body and chewed on it.[19]

The growing military strength of the community of believers posed a threat to the Meccan caravan trade, which depended on safe passage through the Hijaz and Wādī al-Qurā on the way to markets in Gaza, Damascus, and Antioch. As a precautionary measure, the Qurashīs began to use a longer but less traveled route to Syria that passed through Iraq. In the middle of 3 A.H., a Meccan caravan that included the polytheist leader Abū Sufyān was making its way to Syria along this alternate route. Sensing a strategic opportunity, Muḥammad appointed "Zayd" as the commander of a military expedition that traveled north and east in the direction of the Najd, where the small Muslim force intercepted the Meccan caravan at a spring called al-Qarada. Although the Meccans escaped with their lives, Zayd seized silver coins and merchandise and brought the booty to Muḥammad. This was his first victory as a military commander. It would not be his last.[20]

As a military commander, Zayd had to make difficult decisions. In 6 A.H., one of his fellow tribesmen, Diḥya b. Khalīfa al-Kalbī, was sent by the Prophet on a mission to the Byzantine emperor Heraclius. As he was making his way back to the Hijaz, Diḥya was robbed by two Judhamī tribesmen, a father and his son. This provocation demanded a response. Muḥammad appointed Zayd b. Ḥāritha as the commander of a military expedition that was charged with taking revenge on the provocateurs. Zayd led his men to southern Palestine, where—remarkably—they located the two robbers and killed them (along with three other men), took prisoners, and seized cattle as booty. One Judhamī tribesman, Ḥassān b. Milla, tried to save his life by claiming to be a believer. Zayd did spare him, but only after Ḥassān had first recited the short chapter of the Qurʾān that subsequently would come to be known as *Sūrat al-Fātiḥa* ("The Opening").

Zayd also spared the life of Ḥassān's sister, who, in a burst of emotion, is said to have wrapped her arms around her brother's waist and clung tightly to him. When another woman protested, however, Zayd ordered his men to pull the woman away from her brother and to place her with the other female captives until "God should decide what should be done."[21] Once again, Zayd had demonstrated his skill as a military commander. His decision to leave the fate of Ḥassān's sister in the hands of God points to his willingness to defer to God and His prophet on matters of life and death.

The *Sīra* does not always portray Zayd in a positive light. Only one month after the raid to southern Palestine, Muḥammad appointed Zayd as the commander of a military expedition sent against the Banū Fazāra in Wādī al-Qurā, an oasis located approximately seven miles north of Medina. In the resulting battle several Muslims died, and Zayd was wounded. Now it was Zayd's turn to seek revenge. Following his return to Medina, Zayd swore a solemn oath, declaring that he would not have sexual relations with his (here unidentified) wife—a common topos—until he had taken revenge on the Banū Fazāra. After Zayd had recovered from his wounds, Muḥammad put him in charge of a second expedition against the Banū Fazāra. The believers killed one Fazarī tribesman and took several prisoners, including an old woman named Umm Qirfa and her daughter. Here was the opportunity for which Zayd had been waiting. He ordered one of his men to kill the old woman: Her right leg was tied with a rope to one camel and her left leg was tied to another. The camels were then driven in opposite directions until the woman's body had been torn in two.[22] From this episode we learn that Zayd was not invincible on the battlefield and that he could be stubborn, vengeful, and heartless.

On at least one occasion, Zayd's cruel streak had to be corrected by the Prophet. Sometime after the Wādī al-Qurā campaign, Muḥammad appointed Zayd as the commander of a military expedition whose target was the port of Mināʾ on the Red Sea. The believers attacked the town and took many prisoners. After they had returned safely to Medina, Zayd—who was himself a former slave (see Chapter 1)—instructed his men to sell the prisoners in the market. As mothers were being wrenched away from their children, the slaves began to moan and wail. By a stroke of good fortune, their cries reached the ears of the Prophet who, upon learning that Zayd had allowed the prisoners to be sold into slavery without any regard for the integrity of families, intervened, instructing the slave traders not to separate mothers from their children.[23]

The *Sīra* devotes considerable attention to Zayd's participation in the Battle of Muʾtah in 8 A.H. (other sources specify 7 A.H.). In Jumāda I of this year, the Prophet sent three thousand Companions on another military expedition to southern Jordan. At a staging ground outside of Medina, Muḥammad specified the order of command as follows: Zayd was the commander, but if he were killed, then Jaʿfar b. Abī Ṭālib (ʿAlī's older brother) was to take command, and if Jaʿfar were killed, then ʿAbdallāh b. Rawāḥa was to take command. The believers marched off in the direction of Rabbat Ammon. Upon reaching the town of Maʿān, they received news that the emperor Heraclius was waiting for them with 100,000 Byzantine soldiers and 100,000 Arab auxiliaries. The soldiers paused to consider their options. Some wanted to send a letter to Muḥammad in Medina, asking for reinforcements. At this critical moment, ʿAbdallāh b. Rawāḥa stood up and delivered a stirring speech: "Men, what you dislike is that which you have come out in search of, namely, martyrdom. We are not fighting the enemy with numbers, or strength or multitude, but we are confronting them with this religion with which God has honored us. So come on! Both prospects (*al-ḥusnayayn*) are fine: victory or martyrdom."[24]

Ibn Rawāḥa's reference to two excellent prospects draws on the language of the revelation that would become Q. 9:52: "Say: 'Are you waiting for anything but one of the two fairest things (*iḥdā al-ḥusnayayn*) to befall us?'" The believers would be either victorious over the enemy forces, despite overwhelming odds, or rewarded for death on the battlefield with martyrdom and eternal life in Paradise.

Zayd led his men to Mashārif, but then withdrew to the village of Muʾtah, where the believers were overtaken by enemy forces. The battle was engaged. As required by the logic of the narrative, the three commanders fell in the exact order specified by Muḥammad: first Zayd, followed by Jaʿfar, and then ʿAbdallāh b. Rawāḥa. All three men, the *Sīra* informs us, immediately entered Paradise as martyrs.

The death of the three commanders at Muʾtah has been memorialized in poetry, of which three examples may suffice. In the following lines, the poet Ḥassān b. Thābit (d. ca. 40/659) invokes the memory of Muʾtah, the defeat of the Muslim army, and the abandonment of Zayd's body on the battlefield:

> O eye, be generous with the last drop of tears
> And remember in thy ease those in their graves.
> Remember Muʾtah and what happened there
> When they went down to their defeat,
> When they returned leaving Zayd there.[25]

In the following lines, attributed to Jaʿfar b. Abī Ṭālib (the attribution is no doubt spurious), the Companion expresses his eagerness to engage the enemy in battle and his desire for martyrdom:

> Welcome Paradise so near,
> Sweet and cool to drink its cheer.
> Greeks will soon have much to fear
> Infidels of descent unclear
> When we meet, their necks I'll shear.[26]

And in the following lines, attributed to ʿAbdallāh b. Rawāḥa (again the attribution is spurious), the Companion pleads with his soul, urging it to accept death—and martyrdom:

> I swear, my soul, you shall come to the battle;
> You shall fight or be made to fight.
> Though men shout and scream aloud,
> Why should you spurn Paradise?
> Long have you been at ease.
> You are nothing but a drop in a worn-out skin![27]

Considering the reported size of the two opposing armies, it is curious that only eight believers (including the three commanders) are said to have been slain at Muʾtah. Two of the eight casualties, it will be noted, are identified as members of Muḥammad's clan of the Banū Hāshim: Jaʿfar b. Abī Ṭālib and Zayd b. Ḥāritha.[28]

Zayd was survived by his son Usāma. In 11 A.H., according to a terse notice in the *Sīra*, the Prophet appointed Usāma as the commander of a military expedition to Syria, ordering him "to lead his cavalry into the territory of the Balqāʾ and al-Dārūm in the land of Palestine. The men got ready and all the first emigrants went with Usāma."[29] The departure of the military expedition was delayed, however, when the Prophet became ill. During this illness, Muḥammad learned that certain unidentified believers had criticized his decision to put Usāma in command of "the best of the Emigrants and the Helpers."[30] The ailing Prophet rose from his sickbed, walked to the mosque, and climbed to the top of the pulpit, where he chastised his critics, insisting that Usāma's military credentials were as strong as those of his father, Zayd. "Dispatch Usāma's force," the Prophet instructed the believers, before returning to his sickbed.[31] The men resumed their preparations for the military expedition, but their departure was delayed a second time when they received news that Muḥammad had fallen seriously ill. Usāma now paid a visit to the dying leader. Although the Prophet was unable to speak, he did make a gesture, lifting one of his hands in the air and bringing it down upon the young man's head. This gesture was understood by Usāma as a "blessing."[32] Shortly thereafter, the Prophet died. Five men, including Usāma, are said to have prepared the body for burial. It was Usāma, together with the Prophet's *mawlā* Shuqrān, who poured water over the dead man's body.[33]

Recovering Zayd

This is the end of our thought experiment. We have established that a Muslim living in Baghdad in the third/ninth century who had access only to Ibn Hishām's edition of the *Sīra* of Ibn Isḥāq would have known the following about the man named Zayd mentioned in Q. 33:37.

Zayd was the son of a man named Ḥāritha. Under circumstances that are not explained, he became the Prophet's *mawlā*. Zayd was the third person, the second male, and the first adult male to become a believer. He had a son named Usāma. He participated in the hijra to Medina, where he was paired as a "brother" with the Prophet's uncle, Ḥamza b. ʿAbd al-Muṭṭalib, who, before he died, entrusted Zayd with his last will and testament. Zayd served as the commander of many military expeditions. He was trustworthy, reliable, and brave, but he also could be cruel. In 8 A.H. Zayd was slain while fighting in the village of Muʾtah in southern Jordan. As a reward for his willingness to sacrifice his life for the sake of God and His prophet, he immediately ascended to Paradise, where an attractive slave girl with dark red lips is said to have been waiting for him. Zayd was clearly close to Muḥammad and a person of standing and importance within the community of believers.

As for Zayd's son Usāma, the *Sīra* reports that he took care of the Prophet's daughter Ruqayya before she died in 2 A.H., was appointed by the Prophet as the commander of a military expedition to southern Palestine in 11 A.H., received a blessing from the Prophet on the latter's deathbed, and poured water over the Prophet's body after his death.

Otherwise the *Sīra* does not answer any of the questions raised by Q. 33:37. It is striking that the *Sīra* says nothing about the circumstances in which Zayd became Muḥammad's *mawlā* and/or his adopted son. Also striking is the omission of any mention of the episode that would have triggered the revelation of Q. 33:37. On the basis of the information contained in the *Sīra*, our imaginary reader has little sense of how it was that Zayd came to be favored by either God or His prophet or why he alone among the believers is identified by name in the Qurʾān. The reader learns nothing about the identity of the unnamed woman in v. 37 or the circumstances of her marriage to Zayd and the later dissolution of that marriage. Nor does the reader learn anything about the relationship between the unnamed woman and Muḥammad, why Muḥammad kept certain feelings a secret, the source of the Prophet's anxiety or the circumstances of the divine rebuke.[34] Was there perhaps something offensive about this episode that may have prompted Ibn Hishām to remove such information from Ibn Isḥāq's earlier *Sīra*?

To answer this question, I will attempt to recover the figure of Zayd in its literary fullness and complexity. As noted, information about Zayd may be found in a wide range of sources, albeit for the most part in the form of short narrative reports about specific episodes in his life. Once this information has been gathered and arranged in chronological order, it becomes clear that some members of the early community of believers regarded Zayd as a key figure who played a central role in the Islamic foundation narrative.

The contents and formulation of reports about Zayd were shaped by the notion of *sunnat allāh*, an expression that occurs five times in the Qurʾān (Q. 33:38, 33:62, 35:43, 40:85, and 48:23). Verse 38 of *Sūrat al-Aḥzāb* reads as follows: "There is no sin (*ḥaraj*) for the prophet in that which God has ordained for him: God's practice (*sunnat allāh*) concerning those who passed away previously—God's command is a fixed decree." The translation of *sunnat allāh* as "God's practice" does not do justice to this rich and evocative term. I find it helpful to understand *sunnat allāh* by analogy to a theatrical production written, produced, and directed by God. The *sunna* or practice of God is the process whereby the divine playwright inscribes the events of sacred history in a script or text and causes those events to unfold in accordance with His will. The key actors in this dramatic production are the prophets, e.g., Adam, Noah, Abraham, Isaac, Jacob, David, Solomon, Jesus, and, finally, Muḥammad, who was the "seal of prophets." One purpose of this dramatic performance, as related by Muslim storytellers, was to explain the process whereby Muḥammad brought the office of prophecy to an end. As we shall soon discover, the man named Zayd who is mentioned in Q. 33:37 played a central role in this sacred drama.

Chapter 1

Zayd

My son, keep your father's commandment; do not
forsake your mother's teaching.—Prov. 6:20

But the one who says to his parents, "Fie on you both . . ."—Q. 46:17

Do not forsake your fathers, for it is [an act of]
infidelity on your part.—ʿUmar b. al-Khaṭṭāb

Islamic Narratives

The steppe lands between Syria and Iraq served as the grazing grounds of the tribe of Kalb, camel breeders who inhabited oases in the valley formed by Wadi Sirhan in northern Arabia, the gateway to Syria. In the sixth century C.E., Kalbīs could be found living in Salamiyya, Palmyra, Damascus, the Golan, and in the region of Harran. In northern Arabia, they settled in Fadak, Dūmat al-Jandal, Taymāʾ, and al-Ḥīra. The territory of Kalb was controlled by the Ghassanids, vassals of the Byzantines whose capital was Jābiya in the Golan Heights. The Kalbīs, in turn, were clients of the Ghassanids, who used them to defend the Syrian frontier against the Sasanians and the Lakhmids of al-Ḥīra. Like their Ghassanid patrons, they were Monophysite Christians.[1]

1.1 CAPTURE AND ENSLAVEMENT

Sometime in the latter part of the sixth century C.E., a Kalbī tribesman by the name of Ḥāritha b. Sharāḥīl married Suʿdā bt. Thaʿlab. The sources suggest that husband and wife lived in southern Palestine or northern Arabia, without specifying the exact location of their domicile. Circa 580 C.E., Suʿdā gave birth to a son, Zayd, who passed his formative years in the company of his parents, relatives, and fellow tribesmen. Zayd reportedly was short, his nose was flat and wide, and his skin was either white or tawny. When the young man was approximately twenty years old, misfortune struck: Zayd was captured by horse-riding Arabs, transported to Arabia, and sold into slavery.

Several versions of the capture and enslavement of Zayd b. Ḥāritha are preserved in Islamic sources. One account specifies that Zayd was a young man (*ghulām*) when he was seized by members of his own tribe—Kalb—at a place called al-Baṭḥāʾ and transported to a slave market in the vicinity of Mecca. One day, as Muḥammad b. ʿAbdallāh, a member of the clan of Hāshim, was walking through the slave market and examining the merchandise, his eyes happened to fall on Zayd. There was something about the young man, perhaps his sidelock, that set him apart from the other slaves.[2] Later that day, Muḥammad returned to his home, where he said to his wife, Khadīja, "I saw a young man in al-Baṭḥāʾ whose tribe had seized him and offered him up for sale. If only I had the money, I would purchase him." "How much does he cost?" Khadīja asked. "700 *dirhams*," Muḥammad replied. Khadīja now gave her husband 700 *dirhams* with which to purchase the slave. Muḥammad returned to the slave market, purchased Zayd, and brought him home. He was not yet satisfied, however, for he had a feeling that there was something special about this young man. "In truth," he said to Khadīja, "if he were mine, I would give him his freedom." His wife now announced, "He [now] belongs to you, so manumit him."[3] Thus did Zayd become the freedman (*ʿatīq*) of Muḥammad b. ʿAbdallāh al-Hāshimī.

According to another account, Zayd was captured by Tihamī horsemen and sold to Ḥakīm b. Ḥizām b. Khuwaylid, who gave Zayd to his maternal aunt, Khadīja bt. Khuwaylid, who gave him to the Prophet, who manumitted him and adopted him (*tabannāhu*).[4] (On the adoption, see section 1.5, below.)

In another version of the story, Zayd was visiting the family of his maternal grandfather when Fazarī horsemen captured him and sold him in the market town of ʿUkāẓ southeast of Mecca. In this account he was purchased by Khadīja's paternal cousin, a Christian by the name of Waraqa b. Nawfal—not by her paternal nephew, Ḥakīm b. Ḥizām.[5]

A long and detailed account of Zayd's capture and enslavement is preserved by Ibn Saʿd (d. 230/845).[6] In this version of the story, Suʿdā bt. Thaʿlab took her son Zayd to visit her relatives, the Banū al-Maʿn of Ṭayy. During the visit, horsemen of the Banū al-Qayn b. Jasr descended upon the tribal campground. The Arab raiders seized Zayd and carried him off to the Hijaz. In the market of ʿUkāẓ he was sold for 400 *dirhams* to Ḥakīm b. Ḥizām b. Khuwaylid, who was acting on behalf of his paternal aunt, Khadīja bt. Khuwaylid. Shortly thereafter, when Khadīja married Muḥammad, she gave the slave to her husband as a gift.[7]

Despite the variations, these narratives all share a common structure: Following his capture and enslavement by Arab horsemen, Zayd b. Ḥāritha al-Kalbī was transported to a foreign land where he was purchased by or gifted to Muḥammad b. ʿAbdallāh al-Hāshimī, the man who was about to emerge as a prophet and messenger of God and who would soon become the most powerful and important person in Arabia.

1.2 A FATHER LAMENTS THE LOSS OF HIS SON

When Ḥāritha b. Sharāḥīl learned of his son's disappearance and possible death, he was inconsolable. In the following poem, attributed to the Kalbī tribesman, he expressed his feelings as follows:

I weep for Zayd not knowing what has become of him.
Is he alive, is there hope, or has death overcome him?
By God I ask yet do not comprehend.
Was it the plain or the mountain that brought about your end?
I wish that I knew: Will you ever return?
In this world only for your coming back I yearn.
The sun reminds me of him when it dawns,
evoking his memory as the dusk falls.
When the winds blow they stir up memories like dust.
O how long my sorrow and fear for him last!
I shall hasten all my reddish-white camels all over the earth, toiling.
Neither I nor the camels will be weary of wandering
All my life long, until I die,
for every man is mortal, even though hopes lie.
To ʿAmr [b. al-Ḥārith] and Qays do I entrust [Zayd's fate]
and to Yazīd [b. Kaʿb b. Sharāḥīl] and then to Jabal[a b. Ḥāritha].[8]

1.3 A CHANCE ENCOUNTER WITH FELLOW TRIBESMEN

Time passed and life returned to normal—well, as normal as life could be for a young man who had been wrested away from his birth family and sold into slavery. In Mecca, Zayd adjusted to his status as a slave in the household of Muḥammad b. ʿAbdallāh al-Hāshimī.

Mecca was a site of pilgrimage. Once a year, tribesmen from different regions of Arabia would converge on the town in order to circumambulate the Kaʿba and worship their god or gods. One day a group of pilgrims from the tribe of Kalb just happened to spot Zayd near the Kaʿba. What a stroke of good fortune! Or was it perhaps an act of divine providence? The Kalbī tribesmen told Zayd about his family and his father's distress. Curiously, Zayd expressed no concern for either his father or his mother. Indeed, he told his fellow tribesmen that he was not interested in rejoining his family and that he did not want to be found or repatriated.[9] Like his father, he expressed his feelings in verse, asking the Kalbīs to memorize the following lines and convey them to his tribe:

Bear a message from me to my tribe, for I am far away
I reside near the Kaʿba, the place of pilgrimage.
Let go of the grief that has overtaken you;
don't send camels running all over the land.
Praise be to Allāh, I live with the best family,
Maʿadd, from father to son they are the noblest.[10]

After the Kalbī pilgrims had returned home, they told Ḥāritha b. Sharāḥīl what they had learned about his son Zayd, including his whereabouts and the identity of his master. Upon learning that Zayd was alive and well, Ḥāritha exclaimed, "My son, with the Lord of the Kaʿba!" Determined to recover Zayd, Ḥāritha traveled to Mecca, accompanied by his brother Kaʿb (cf. Heb. Yaʿqôb = Jacob).[11]

A longer version of the encounter between Zayd and the Kalbīs is preserved in Qurṭubī's commentary on Q. 33:37, where it is not unidentified Kalbī pilgrims who locate Zayd in Mecca but rather his uncle, Kaʿb, who was in Mecca on business. Upon entering the market, Kaʿb encountered a young man (*ghulām*) who bore a striking resemblance to his missing nephew. In an effort to determine the identity of this young man, Kaʿb interrogated him, as follows:

"What is your name, O young man?"
"Zayd."
"The son of whom?"
"The son of Ḥāritha."
"The son of whom?"
"The son of Sharāḥīl al-Kalbī."
"What is your mother's name?"
"Suʿdā—and I was with my maternal aunts of Ṭayy [when I was captured]."

Kaʿb embraced Zayd, who no doubt returned the gesture—even if the sources are silent about Zayd's reaction to being found. Kaʿb then sent a message with the good news to his brother Ḥāritha and the tribe of Kalb. It was not long (in the narrative, that is) before Ḥāritha arrived in Mecca determined to ransom Zayd from his master and to reunite him with his birth family. The two brothers asked Zayd a question, "To whom do you belong?"—the same question posed by Muḥammad to the houri in Paradise (see Introduction). "To Muḥammad b. ʿAbdallāh," Zayd responded.[12]

1.4 A TEST

Ḥāritha and Kaʿb, the two sons of Sharāḥīl al-Kalbī, now sought out Muḥammad b. ʿAbdallāh al-Hāshimī, who, they were told, might be found in the *masjid* or house of prayer. The Kalbīs entered the *masjid* and introduced themselves to Muḥammad—who, it should be kept in mind, had not yet received his first revelation or emerged as a prophet. They addressed Muḥammad as follows: "O son of ʿAbdallāh, O son of ʿAbd al-Muṭṭalib, O son of Hāshim, O son of the Lord of his tribe, you (pl.) are the people of the Sacred Precinct (*al-ḥaram*) and you are its protectors. In the name of the [Lord of the] House, you free the captives and feed the prisoners. We have come to you in the matter of our son who is in your possession. Trust us (*fa-ʾmun ʿalaynā*) [viz., with our son] and deal kindly with us in the matter of his ransom, for surely we will pay you a large ransom."[13]

In this carefully crafted speech, the Kalbīs honor Muḥammad by acknowledging his noble lineage and his membership in the Hāshimī clan. As guardians of the Sacred Precinct, the Hāshimīs had important duties, including the obligation to "free the captives and feed the prisoners." The language attributed to the two men echoes that of Ps. 102:21 ("to hear the groans of the prisoner, to release those condemned to death") while at the same time anticipating that of Q. 90:13–14 ("the freeing of a slave or the feeding on a day of hunger"). Only after acknowledging Muḥammad's impressive genealogy and high social status do the Kalbīs mention an unnamed "son" who was his slave. Appealing to the virtues of mercy, kindness, and fair play, they implore Muḥammad to trust them (*fa-ʾmun ʿalaynā*), an ironic allusion to Q. 12:11, where Joseph's brothers ask Jacob, "Father, how is it that you do not trust us with Joseph?" (*mā laka lā taʾmunnā ʿalā Yūsuf*). When the Kalbīs offer Muḥammad a large sum of money so that they might ransom Zayd and reunite him with his mother, he feigns ignorance and asks them which of his slaves they have in mind. "Zayd b. Ḥāritha," they reply.

Zayd b. Ḥāritha was the slave who had been purchased by Khadīja for either 400 or 700 *dirham*s and gifted to Muḥammad. Miraculously, Zayd's father and uncle had tracked him down and they wanted to take him back to his tribal homeland. How could anyone criticize Muḥammad for facilitating Zayd's reunification with his birth family? Surely this was the proper course of action; indeed, it was arguably the only ethical and humane thing to do. But Muḥammad had a better idea. He informed the Kalbīs that he would summon Zayd and let the young man make the decision himself of his own free will. If Zayd chose to return home with his father and uncle, he was free to do so, and no ransom would be taken; if, however, he chose to remain a slave in Mecca then, Muḥammad explained, "by God the decision will have been his alone and I will have had no part in it." The Kalbīs, who could not imagine that Zayd would choose to remain a slave, readily agreed to the proposal.[14]

Muḥammad now summoned Zayd and asked him if he recognized the two visitors. "Yes," Zayd said, gesturing with his hand. "That one"—pointing at Ḥāritha—"is my father," he announced, "and that one"—pointing at Kaʿb—"is my paternal uncle." Stung by Zayd's identification of Ḥāritha as his father, Muḥammad exclaimed, "But I am the one whom you have known, and you know [the nature of] my companionship with you" (*raʾayta ṣuḥbatī laka*).[15] Clearly, the relationship between Zayd and Muḥammad was a close one. On the surface, Muḥammad's reference to his "companionship" with Zayd may be nothing more than an allusion to the excellent treatment the slave had received from his master (*ṣāḥib*). As we will learn in the Conclusion, however, *ṣuḥba* or companionship is a highly charged term that played a prominent role in sectarian disputes over the right to succeed Muḥammad as leader of the community.

This was a decisive moment for Zayd, a major turning point in his life. One imagines that his heart was torn between his love for his father and his loyalty to his master. As we read in Q. 33:4, "God has not put two hearts inside any man."[16] In Qurṭubī's version of the episode, Muḥammad asks Zayd, "What kind of a master/companion have I been to you?" (*fa-ayyi ṣāḥib kuntu laka*?), whereupon the slave breaks out in tears and responds, "Why have you asked me this [question]?"[17]

Muḥammad explained to Zayd that the decision was his to make: If he wished, he could return to his homeland with his father and uncle; alternatively, if he wished, he could remain in Mecca with his master, the man who, unbeknownst to Zayd or any other human being, would soon emerge as a prophet and messenger of God. Muḥammad was testing Zayd to determine whether his loyalty to his master was as great as—indeed, greater than—his love for his birth family. This was Zayd's first opportunity to demonstrate that his devotion to Muḥammad was absolute and unconditional. Without a moment's hesitation, he announced, "I would not choose anyone over you." To this he added, "In my mind, you have the status of both father and mother."[18]

The Kalbīs were dumbfounded. "Woe to you, O Zayd," they exclaimed. "Would you choose slavery over freedom and would you choose your master over your father, paternal uncle, and family?" To this question Zayd responded, "Yes, I would. Having seen what I have seen in this man, I would never choose anyone over him."[19]

Just as Muḥammad knew, instinctively, that there was something special about Zayd, so too Zayd knew, instinctively, that there was something special about Muḥammad. By choosing of his own free will to remain with his slave master rather than be reunited with his birth family—thereby inverting the biblical topos of deliverance from slavery to freedom—Zayd demonstrated that his loyalty to Muḥammad was absolute and unconditional, thereby passing the test, the first of several that he would undergo over the course of the next two decades. One wonders how events would have unfolded had Zayd chosen freedom over slavery rather than slavery over freedom.

1.5 ADOPTION

The sources are silent about Muḥammad's reaction to Zayd's decision to choose continued slavery with his master over freedom with his birth family, but he no doubt was pleased. To mark the special bond between the two men, Muḥammad now made a very important decision: He would adopt Zayd as his son. The adoption must have taken place sometime after 605 C.E., the year in which Muḥammad is said to have married Khadīja, and before 610 C.E., the year in which he received the first revelation. At the time of the adoption, Muḥammad would have been between thirty-five and forty years old and Zayd would have been between twenty-five and thirty years old—clearly a grown man.

Adoption had been practiced in the Near East since ancient times. In Arabia, the institution was called *al-tabannī*, literally, to take someone as a son. It was customary to celebrate the event at a special ceremony in which the terms of the new relationship were formally announced in the presence of witnesses. Zayd's adoption by Muḥammad was performed in front of the Kaʿba in the presence of an unspecified number of members of the tribe of Quraysh. Also present were Zayd's father and uncle.[20]

Several versions of the adoption ceremony are preserved in the sources. In one Muḥammad proclaims, "O you who are present, bear witness that Zayd is my son. I will inherit from him and he will inherit from me."[21] In another Muḥammad says, "Bear witness that I am his heir and he is mine."[22] But that was not all. The adoption also entailed a name change. Zayd was no longer Zayd b. Ḥāritha al-Kalbī but rather Zayd b. Muḥammad al-Hāshimī, a name that he would bear with pride for the next fifteen or twenty years.[23] In the eyes of the Meccans, Zayd was now Muḥammad's son (*ibn*), his heir (*wārith*), and a member of the noble clan of Hāshim. The Kalbī slave had come a long way in a short time.

1.6 FATHER AND SON

After witnessing the ceremony and acknowledging their consent to the adoption, Zayd's father Ḥāritha b. Sharāḥīl and his uncle Kaʿb returned to their homeland, empty-handed, albeit satisfied (*ṭābat anfusuhumā*).[24]

The Islamic narratives about Zayd's capture and enslavement, his relations with his birth family, and his eventual adoption by Muḥammad draw on several biblical themes and motifs relating especially to the figures of Joseph and Dammesek Eliezer. We now turn to the relevant biblical models, after which we will analyze the textual encounters.

Biblical Models

Joseph

1.1 CAPTURE AND ENSLAVEMENT

Jacob loved Joseph, a son of his old age, more than his other sons. When Joseph was seventeen years old, his jealous brothers plotted to kill him, but Judah persuaded his other siblings to sell Joseph to Ishmaelite traders for twenty silver coins. The Ishmaelites transported Joseph to Egypt, where he was purchased by Potiphar, chief steward of Pharaoh (Gen. 37). Despite his mistreatment by his brothers and enslavement, "the Lord was with Joseph" (Gen. 39:2), whose apparent misfortune was part of a divine plan.

1.2 A FATHER LAMENTS THE LOSS OF HIS SON

After selling Joseph to Ishmaelite traders, his brothers tricked Jacob into thinking that his son had been killed by a wild beast. Jacob was inconsolable. "Now I will go down mourning to my son in Sheol," he lamented (Gen. 37:35).

1.3 A CHANCE ENCOUNTER WITH MEMBERS OF HIS FAMILY

Joseph's apparent misfortune continued when Potiphar's wife falsely accused him of making a sexual advance. Although Joseph was imprisoned, the Lord was still with him (Gen. 39:21). After demonstrating his skill as a dream interpreter, Joseph was summoned by Pharaoh and interpreted the ruler's dreams. As a reward, Pharaoh put Joseph in charge of his court, second in command only to the king himself. As Joseph had predicted, seven years of plenty were followed by seven years of famine. "So all the world came to Joseph in Egypt to procure rations" (Gen. 41:57). In Canaan, famine compelled Jacob to send ten of his sons to Egypt—the youngest, Benjamin, remained with his father, lest he too meet disaster. In Egypt, the brothers humbled themselves before the vizier, seeking food. They did not recognize Joseph, although he recognized them.

1.4 A TEST

Eager to acquire news about Jacob and Benjamin, Joseph pretended not to know his brothers (Gen. 42:7–8). He interrogated them and accused them of being spies. Keeping his brother Simon as a hostage, Joseph demanded that the brothers travel to Canaan and return with their youngest brother. In Canaan the brothers tried to persuade their father to allow them to transport Benjamin to Egypt. Jacob refused, but when the famine intensified, he had no choice. Upon their arrival in Egypt, the brothers presented themselves to Joseph, who instructed his steward to take them to his house, where he learned that his elderly father was in good health and that the youngest of the brothers was Benjamin. Overwhelmed, Joseph hurried to another room, where he wept (Gen. 43:30). After further machinations, Joseph revealed his true identity to his brothers and asked about the welfare of his father. To ease their distress, Joseph explained that it was God who had sent him to Egypt ahead of them "to insure your survival on earth, and to save your lives in an extraordinary deliverance" (Gen. 45:5).

1.5 ADOPTION

1.5.1 Dammesek Eliezer

As Abram approached the end of his life he remained childless, notwithstanding God's promise to make him the father of a great nation (Gen. 12:2).

God later appeared to the patriarch in a vision and promised that He would protect and reward him (Gen. 15:1). In response to this divine promise, Abram delivered a lament over his childlessness and its consequences: "O Lord Yahweh, to what purpose are your gifts, when I continue childless, and the successor to my house is Dammesek Eliezer?" (Gen. 15:2). Abram continued: "Since you have granted me no offspring, a member of my house will become my heir" (*ben beitî yôresh otî*) (Gen. 15:3). God now corrected Abram, "That one shall not be your heir; none but your own issue shall be your heir" (Gen. 15:4). And He promised Abram that his descendants would be as numerous as the stars in the sky (Gen. 15:5). The member of Abram's house who, the patriarch feared, would be his heir is the man identified in

Genesis 15:2 as Dammesek Eliezer. Some modern scholars have suggested that Abram adopted Dammesek Eliezer as his son, although the point is contested.[25]

1.5.2 Joseph

After demonstrating his skill as a dream interpreter, Joseph advised Pharaoh to "find a man of discernment and wisdom, and set him over the land of Egypt" (Gen. 41:33). Pharaoh appointed Joseph as his vizier. To mark the change in his status, Pharaoh gave Joseph a new name—Zaphenath-paneah or "creator of life"—and he arranged for him to marry Asenath, the daughter of Poti-phera, the priest of On (Gen. 41:45). Indeed, as Joseph would later boast to his brothers, God had made him "a father to Pharaoh, lord of all his household, and ruler over the whole land of Egypt" (Gen. 45:8). Asenath bore Joseph two sons: Menasseh ("God has made me forget completely my hardship and my parental home") and Ephraim ("God has made me fertile in the land of my affliction") (Gen. 41:50–51). Joseph appears to have become an Egyptian.

1.6 FATHER AND SON ARE REUNITED

After revealing his identity to his brothers, Joseph instructed them to return to Canaan so that they might bring Jacob to Egypt, where he would live in the land of Goshen, near Joseph. When Pharaoh learned of Joseph's plan to bring his family to Egypt, he was pleased and offered wagons and provisions (and a change of clothing) for the return trip to Canaan. Upon their arrival in Canaan, the brothers gave Jacob the good news: Joseph was alive. The patriarch was incredulous, but when he heard the entire story, he said, "Enough! . . . My son Joseph is still alive! I must go and see him before I die" (Gen. 45:17). Jacob and his household—seventy persons—traveled to Egypt, where they were met by Joseph at Goshen. Joseph embraced his father and wept (Gen. 46:29). "Now I can die," Jacob said to Joseph, "having seen for myself that you are still alive" (Gen. 46:30).

Textual Encounters

Joseph

The names Yosef (Heb.) and Zayd (Ar.) are both derived from a root that signifies *to add* or *to increase*. The onomastic equivalence is only one of numerous parallels between these two figures. It is perhaps no coincidence that in the Hebrew Bible Joseph is described as *yefeh to'ar* or good-looking (Gen. 39:6), while in Islamic sources Zayd is described as *ghulām yafʿa* or a youth who has attained physical maturity (Heb. *yafeh* and Ar. *yafʿa* are homonyms).[26] Each man was born in Syria-Palestine, separated from his birth family, and sold into slavery in a foreign land. In each case, the youth was captured while in the care of someone other than his father. Whereas the biblical narrative portrays Joseph as a young man whose pride triggered the jealously of his brothers, the Islamic narrative portrays Zayd as an innocent victim of circumstance. Each youth was captured by Arab tribesmen and taken to a foreign land where he entered the house of a powerful master: Joseph was acquired by Potiphar and subsequently entered the service of Pharaoh; Zayd was acquired by Khadīja and subsequently entered the household of Muḥammad. Each man developed a special filial bond with his master: Joseph proudly claimed that God had made him a father to Pharaoh (Gen. 45:8); Zayd regarded Muḥammad as both his father and mother.

The father of each man was inconsolable following the disappearance and apparent death of his son. Jacob's lament in Genesis 37:35 ("No, I will go down mourning to my son in Sheol") is echoed by Ḥāritha's ode to Zayd ("I weep for Zayd not knowing what has become of him / Is he alive, is there hope, or has death overcome him?"). In both cases, the missing person and one or more of his relatives are reunited by an act of divine providence. Famine compelled Jacob to send his sons to Egypt, where Joseph was eager to acquire news of his father and younger brother (Gen. 42). Pilgrimage brought Kalbī tribesmen to Mecca (alternatively, business brought Zayd's uncle to the town). But whereas Joseph was eager to acquire news about his father and youngest brother, Zayd let it be known that he did *not* want to be reunited with his family and advised the Kalbīs not to grieve for him. In both cases, there is a recognition scene: In the biblical narrative, Joseph immediately recognizes his brothers but pretends not to know them, while his brothers do not at first recognize him (Gen. 42:7–8). In Qurṭubī's version of the Islamic narrative, Kaʿb b. Sharāḥīl recognizes Zayd although Zayd does not at first recognize his uncle. In each instance, the recognition scene is preceded by an interrogation: In the biblical narrative Joseph interrogates his brothers; in the Islamic narrative, Kaʿb interrogates his nephew. In both cases, the decision about whether or not to reunite is the result of a test: In the biblical narrative, it is Joseph who tests his brothers; in the Islamic narrative, it is Muḥammad who tests Zayd. Both Joseph and Zayd shed tears. Joseph cries four times, twice in private and twice in public.[27] By contrast, Zayd does not shed any tears when he is reunited with either his uncle or his father, but he does cry in public after hurting his master's feelings by identifying Ḥāritha b. Sharāḥīl as his father.

Joseph's status as vizier made it possible for him to bring his entire family to Egypt, where he made peace with his brothers and was reunited with his father. Pharaoh was happy for Joseph and the reunification of the family (Gen. 45–46). Thus, Joseph was able to maintain his relationship with both Pharaoh and his birth family. Zayd was unable to achieve this balance: If he chose to be reunited with his family and to return to Syria, he would have to abandon his master; if he chose to remain with his master in Mecca, he would have to abandon his birth family. Unlike Pharaoh, who was pleased by the arrival of Joseph's family (Gen. 45:16–20), Muḥammad was threatened by the arrival of Ḥāritha and his brother in Mecca. In the biblical narrative Joseph's family joins him in Egypt, temporarily abandoning their homeland. In the Islamic narrative, Zayd's family returns to their homeland empty-handed but satisfied. Presumably, they never saw Zayd again.

Just as "the Lord was with Joseph" (Gen. 39:2 and 21), Zayd was favored by both God and His prophet (Q. 33:37). Both men were instruments of divine will. We know that God sent Joseph to Egypt to ensure the survival of the Israelites and to save their lives in "an extraordinary deliverance" (Gen. 45:5). But why did God send Zayd to Arabia? The answer to this question will emerge as we follow the course of Zayd's life (and death).

Dammesek Eliezer

In section 1.5 ("Adoption"), the figure of Zayd resembles that of the biblical Dammesek Eliezer. Each was born in Syria, enslaved, and entered the household of a man who would soon become the founder of a new religion.

Each became his master's trusted servant. Just as Dammesek Eliezer was for a time Abram's heir, Zayd was—for more than fifteen years—Muḥammad's heir. Dammesek Eliezer's status as Abram's heir was eliminated first by the birth of Ishmael and then by the birth of Isaac; the competition between the two natural sons was ended by Abram's expulsion of Ishmael and his decision not to sacrifice Isaac. Zayd's status as Muḥammad's heir was eliminated under circumstances that will be treated in Chapter 2.

Chapter 2

Zaynab

We gave her to you in marriage.—Q. 33:37

Islamic Narratives

INTRODUCTION: THE BELOVED OF THE MESSENGER OF GOD AND HIS SON

Muḥammad is said to have received his first revelation in 610 C.E., shortly after adopting Zayd. The identity of the first person to become a believer is a matter of dispute. It stands to reason that the first converts would have been his wife, children, and close relatives. As ʿAlī b. Abī Ṭālib would later recall, "When Muḥammad called for faith in God and for proclamation of His unity we, the People of his House (*ahl al-bayt*), were the first to have faith in him and to hold true what he brought."[1] In the *Sīra*, it will be remembered, the first four persons to become believers are identified as the Prophet's wife Khadīja, his cousin ʿAlī b. Abī Ṭālib, "Zayd the *mawlā* of the Messenger of God," and Abū Bakr—in that order.[2] It is reported on the authority of al-Zuhrī, however, that Zayd was the first person to become a Muslim: "We are not aware of anyone who became a Muslim before Zayd b. Ḥāritha [*sic*]."[3]

In Islamic sources, Zayd is invariably identified as either "the *mawlā* of the Messenger of God" or as "Zayd b. Ḥāritha al-Kalbī." His identification as "the son of Ḥāritha" merits attention. Muḥammad, it will be recalled, had first manumitted Zayd and then adopted him as his son. As a consequence of the adoption, Zayd b. Ḥāritha al-Kalbī became Zayd b. Muḥammad al-Hāshimī. Furthermore, the adoption ceremony took place *before* Muḥammad received his first revelation and emerged as a prophet. Thus, at the moment on which Zayd became a believer he was Muḥammad's son and heir—a powerful combination. One wonders why neither Ibn Isḥāq nor al-Zuhrī identifies him as "Zayd b. Muḥammad." We will return to this issue in the Conclusion. Be that as it may, as the first adult male to embrace Islam, Zayd b. Muḥammad would have been a person of standing within the community of believers.[4]

The special relationship between Muḥammad and Zayd is reflected in Zayd's nickname: He was known as "The Beloved Zayd" (Zayd al-Ḥibb) or as "The Beloved of the Messenger of God" (Ḥibb Rasūl Allāh),[5] a term with strong theological overtones.[6] On several occasions, Muḥammad is said to have singled out Zayd as "the person most loved by me" (*aḥabbu 'l-nās ilayya*) or as "one of the persons most loved by me" (*min aḥabbi 'l-nās ilayya*).[7] In addition, it is reported on the authority of ʿAlī b. Abī Ṭālib that the Prophet said to Zayd, "You are our brother and our *mawlā*."[8] Similarly, it is reported on the authority of Usāma b. Zayd that the Prophet said to his father, "You are my *mawlā*, part of me, and the person most beloved to me."[9]

At the time of his adoption, Zayd, who would have been between twenty-five and thirty years old, had not yet married. It was not long before Muḥammad identified a believing woman who would be a suitable wife for his son. Muḥammad was an orphan: His father ʿAbdallāh is said to have died shortly before he was born and his mother Āmina bt. Wahb is said to have died when he was approximately six years old. One of Muḥammad's caretakers as a child was a black Ethiopian slave by the name of Baraka ("Blessed") who was approximately ten years older than him. After Āmina died, Muḥammad inherited Baraka.[10] It is said that he used to refer to Baraka as "the remainder of my family" and as his "mother." Muḥammad later manumitted Baraka and she became his client. She married and gave birth to a son named Ayman—hence her matronymic, Umm Ayman ("Lucky" or "Auspicious").[11] Subsequently, her husband either died or divorced her.

What better partner could there be for Muḥammad's adopted son than the Prophet's surrogate mother? When Muḥammad informed his son that he had chosen Umm Ayman as his bride, however, Zayd was not enthusiastic. Perhaps he was reluctant to marry a dark-skinned woman. Or perhaps he was concerned about Umm Ayman's age and potential fertility. After all, she would have been between forty and forty-five years old at the time. As an incentive, the Prophet is reported to have said, "Whoever wants to experience the pleasure of marrying one of the women of Paradise, let him marry Umm Ayman."[12] Just as Zayd had been assured entry to Paradise—recall the attractive woman with dark red lips who was waiting for him there—so too Umm Ayman had been guaranteed entry to Paradise. A narrative arch had been sealed.

Whatever fears Zayd may have had about Umm Ayman's fertility were put to rest when she gave birth to a son circa 613 C.E. The infant, who was named Usāma, was Zayd's son and the Prophet's grandson.[13] He was arguably the first child born into the new community of believers (ʿĀʾisha bt. Abī Bakr is said to have been born in 614).

2.1 A MARRIAGE PROPOSAL

All three members of Zayd's immediate family had a special relationship with Muḥammad: Zayd was the Prophet's adopted son and heir, Umm Ayman was his surrogate mother, and Usāma was a beloved grandson (see Chapter 4). It should come as no surprise that Zayd, Umm Ayman, and Usāma all participated in the hijra to Medina, where they lived in close proximity to the Prophet.

Shortly after arriving in Medina in 1 A.H., Zayd told his father that he wanted to take a second wife. "Who is the woman that would you like to marry?" Muḥammad asked. "Zaynab bt. Jaḥsh," Zayd replied.[14] Note well: Zaynab bt. Jaḥsh is the woman who is referred to—albeit without mention of her name—in Q. 33:37 (see Introduction). Zaynab was the daughter of Jaḥsh (literally "young ass") b. Riʾāb al-Asadī and of Umayma bt. ʿAbd al-Muṭṭalib. Thus, Zaynab and Muḥammad were paternal cross-cousins: Both were grandchildren of ʿAbd al-Muṭṭalib, she through her mother Umayma and he through his father ʿAbdallāh. In addition to her noble lineage, Zaynab is said to have been a beautiful woman. She had two brothers, ʿUbaydallāh and ʿAbdallāh, both of whom are said to have participated in the hijra to Abyssinia circa 615. ʿUbaydallāh reportedly died in Abyssinia after converting to Christianity. ʿAbdallāh is said to have returned to Mecca sometime before 622 C.E.—a key narrative detail—and, together with his sister, participated in the hijra to Medina.

Muḥammad rejected Zayd's request for permission to marry Zaynab, while at the same time assuring his son that he would secure a beautiful wife for him. It would be inappropriate, he explained, for Zayd to marry this noble Qurashī woman. (Note the literary inversion: Whereas in Mecca Zayd had been reluctant to marry Umm Ayman, in Medina Muḥammad was reluctant to give Zayd permission to marry Zaynab.) Zayd stood his ground. He pressed his father to approach Zaynab, suggesting that he say to her, "Zayd is the most noble of men in my eyes." To this Zayd added, "She is indeed a beautiful woman, and I fear that she will reject any proposal that comes from me, although I am determined to marry her." Muḥammad likewise stood his ground. Undeterred, Zayd approached ʿAlī b. Abī Ṭālib, the Prophet's cousin who recently had married his daughter Fāṭima, and asked him to intercede with the Prophet on his behalf. "Surely," Zayd said, "he will not turn you down." The two men approached Muḥammad, who now relented and agreed to pursue the matter, despite his initial misgivings.[15]

The Prophet sent ʿAlī—his cousin and son-in-law and a trusted agent—to convey the marriage proposal to the House of Jaḥsh. When ʿAlī arrived, however, Jaḥsh was nowhere to be seen. One suspects that he was dead.[16] Technically, Zaynab was an orphan, and her brother ʿAbdallāh (who, conveniently, had recently returned from Abyssinia) took her father's place as her marriage guardian.[17] Just as Zayd had been reluctant to marry Umm Ayman, so too Zaynab was now reluctant to marry Zayd. She protested, "I don't want Zayd for myself, for I am the most perfect woman of Quraysh." Similarly, her brother ʿAbdallāh refused to give his sister in marriage to a man who only recently had been a slave.[18] At this crucial juncture, God intervened in history to resolve the impasse by sending down the revelation that would become v. 36 of *Sūrat al-Aḥzāb*: "When God and His messenger have decided a matter, it is not for any believing man or woman to have any choice in the affair." That is to say, God and His prophet had chosen Zayd for Zaynab and had ordered ʿAbdallāh to give his sister in marriage to the Beloved of the Messenger of God. As believers, ʿAbdallāh and Zaynab had no choice but to obey God and His prophet by consenting to the marriage.[19] As a marriage gift, Muḥammad sent the family ten *dinars*, sixty *dirhams*, a cloth headcovering, a nightgown, a housedress, a wrapper, fifty liters of food, and ten liters of dates.[20]

2.2 AN EXTRAORDINARY ENCOUNTER

In compliance with a divine command—albeit *not* of her own free will—Zaynab bt. Jaḥsh was married to Zayd b. Muḥammad, the Beloved of the Messenger of God, the Prophet's son and heir. It may come as no surprise that the marriage was not a success. It was not long before Zayd began to complain to his father about flaws in his wife's character and behavior. As Zayd's father and Zaynab's father-in-law, it was Muḥammad's responsibility to promote domestic harmony. In addition, the Prophet had a strong interest in the success of the marriage, for any son born to the couple would have been his grandson and potential heir. Confident that he could correct Zaynab's behavior, Muḥammad paid a visit to the couple at their home. When he arrived, Zayd was away on an unspecified task and only Zaynab was there. The stage was set for an extraordinary encounter between Muḥammad and Zaynab, several versions of which are preserved in Islamic sources.

According to one version, just as the Prophet began to speak with his daughter-in-law, God ordained that he be smitten by her beauty, grace, and form. Even after Muḥammad had returned home, God caused these feelings to linger in his heart. Sometime later, when Muḥammad asked Zayd about his relationship with his wife, his son repeated his complaint about Zaynab's behavior and reiterated his desire to divorce her. Although the Prophet was in love with Zaynab, he kept his feelings a secret, instructing Zayd to "keep your wife to yourself and fear God."[21]

In another version of the encounter, Muḥammad's reaction to Zaynab is formulated in the language of human passion and sexual desire. Sometime after the marriage between Zayd and Zaynab, Muḥammad went to visit his son, who was not at home. But Zaynab was there. Somehow—the storyteller leaves the details to the imagination of his audience—the Prophet caught a glimpse of Zaynab as she was in the act of rising to her feet (*fa-abṣara Zaynab qāʾimat^an^*). "She was beautiful and white of skin, one of the most perfect women of Quraysh. The Prophet—may God bless him and grant him peace—immediately experienced sexual desire for her (*hawiyahā*), and he exclaimed, 'Praise be to God who has the power to transform a man's heart [in an instant].' "[22]

In a third version, which makes no reference to poor relations between husband and wife, the extraordinary encounter is a product of serendipity. Again the incident is said to have taken place shortly after the Prophet had arranged for Zaynab to marry Zayd. One day, the Messenger of God went out looking for Zayd. He arrived at the couple's residence and stood at the entrance, which was covered with a curtain made of animal hair—surely a sexual symbol. Suddenly, the wind lifted the curtain, exposing Zaynab, in her chamber, uncovered. "Immediately, the Prophet's heart was filled with love for her."[23] A variant of this narrative makes God responsible for the act of nature: "God sent a wind that lifted up the curtain to reveal Zaynab wearing a single apron in her quarters. When the Prophet saw Zaynab, she sank into his heart." As Muḥammad retreated, dumbfounded, he is again said to have muttered, "Praise be to God who has the power to transform a man's heart [in an instant]."[24]

2.3 A FAILED MARRIAGE

Later that same day, after Zayd had returned home, Zaynab told her husband about the extraordinary encounter with her father-in-law. When she was done, she asked him if he wanted to hear the story again, and again, and again. Relations between the couple went from bad to worse. The two ceased having sexual relations—although Zaynab was careful to specify that she did not refuse to make herself available to her husband for sexual intercourse. Rather, she explained, Zayd had lost interest in her and, she suggested, suffered from a sexual dysfunction.[25]

In a curious reversal, the man who had begged his father for permission to marry the beautiful Zaynab now pleaded with him for permission to divorce his haughty, condescending, and sharp-tongued wife. Again, Muḥammad kept his feelings a secret and told his son, "Keep your wife to yourself and fear God."[26]

One wonders about Muḥammad's behavior. The sources report that he was in love with Zaynab, and that Zayd wanted to divorce his wife. If Zayd were to divorce Zaynab, surely Muḥammad could marry her. Apparently not, for the noble and beautiful Qurashī woman was not only the Prophet's paternal cross-cousin but also his daughter-in-law. Among the Israelites, and no doubt throughout the Near East, sexual relations between a man and his daughter-in-law are prohibited: "Do not uncover the nakedness of your daughter-in-law: she is your son's wife" (Lev. 18:15). Anyone who committed one of these abhorrent acts was to be cut off from his people (Lev. 18:29). Apparently, Muḥammad and the community of believers regarded themselves as bound by this biblical rule—or its Arabian equivalent. If so, the Prophet now found himself standing on the edge of a steep precipice: If he listened to his heart, he would be committing a sin. He must have suspected that if he did have sexual relations with Zaynab, even within the framework of a valid marriage, he would expose himself to public ridicule not only from fellow believers, but also from the Jews and Hypocrites of Medina.

2.4 DIVINE INTERVENTION

It was precisely at this moment that God again intervened in history to make sure that this prophet would not commit the same sin—illicit sexual relations—that is attributed to earlier prophets in the Hebrew Bible and New Testament. According to II Samuel 11, King David—who is identified as a prophet in the Qurʾān—fell in love with Bathsheba and, acting in secret, engaged in sexual relations with the woman, despite her being married to one of the king's soldiers, Uriah the Hittite. Similarly, according to Matthew 1:18, Mary, the mother of Jesus—the latter is also identified as a prophet in the Qurʾān—appears to have engaged in illicit sexual relations with an unidentified third party prior to the consummation of her marriage with Joseph. Now, some six hundred years later, history—or its sacred counterpart—was about to repeat itself. Another prophet, Muḥammad, was poised to commit a sin. Surely, this is the unstated anxiety to which allusion is made in Q. 33:37 (see Introduction).

One wonders how the events of early Islamic history would have unfolded had God chosen not to intervene at this particular moment in time. Be that as it may, God removed Muḥammad's anxiety by introducing a distinction between two types of daughter-in-law: the wife of a biological son and the wife of an adopted son. It had been a sin in the past, and it remained a sin in the present, to have sexual relations with the wife of one's biological son (see Q. 4:23: "Forbidden to you are . . . the licit wives of your natural sons"). Henceforth, however, it would not be a sin for a man to have sexual relations with the former wife of his adopted son, albeit on the condition that the adopted son no longer had any sexual desire for the woman in question, as we know to have been the case with Zayd. It was only after the Divinity had introduced this critical legal distinction in the revelation that would become v. 37 of *Sūrat al-Aḥzāb* that He was able to proclaim: "We gave her to you in marriage." That is to say, God ("We") gave Zaynab ("her") to Muḥammad ("you") in marriage. Zaynab herself is reported to have said that her marriage to Muḥammad was unique in three respects: First, both she and Muḥammad were descendants of ʿAbd al-Muṭṭalib; second, God served as Zaynab's marriage guardian; and, third, the angel Gabriel served as God's agent.[27] It may come as no surprise that the haughty and boastful Zaynab would later flaunt the circumstances of her marriage to Muḥammad in the faces of the Prophet's other wives: "You were given in marriage to the

Prophet by men, but I was given in marriage to the Prophet by God—may He be magnified and exalted."[28]

The marriage between Muḥammad and Zaynab bt. Jaḥsh was made possible by a distinction introduced by the Divinity between wives of natural sons and wives of adopted sons. Almost immediately, however, this distinction would become the proverbial distinction without a difference.[29]

2.5 THE REPUDIATION OF ZAYD AND THE ABOLITION OF ADOPTION

The revelation of Q. 33:37 was followed by a momentous act: Muḥammad repudiated Zayd as his son and disinherited him. "I am not your father," the Prophet said, uttering a linguistic formula that parents who wanted to dissolve an adoptive relationship had been using for two thousand years. To this he might have added, "You are no longer my son or my heir."[30]

In fact, Zayd had done nothing that would have justified his repudiation. Again, he was being tested. Was the man who some twenty years earlier had chosen slavery with his master over freedom with his family willing to give up his name, Zayd b. Muḥammad, and his status as Muḥammad's sole heir, so that the Prophet might marry his former wife, the beautiful Zaynab bt. Jaḥsh? Without a moment's hesitation, Zayd is reported to have said, "O Messenger of God, I am Zayd b. Ḥāritha and my genealogy is well-known."[31] To this declaration the Qurʾān commentator Muqātil b. Sulaymān (d. 150/767) adds, "Indeed, he was Zayd b. Ḥāritha b. Qurra b. Sharāḥīl al-Kalbī, one of the Banū ʿAbd Wadd."[32] The specification of his ancestors and tribe established that there were no blood ties between Zayd and Muḥammad.

Muḥammad's repudiation of Zayd as his son was followed by an equally momentous legal change: the abolition of the institution of adoption. It must have been shortly after Zayd's repudiation that God delivered a cluster of revelations that would become vv. 4–6 of *Sūrat al-Aḥzāb*. These three verses read as follows:

> 4 God has not put two hearts inside any man, nor has He made your wives whom you declare to be as your mothers' backs your [real] mothers; nor has He made your adopted sons your [real] sons. That is what you say with your mouths, but God speaks the truth and guides to the [right] way.
>
> 5 Call them after their fathers. That is fairer with God.

> If you do not know their fathers, they are your brothers in religion and your wards (*mawālīkum*). There is no sin for you in any mistakes you have made but there is in what your hearts have intended. God is Forgiving and Compassionate.
>
> 6 The prophet is closer to the believers than they are themselves, and his wives are their mothers; but blood relations are nearer to one another in God's decree than the believers and the emigrants, though you should act in a way recognized as proper towards your friends. That is written in the decree.

Our immediate concern here is with vv. 4–5, which signal the abolition of adoption (we will attend to the opening clause of v. 6 in section 2.7 below). Verse 4 opens with the pronouncement that "God has not put two hearts inside any man"—the image points to the issue of dual loyalty. A man cannot have two fathers, one biological, the other adoptive, the Qurʾān suggests. God created only one heart in the breast of a man. Later in the verse we read: "nor has He made your adopted sons your [real] sons." This clause is universally understood by Muslim scholars as signaling the abolition of adoption. Lest there be any doubt about the matter, the Prophet himself is reported to have said, "There is no adoption in Islam: the custom of the Age of Ignorance (*jāhiliyya*) has been superseded."[33] On the strength of this *sunna*ic pronouncement and vv. 4–5 of *Sūrat al-Aḥzāb*, the institution of adoption was abolished.

Verse 5 addresses naming practices. It opens with: "Call them after their fathers. That is fairer with God." That is to say, children should be identified as the sons (or daughters) of their biological fathers. The verse concludes with a warning to believers: "There is no sin for you in any mistakes you have made but there is in what your hearts have intended. God is forgiving and Compassionate." This warning serves as an instruction delivered by the Divinity to the community of believers. Following the abolition of adoption circa 5 A.H., it was a sin for one believer to refer to another as the son (or daughter) of anyone other than his (or her) biological father. Although Zayd had been known as "the son of Muḥammad" for more than fifteen years, henceforth, any believer who referred to Zayd as "the son of Muḥammad" would be committing a sin. This is why, in Q. 33:37, the doubly favored man is identified only as *Zayd*, despite the fact that at the moment this verse is said to have been revealed he was known as *Zayd b. Muḥammad*. And this is why, in the *Sīra*—indeed, in virtually every Islamic source ever written—the "Zayd" of Q. 33:37 is identified as either the *mawlā* of the Messenger of God or as Zayd b. Ḥāritha al-Kalbī—but never as Zayd b. Muḥammad. *Nomen est omen.*

These two verses suggest that the institution of adoption had been abolished and that Zayd was no longer "the son of Muḥammad" but rather, once again, "the son of Ḥāritha." The question arises: If Zayd was no longer Muḥammad's son, what was his relationship with the man who for the past fifteen or twenty years had been his father? The answer to this question is suggested by the third sentence in v. 5: Members of the community who are fatherless "are your brothers in religion and your *mawālī*." The word *mawālī* is the plural form of *mawlā*, which, as we have seen in the Introduction, signifies "ally," "friend," "ward," or "protégé." As the Prophet's *mawlā*, Zayd was Muḥammad's ward or protégé. And this is how he has been remembered by posterity: Zayd b. Ḥāritha, the *mawlā* of the Messenger of God.

2.6 A DISTASTEFUL MISSION

Shortly after Zayd had divorced Zaynab, Muḥammad instructed him to inform his former wife that he, that is to say, the Prophet, was now going to marry her. Why Zayd, of all people? "By my soul," Muḥammad confided to Zayd, "there is no one whom I regard as more trustworthy than you."[34] Zayd may no longer have been Muḥammad's son and heir but he was still his trusted servant.

Zayd was understandably reluctant to carry out this assignment. As a believer, however, he had no choice in the matter (just as, previously, Zaynab, as a believer, had no choice but to marry Zayd). Zayd now made his way to Zaynab's apartment, where, at the time of his arrival, she was kneading dough to make bread. This was another decisive moment for Zayd. The very sight of Zaynab caused him great emotional distress and he could not bear to look at the woman. He turned his back on his former wife and began to walk away from her. Would Zayd disobey a direct order from the Prophet? As he was retreating, Zayd looked backward and managed to utter the following words, "O Zaynab, the Messenger of God has sent me to ask for your hand in marriage on his behalf." To this, Zaynab responded, "I do not make any decision before consulting with my Lord." The narrator continues: "Zaynab stood up and walked to her place of prayer. And the Qurʾān was revealed"—without identifying the verse that was revealed on this occasion. "Then the Messenger of God came and entered without [asking for] permission."[35]

Again Zayd was being tested. The purpose of this test was to measure his patience, submissiveness, and obedience.[36] Again Zayd passed the test. For this he was surely rewarded.

2.7 ZAYD AND ʿALĪ

In his new capacity as the *mawlā* of the Messenger of God, Zayd continued to enjoy Muḥammad's confidence. In the year 6 A.H. alone, for example, the Prophet is said to have appointed Zayd as the commander of six military expeditions.

The close relationship between Muḥammad and Zayd appears to have antagonized ʿAlī b. Abī Ṭālib. On one occasion, it is reported, angry words were exchanged between Zayd and ʿAlī. Although the date of the exchange is not specified, it must have taken place shortly after Zayd had become the Prophet's *mawlā* in 5 A.H. but before he died in either 7 or 8 A.H. (see Chapter 3). Apparently, the Prophet's cousin and son-in-law took offense at an unidentified statement made to him by Zayd. In response to this statement, ʿAlī retorted, "Is that how you speak to your master (*a-taqūl hādhā li-mawlāka*)?" (The word *mawlā* here is used in its technical, legal sense of "master" or "client"; as noted in the Introduction, it can refer to either side of this relationship). To this Zayd replied, "You are not my master (*lasta mawlāya*)! Rather, my master is the Messenger of God." The dispute between the two men was brought to the attention of the Prophet, who sought to resolve it by making the following statement: "Of whomever I am the master, ʿAlī is the master (*man kuntu mawlāhu fa-ʿAlī mawlāhu*)." One might ask: Of whom was the Prophet the master? Surely, the answer to this question is Zayd the *mawlā* of the Messenger of God. If so, then this report would appear to serve the interests of the ʿAlids against supporters of Zayd. As one might expect, the report was recorded by the Shiʿi scholar al-Sharīf al-Murtaḍā (d. 460/1067–8); two centuries earlier, it also was recorded by the Muʿtazilī scholar al-Iskāfī (d. ca. 220/835).[37]

It sometimes happens that a statement attributed to Muḥammad may "migrate" from one time, place, and context to another time, place, and context—with a concomitant change of meaning. Such was the case with "*man kuntu mawlāhu fa-ʿAlī mawlāhu*." In most Shiʿi sources, this statement is said to have been made in the year 10 A.H., as the Prophet was returning from Mecca to Medina after performing the Farewell Pilgrimage. Approximately halfway between these two towns, there is a pond or pool (*ghadīr*) surrounded by bushes or trees in an area known as Khumm. The Prophet and his Companions are said to have reached this spot on 18 Dhū al-Ḥijja. Taking ʿAlī by the hand—a key gesture—Muḥammad asked his followers if he was not "closer to the believers than they are themselves" (*awlā bi'l-muʾminīn min anfusihim*). This utterance, it will be noted, draws directly on the opening clause of Q. 33:6 (see above). When the throng gathered around him concurred, Muḥammad announced: "Of whomever I am the master, ʿAlī is the master." In this context, the purpose of the Prophet's statement was not to resolve a dispute between Zayd and ʿAlī but rather to establish that there was no one within the community of believers who was closer to Muḥammad than ʿAlī was. According to Shiʿis, the Prophet's statement, uttered in the presence of as many as 1,300 witnesses, established his desire or intent that ʿAlī succeed him as leader of the community.[38] Thus was a statement that began as polemic against Zayd transformed into polemic in favor of ʿAlī.

The Islamic narratives relating to Zayd's marital career—the circumstances of his marriage to Zaynab, the extraordinary encounter between his wife and his father, his repudiation by his father, and Muḥammad's selection of Zayd to inform his former wife of her upcoming marriage to the Prophet—draw on biblical themes and motifs associated with Dammesek Eliezer, Ishmael, Isaac, and Uriah the Hittite. Let us first examine the relevant biblical models and then analyze the textual encounters.

Biblical Models

2.1 A MARRIAGE PROPOSAL

At the end of his life, Abraham made arrangements for the marriage of his son Isaac. He ordered his senior servant—perhaps the Dammesek Eliezer of Genesis 15 (see Chapter 1)—to swear a solemn oath to secure a wife for Isaac from among the women of Mesopotamia. Under no circumstance was Isaac to return to the patriarch's homeland, even if the woman chosen for Isaac by the servant refused to follow him to Canaan. The servant swore the oath and then traveled to Aram Naharaim, heading for the town in which Abraham's brother Nahor resided. Upon arrival the servant made his way to a spring, where he prayed to God that the first woman who offered water to him and to his camels would be the woman chosen by God for Isaac. No sooner had he finished praying than he was approached by Rebecca, the daughter of Bethuel (lit. "house of God") the son of Milcah (who was the wife of Abraham's brother Nahor). Thus, Rebecca was the great-granddaughter and Isaac was the grandson of Abraham's father, Terah. Rebecca was "very beautiful" and "a virgin whom no man had known" (Gen. 24:16). The young woman offered water to the senior servant and to his camels and offered him home hospitality. By a stroke of good fortune—or perhaps it was divine providence—the servant had found his way to the house of his master Abraham's relatives.

Rebecca brought the news of the Canaanite emissary to the house of her mother; her father Bethuel was nowhere to be seen. When her brother Laban heard the story, he rushed to the spring and reiterated his sister's offer of hospitality. Upon arriving at the house, the servant explained the purpose of his mission and specified the details of the oath he had sworn to his master. In the absence of Bethuel, Rebecca's brother Laban served as her marriage guardian. Laban welcomed the marriage proposal. Indeed, he acknowledged, "the matter was decreed by the Lord" (Gen. 24:50). This was a marriage made in heaven. As a marriage gift, Abraham's trusted servant gave Rebecca silver, gold, and garments, and he gave her brother and mother unspecified presents. The next morning, Laban asked for a delay of ten days before the departure of his sister, but the servant was eager to return to his master. The family put the question to Rebecca. "Will you go with this man?" they asked. "I will," she responded (Gen. 24:58). Thus did Rebecca choose—of her own free will—to leave her homeland and her family and migrate to the land of Canaan, where she would marry Isaac (Gen. 24:61).

2.2 AN EXTRAORDINARY ENCOUNTER

2.2.1 David, Bathsheba, and Uriah the Hittite (II Samuel 11–12)

Late one afternoon, as King David was walking on the roof of the royal palace, he caught a glimpse of a beautiful woman as she was bathing (*va-yar' ishâ roḥetset*). Inquiries were made, and the woman was identified as Bathsheba, daughter of Eliam and wife of Uriah the Hittite, a foreigner who was one of the king's soldiers. Disregarding the woman's marital status, and acting in secret, the king instructed his agents to bring the woman to the royal palace, where he sinned by engaging in sexual relations with her. Bathsheba—who had completed a menstrual cycle immediately prior to the sexual encounter—became pregnant. The birth of a child would expose the king's sin.

Fearing public condemnation, David summoned Uriah from the battlefront and ordered the soldier to go home so that he might sleep with his wife, thereby concealing his sin. Uriah refused. In an act of cunning desperation, David ordered Uriah to carry a sealed letter from the king to his general Joab. In the letter, David instructed Joab "to place Uriah in the front line of battle, where the fighting is fiercest" (II Sam. 11:15). In the ensuing battle, Uriah was killed outside the walls of Rabbat Ammon. Bathsheba was now a widow. After she had completed the period of mourning for her husband, David married her. Several months later, she gave birth to a son.

"The Lord was displeased with what David had done" (II Sam. 12:1) and He sent the prophet Nathan to rebuke the king for his sin. Eventually, David repented, whereupon his sins were forgiven, although he did not go unpunished. God declared that he would "make a calamity rise against you from within your house" (II Sam. 12:11). In addition, Nathan informed the king that Bathsheba's child would die in infancy (II Sam. 12:14). This prophecy was fulfilled.

Subsequently, Bathsheba bore David a second son to whom she gave the name of Solomon. This son was loved by the Lord (*ve-yahweh ahevô*), who let it be known through the prophet Nathan that the child's true name was Yedidiah or "Friend of God" (II Sam. 12:24–25). Bathsheba played an instrumental role in securing the throne for Solomon, who succeeded his father as King of Israel, ensuring the continuation of the Davidic line (I Kings 1:11–31).

2.2.2 Abraham, Ishmael, and the Latter's Wives

The rabbis taught that the expulsion of Hagar and Ishmael in Genesis 21 was the ninth of ten trials experienced by Abraham during his lifetime. One finds a midrashic elaboration of the biblical narrative in *Pirkei de Rabbi Eliezer* (PRE) 30. The rabbis asked: "Did Abraham still love Ishmael even after sending him into the wilderness?" In the narrative response to this question, Abraham has an encounter with first one and then a second daughter-in-law. The story is as follows:

Three years after expelling Ishmael, Abraham went to see his son, but only after swearing to Sarah that when he reached Ishmael's dwelling, he would not dismount from his camel.[39] Upon Abraham's arrival, Ishmael and Hagar were off in the desert gathering fruit. Thus, the aged patriarch was greeted by Ishmael's wife, presumably the Egyptian woman who, according to the biblical narrative, had been chosen for Ishmael by Hagar (Gen. 21:21). When the woman refused Abraham's request for bread and water, the patriarch instructed her to inform her husband that an old man from the land of Canaan had come to visit him and that the man had recommended that he replace the doorsill of his house. This was a coded message that signified: divorce your wife. When Ishmael returned, his wife conveyed the message to him, whereupon he divorced her. Hagar now secured a new wife for her son, a woman named Fatimah who was related to Hagar's father.

Three years later, Abraham once again asked Sarah for permission to visit Ishmael. Again Sarah made her husband swear an oath that he would not dismount his camel. Again Ishmael and Hagar were off in the desert (on this occasion they were tending to camels) when Abraham arrived at his son's house. Again the patriarch found only Ishmael's new wife, his daughter-in-law, Fatimah. Abraham asked the woman for bread and water, and she brought it out to him. When Ishmael returned, his wife conveyed another coded message. Ishmael kept this wife. Thus did the son who had been expelled learn that his father still loved him and that his house was blessed.[40]

2.3. A FAILED MARRIAGE

2.4. DIVINE INTERVENTION

No biblical models.

2.5 REPUDIATION

In Genesis 21:10, Sarah instructs Abraham to "cast out that slave-woman and her son, for the son of that slave shall not share in the inheritance with my son Isaac."

2.6 A DISTASTEFUL MISSION

Whereas in Genesis 24 Abram's senior servant is completely devoted to his master, in later midrashic sources, where the servant is identified as Eliezer, his relationship to his master is more complex. According to *Genesis Rabbah* 59:9, Eliezer had a daughter who might have become Isaac's wife in the event that her father's mission to Mesopotamia failed. When Abram learned of Eliezer's hope that his daughter would marry Isaac, he cursed his servant, who nevertheless carried out his mission, placing the interests of his master over his own interests and those of his daughter. According to PRE 16, Abraham rewarded his servant for successfully completing his mission and securing a wife for Isaac by granting him his freedom. Eliezer later became the king of Bashan, ruling under the name of Og. According to *Derekh Eretz Zuta* 1:9, the Lord found Eliezer to be a worthy man, despite his having been born to the accursed Canaanite nation, for which reason he was allowed to enter Paradise before he died.

2.7 ZAYD AND ʿALĪ

No biblical model.

Textual Encounters

2.1 A MARRIAGE PROPOSAL

Following the hijra to Medina, Muḥammad sent ʿAlī b. Abī Ṭālib to arrange a marriage between the Prophet's adopted son Zayd and his paternal cross-cousin Zaynab bt. Jaḥsh. The Islamic narrative is modeled on Genesis 24, in which Abraham sends his senior servant to secure a wife for Isaac.

Unlike Abraham, who was determined that Isaac, his natural son and heir, marry within the family (Gen. 24:1 ff.), Muḥammad was determined that Zayd, his adopted son and heir, not marry a member of his family—although the Prophet eventually changed his mind. Abraham sent his senior servant to Mesopotamia to secure a wife for Isaac (the servant was concerned that the woman he selected would reject his proposal); Muḥammad sent his cousin and son-in-law, ʿAlī b. Abī Ṭālib, to secure a wife for Zayd (who feared that the woman he wanted to marry would reject a proposal that emanated directly from him).

The respective genealogical positions of the bride and groom in the biblical and Islamic narratives are mirror images of one another. In the biblical narrative, Isaac is Terah's grandson, and Rebecca is Terah's great-granddaughter. In the Islamic narrative, Zayd is ʿAbd al-Muṭṭalib's great-grandson (through adoption), and Zaynab is ʿAbd al-Muṭṭalib's granddaughter (through her mother). In both cases, the bride's father is conspicuously absent: In Genesis 24, Rebecca's father, Bethuel, is nowhere to be seen and is presumably dead;[41]

in the Islamic narrative, Zaynab's father, Jaḥsh, is nowhere to be seen and is presumably dead. In each case, the brother of the bride, Laban and ʿAbdallāh b. Jaḥsh, respectively, serves as her marriage guardian.

Like Rebecca, who was "very beautiful, a virgin whom no man had known" (Gen. 24:16), Zaynab was, by her own testimony, "the most perfect woman in the tribe of Quraysh." Unlike Rebecca and her family, who welcomed the marriage proposal, Zaynab and her brother initially rejected the marriage proposal. In both cases, the groom's family paid handsomely for the bride: As a marriage gift, Rebecca received silver, gold, and garments, and her brother and mother received unspecified presents; similarly Zaynab received silver, gold, and garments, and her family received food and dates.

In both cases, the marriage depended on the willingness of each woman to leave her birthplace and migrate to another land or town: Rebecca agreed—of her own free will—to leave Mesopotamia and travel to Canaan in order to marry Isaac (Gen. 24:57); similarly, Zaynab left her birthplace in Mecca and traveled to Medina, where she married Zayd.

In both instances, God was responsible for the marriage: The marriage between Rebecca and Isaac was "decreed by the Lord" (Gen. 24:44, 50); the marriage between Zaynab and Zayd was decided by both God and His prophet (Q. 33:36).

2.2 AN EXTRAORDINARY ENCOUNTER

2.2.1 Zayd Is Uriah the Hittite

The amorous episode involving Muḥammad and Zaynab is modeled on the story of David and Bathsheba in II Samuel 11–12, as noted by the Qurʾān commentator Muqātil b. Sulaymān in the first half of the second century A.H.[42]

Just as King David caught a glimpse of the beautiful wife of Uriah the Hittite while she was in the act of bathing (*va-yarʾ ishâ roḥetset*; II Sam. 11:2), so too Muḥammad caught a glimpse of the beautiful wife of Zayd b. Muḥammad while she was in the act of rising to her feet (*abṣarahā qāʾimat*^{an}). Whereas Uriah's wife exposed herself in public, the exposure of Zayd's wife took place within the privacy of her home. David was unable to control his sexual impulses, and, acting in secret, sinned by engaging in sexual relations with Uriah's wife—but only after she had purified herself (II Sam. 11:4). By contrast, Muḥammad did exercise restraint, keeping his desire for his daughter-in-law a secret until God intervened in history to make it possible for him to have sexual relations with Zaynab within the framework of a legal marriage—but only after the expiration of her waiting period. Both men feared public disapproval. And just as Uriah the Hittite ceased to have sexual relations with Bathsheba after she had been impregnated by David (II Sam. 11:8–11), so too Zayd ceased to have sexual relations with Zaynab after his father had fallen in love with his wife.

Unlike David, who did not understand that he had committed a sin (II Sam. 12:1ff.), Muḥammad struggled to avoid committing a sin. Just as David was rebuked by the prophet Nathan (II Sam. 12:1–14), Muḥammad was rebuked by God ("you feared the people when God had better right to be feared by you"). Just as David took Uriah's wife before the very eyes of the Israelite community, Muḥammad took Zayd's wife before the very eyes of the community of believers (thus appearing to fulfill the Lord's threat to David in II Sam. 12:11). Whereas Bathsheba became pregnant with David's child, Zaynab did not become pregnant with Muḥammad's child—albeit for a very good reason (see the Conclusion).

The biblical narrative and its Islamic counterpart share the motifs of illicit sexual relations, a secret, fear of public opinion, sin, and rebuke.

2.2.2 Zayd Is Ishmael

The story of Muḥammad's extraordinary encounter with his daughter-in-law also bears a striking resemblance to an encounter between Abraham and two of his daughters-in-law, as related in *Pirkei de Rabbi Eliezer*, a postbiblical text. Whereas Abraham paid a visit to Ishmael (and his wife) after repudiating his son, Muḥammad paid a visit to Zayd (and his wife) prior to the repudiation. Sarah made her husband swear an oath that he would not dismount his camel, perhaps for fear that he would have sexual relations with his daughter-in-law; Muḥammad was subject to no such constraint. When each man arrived at his respective destination, he found only his daughter-in-law at home. Unlike Abraham, who remained on his camel, Muḥammad entered his daughter-in-law's house and fell in love with the woman, although he did not yet have sexual relations with her. Whereas Abraham advised Ishmael to divorce his first wife after she treated her father-in-law inappropriately, Muḥammad ordered his son not to divorce his wife despite the fact that she was treating her husband inappropriately. In the rabbinic narrative one man marries two women in succession but only the second marriage is successful; in the Islamic narrative one woman marries two men in succession but only the second marriage is successful. Just as Abraham continued to love Ishmael after expelling him, so too Muḥammad continued to love Zayd after repudiating him.

2.3. A FAILED MARRIAGE

2.4. DIVINE INTERVENTION

No textual encounter.

2.5 REPUDIATION

As his father's firstborn son, Ishmael was Abraham's heir until his father repudiated him and sent him into the desert; as Muḥammad's adopted son, Zayd was the Prophet's heir until his father repudiated him.

2.6 A DISTASTEFUL MISSION

Shortly after divorcing Zaynab, Zayd was instructed by Muḥammad to inform his former wife of her impending marriage to the Prophet. Once again, the figure of Zayd brings to mind that of Dammesek Eliezer (see Chapter 1). In this instance, however, the modeling is based on a postbiblical midrash.

In Genesis 24, Abram sends his trusted servant to Mesopotamia to secure a wife for Isaac. According *Genesis Rabbah* 59:9, the mission was distasteful because the servant, identified here as Eliezer, hoped that *his* daughter would marry Isaac. Eliezer had to suppress his own personal interests in order to carry out the mission. Similarly, after he had divorced Zaynab, Zayd was ordered by Muḥammad to inform his former wife of her upcoming marriage to the Prophet. Although Zayd found the order distasteful, he nevertheless carried it out. Each man was being tested, each passed the test, and each was rewarded with the gift of eternal life in Paradise: Dammesek Eliezer ascended to heaven *before* he died. As we shall see in Chapter 3, Zayd entered the Garden the moment he was martyred on a battlefield in southern Jordan.

Dammesek Eliezer's name is mentioned once in the Hebrew Bible; Zayd's name is mentioned once in the Qurʾān. Each name is a *hapax legomenon.*

2.7 ZAYD AND ʿALĪ

No textual encounter.

Chapter 3

Mu'tah

But among the people are those who sell themselves in seeking God's approval. God is gentle towards His servants.—Q. 2:207

Do not reckon those who were killed in God's way as dead: No! They are alive with their Lord. They have provision [from him].—Q. 3:169

Islamic Narratives

INTRODUCTION

In the *Sīra* of Ibn Isḥāq the Muslim community's memory of Zayd centers largely on his role as a military figure (see Introduction). Even if the sources do not identify him as Zayd b. Muḥammad, it would have been under that name that he participated in the Battles of Badr (2 A.H.), Uḥud (3 A.H.), and, perhaps, the Battle of the Ditch, fought in 5 A.H., the year in which he was repudiated by Muḥammad, reverted to his birth name of Zayd b. Ḥāritha al-Kalbī, and became the *mawlā* of the Messenger of God.

Following his repudiation, Zayd was no longer the Prophet's son and heir but he was still regarded as a member of the House of Hāshim. As another Hāshimī, ʿAlī b. Abī Ṭālib, would later recall, "Whenever matters got tough and the battle cry was sounded, [Muḥammad] used to put the People of his House up in the front rank and protected his Companions from the heat of the lances and the sword."[1] Indeed, the Prophet's repudiation of Zayd seems only to have increased his confidence in the man. In the year 6 A.H. alone, Muḥammad appointed Zayd as the commander (*amīr*) of no less than six military expeditions.[2] The dangers were great. In 7 or 8 A.H.—the exact date is disputed—Zayd died on a battlefield in southern Jordan. The circumstances of his death, treated briefly in our Introduction, merit closer attention.

3.1 A PROVOCATION

In either 7 or 8 A.H., Muḥammad instructed one of his Companions, an Azdī by the name of al-Ḥārith b. ʿUmayr, to take a letter to the governor of Provincia Arabia, who resided in Bostra in southern Syria.[3] The letter presumably contained an invitation to accept Islam. Al-Azdī set out on his mission, but when he reached the village of Muʾtah in southern Jordan, he was captured, incarcerated, and beheaded by a Christian Arab by the name of Shuraḥbīl b. ʿAmr al-Ghassānī. This was the first time that an emissary (*rasūl*) of the Messenger of God had been killed by an agent of a foreign power. Thus did the king of Provincia Arabia incur the wrath of the Messenger of God, who was determined to seek revenge. This provocation would soon lead to the battle in which Zayd was killed.

3.2 SACRIFICE: A FATHER AND HIS SON

Muḥammad now raised a force of 3,000 fighters who gathered at al-Jurf, a military staging ground located approximately three miles north of Medina. Upon his arrival at the military camp, the Prophet did not at first issue any instructions regarding the order of command or rules of engagement. It was only after he had performed the noon prayer that he and his Companions formed a circle and began to deliberate on military matters. The Prophet issued the following instructions to the soldiers: "Zayd b. Ḥāritha is the commander of the army. If Zayd b. Ḥāritha is killed, then Jaʿfar b. Abī Ṭālib is the commander. If Jaʿfar is killed, then ʿAbdallāh b. Rawāḥa is the commander. If ʿAbdallāh b. Rawāḥa is killed, then let the Muslims choose a man from among themselves and make him their commander."[4]

It is curious that the Prophet should have named not one commander of the military expedition but three successive commanders. Be that as it may, all three of the men whose names were mentioned by the Prophet had outstanding leadership credentials:

1. Zayd b. Ḥāritha was—or had been until 5 A.H.—the Prophet's adopted

son and heir, the first adult male believer, the Beloved of the Messenger of God, and the only believer apart from Muḥammad whose name was mentioned by God in a revelation that would become part of the Qurʾān.

2. Jaʿfar b. Abī Ṭālib was the Prophet's paternal cousin and the older brother—by ten years—of ʿAlī b. Abī Ṭālib. Like Zayd he was an early convert and, like Zayd, he was already an adult at the time of his conversion. Jaʿfar married Asmāʾ bt. ʿUmays, who bore him three sons: ʿAwn, Muḥammad, and ʿAbdallāh.[5] Circa 615 C.E. Jaʿfar participated in the hijra to Abyssinia, where he served as the leader of the community of believers-in-exile for approximately thirteen years. He returned to Medina in 7/628, just after the capture of Khaybar, at which time the Prophet is said to have embraced him, kissed him between the eyes, and announced, "I do not know what gives me greater pleasure, my conquest [of Khaybar] or the return of my brother Jaʿfar." On another occasion, Muḥammad reportedly told Jaʿfar, "You look like me and you act like I do."[6] Clearly, Jaʿfar was a person of standing within the community of believers.[7]

3. ʿAbdallāh b. Rawāḥa al-Khazrajī was one of the twelve representatives (*naqībs*) of the Medinese clans who met with the Prophet just prior to the hijra to Medina at what is known as the second ʿAqaba meeting. In the years following the hijra, ʿAbdallāh distinguished himself as an energetic champion of the new community of believers. Like Zayd he was a soldier and like Zayd he was entrusted with important missions by the Prophet. When the believers defeated the polytheists at Badr in 2/623, it was ʿAbdallāh b. Rawāḥa and Zayd who were dispatched to Medina with the good news (see Introduction). Two years later, in 4 A.H., Muḥammad appointed Ibn Rawāḥa as his *khalīfa* or deputy ruler of Medina during one of his absences from the city. The Medinese Companion's leadership skills no doubt were connected to his facility with the Arabic language: He was one of the Prophet's secretaries, a respected storyteller, and a poet whose artistry is said to have been comparable to that of Ḥassān b. Thābit and Kaʿb b. Mālik.[8]

The circle of men who had gathered around Muḥammad when he issued the order of command included a Jew identified as al-Nuʿmān b. Funḥuṣ. When this Jew heard the Prophet's statement—Zayd is the commander, then Jaʿfar, then ʿAbdallāh b. Rawāḥa—he turned to Muḥammad and said: "[O] Abū al-Qāsim, if you are a true prophet, then the men whose names you have specified, however many or few, will all be killed. Verily, whenever an Israelite prophet would appoint a man as the leader of an army, and say, 'If so-and-so is killed,' all of them would be killed, even if he specified the names of one hundred men."[9]

In this narrative, an otherwise unknown Jew by the name of al-Nuʿmān b. Funḥuṣ plays the role of the intimate adversary. One might say that he is Satan, albeit in disguise (see Section 3.5, below). Words have power, and that power is sometimes lethal. In the minds of the biblical Israelites, the verbal utterance (*dābār*) of a true prophet is the very essence of future history and historical reality.[10] If Muḥammad was in fact a true prophet, then the very words he had just uttered constituted a death sentence for the three commanders—including his former son Zayd, the Beloved of the Messenger of God, and his nephew Jaʿfar, who was the Prophet's spitting image. The Jew was clearly appealing to Muḥammad's familial instincts as Zayd's erstwhile adoptive father and as Jaʿfar's uncle.

Al-Nuʿmān b. Funḥuṣ was testing Muḥammad, trying to dissuade him from sacrificing the three commanders. The validity of the test depended on Muḥammad's understanding that his battle instructions—the very words that he had just uttered—meant that Zayd, Jaʿfar, and Ibn Rawāḥa were heading to certain death on the battlefield. Muḥammad, however, paid no heed to the Jew's advice, no doubt because he regarded himself as true prophet, even if that meant that Zayd and his two co-commanders must die. Muḥammad passed the test. The respective fates of Zayd, Jaʿfar, and Ibn Rawāḥa had been sealed by the Prophet and no doubt by God as well.

Al-Nuʿmān b. Funḥuṣ now turned to Zayd—according to our source, he expressed no interest in either Jaʿfar or Ibn Rawāḥa—and told him that his fate was inextricably linked to the truth of Muḥammad's claim to be a prophet. "Prepare your last will and testament," the Jew advised, "for you will never return to Muḥammad if he is a true prophet!" Now it was Zayd who was being tested. In a very real sense, Zayd's life had unfolded in anticipation of this moment when he would be asked to surrender his life for the sake of God and His prophet. This was the man who had chosen slavery with Muḥammad over freedom with his family, the first adult male believer, the

Beloved of the Messenger of God, the man who was favored by both God and His prophet, and the only believer apart from Muḥammad whose name was mentioned by God in a revelation that would become part of the Qur'ān. Even if Zayd was no longer Muḥammad's son and heir, he remained his *mawlā*—that is to say, his ally, friend, or protégé. Unlike Muḥammad, Zayd did respond to the Jew. True to form, he rose to the occasion by uttering words that are recognizable as a short version of the testimony of the faith, "I bear witness that Muḥammad is a prophet." To which he added, "He speaks the truth [and] is veracious *(bārr)*"[11]—alluding perhaps to Q. 3:92, "You will not attain piety *(birr)* until you spend some of what you love; and whatever you spend, God is aware of it." In the present instance, Muḥammad attained piety by "spending" Zayd, the Beloved of the Messenger of God.[12] Note well: Zayd is portrayed as a willing participant in the sequence of events that would result in his death and martyrdom. He was fully prepared to die for the sake of God and His Prophet. And Muḥammad was fully prepared to sacrifice the Beloved of the Messenger of God.

3.3 RULES OF ENGAGEMENT—AND THE STANDARD

After specifying the order of command, the Prophet gave the soldiers clear instructions regarding the purpose of the military mission and the rules of engagement: "Wage war in the name of God [and] on the path of God, kill those who deny God; do not act treacherously or unfaithfully, and do not slay a child." The Prophet also instructed the soldiers to invite combatant polytheists to accept Islam and to treat enemy soldiers in accordance with their response to this invitation. There were three options:

1. If the enemy accepted the invitation to Islam, then the soldiers should cease hostilities and do them no harm. Those who accepted Islam should be invited to relocate to the Abode of the Emigrants, where they would have the same rights and obligations as the Emigrants themselves; those who chose to remain in their homelands would acquire the same status as Bedouin who had submitted; that is to say, they would be subject to God's judgment but would not be entitled to a share of the booty or spoils.

2. If the enemy rejected the invitation to Islam, they were to be given the option of paying the *jizya* or poll tax. If they agreed, then the sol-

diers were to cease hostilities and do them no harm; if they refused, then the soldiers were to continue the fight.

3. As for the inhabitants of a fortress or town that was subjected to a siege, if they sued for peace, they were to be given "the protection of your father and the protection of your companions" but not "the protection of God and the protection of His Prophet."[13]

After issuing these instructions, the Prophet placed a white standard—a symbol of authority—in the hands of Zayd b. Ḥāritha, whereupon the army broke camp. The Prophet accompanied the soldiers to a spot known as Thaniyyat al-Wadāʿ or the Farewell Pass,[14] where the noncombatants took leave of the soldiers,[15] imploring God to defend the men and bring them back safe and sound. Upon hearing these supplications, Ibn Rawāḥa is said to have recited a verse of poetry in which he asked God to forgive him for certain unspecified sins and to make sure that he received "a sword blow that makes a deep wound that shoots out frothing blood"—a harbinger of things to come.[16]

3.4 A MOTIVATIONAL SPEECH

The believers now began the march toward the village in southern Jordan where the Prophet's emissary al-Ḥārith b. ʿUmayr al-Azdī had been slain. They were marching toward Muʾtah, a word that evokes notions of madness (*mūta*) and death (*mawt*). Ironically, as Zayd led his men to their destination, he no doubt passed through or near the territory of Kalb, where his father, mother, and uncle—if they were still alive—would have resided. If he did, the sources are silent about the matter.

As the soldiers made their way northward, Bedouin Arab mercenaries became aware of their presence. The Bedouin gathered an army of their own that was commanded by a man with the same name—Shuraḥbīl—as that of the Christian Arab who had slain the Prophet's emissary al-Ḥārith b. ʿUmayr. This Shuraḥbīl, who was from the tribe of Azd, dispatched scouts to gather intelligence on the invaders. Upon reaching Wādī al-Qurā, at the northern edge of the Hijaz, the believers set up camp for several days, after which they advanced to Maʿān, south of Kerak. Here they learned that the Byzantine emperor Heraclius[17] had assembled an army of 100,000 soldiers that included contingents from the tribes of Bahrāʾ, Wāʾil, Bakr, Lakhm, and Judhām, commanded by a certain Mālik from the tribe of Balī. Scouts sent ahead by Zayd reported that the imperial army had reached Maʾāb in the province of Balqāʾ.

Upon receiving this disconcerting news, the believers paused for two days to consider their next move. Some recommended sending a letter to Muḥammad so that the Prophet might either recall them to Medina or send reinforcements. This option was vigorously opposed by ʿAbdallāh b. Rawāḥa, who, it will be recalled, appears to have had a death wish. Ibn Rawāḥa stood up and delivered a stirring speech. Assuming his audience's familiarity with the revelations received by Muḥammad, he skillfully incorporated the language of scripture into his words.[18] He urged his comrades to engage the enemy in battle, instructing them that there were only two possible outcomes, victory or martyrdom:

> By God, we have not been fighting armies on the strength of superior numbers, superior weapons, or superior horses, but rather on the strength of this religion by means of which God has honored us. Be off with you [and fight]. By God, at Badr I saw that we had only two horses and at Uḥud we had only one. There are only two possibilities, both good (*iḥdā al-ḥusnayayn*): victory over them—as God promised us and as His Prophet promised us, a promise that will not be broken—or martyrdom (*al-shahāda*), in which case we will join our brothers as their companions in the Garden.[19]

3.5 MARTYRDOM

The two armies met in or near the village of Muʾtah. After the believers had arranged themselves in rows, each of the three commanders dismounted his horse and fought on foot in hand-to-hand combat. The first to seize the standard and attack the enemy was Zayd b. Ḥāritha, who was killed by the thrust of a spear. After Zayd was slain, Jaʿfar b. Abī Ṭālib seized the standard, dismounted, and, in a heroic gesture, hamstrung his horse so that there would be no escape from the battlefield. Without hesitating, Jaʿfar attacked. He too was killed, slain by a Byzantine soldier who cut his body in two.

According to ostensible eyewitnesses, Jaʿfar received thirty or more wounds on the lower part of his body and exactly seventy-two[20] sword blows and one spear wound on the upper part of his torso.[21]

At the very moment that the battle was being fought in southern Jordan, the Prophet was sitting on the pulpit of the mosque in Medina. Miraculously, Muḥammad began to receive visual images of the events as they were unfolding on the battlefield more than five hundred miles away. The identification of the Prophet as the primary witness to the battle is a literary device employed by the storytellers.[22] Who could contest the authenticity of an event witnessed by the Prophet himself with his very eyes in a vision that could have been granted to him only by God!

As the images from the distant battlefield flashed before his eyes, Muḥammad relayed the news to his Companions in the mosque. The Prophet reported that at the very moment that Zayd b. Ḥāritha seized the standard but before he attacked, he was approached by Satan, who attempted to entice him with the trappings of this world and to repel his desire for death. Zayd resisted Satan's entreaties, proclaiming, "Now that belief has been firmly established in the hearts of the believers, you seek to entice me with the pleasures of this world!" After making this proclamation of his faith—arguably his last words—Zayd attacked the enemy and was slain. At that very moment, in Medina, the Prophet uttered a prayer for Zayd: "Ask God to forgive him, for he has entered the Garden, running."[23] Upon entering the Garden, Zayd no doubt was greeted by an attractive slave girl with dark red lips. Thus was sealed a narrative arc that began with the Prophet's Ascension to heaven (see Introduction).

In Medina the Prophet continued to relate the details of the battle: Jaʿfar b. Abī Ṭālib now seized the standard. He too was approached by Satan, who tried to arouse his desire for this world and to repel his desire for death. Like Zayd, Jaʿfar resisted Satan's entreaty, proclaiming, "Now that belief has been firmly established in the hearts of the believers, you seek to stimulate my desire for this world!" Following this proclamation of faith, Jaʿfar advanced until he too was slain. At that very moment, in Medina, the Prophet uttered the following prayer for Jaʿfar: "Ask God to forgive your brother, for he is now a martyr." Like Zayd, Jaʿfar immediately entered the Garden. But whereas Zayd entered the Garden running, Jaʿfar entered the Garden flying. Miraculously he sprouted two wings made of precious stones that made it possible for him to fly at will.[24] Thus did Jaʿfar come to be known as al-Ṭayyār or "the Flier."

The Prophet continued his account of the battle: After Zayd and Jaʿfar had fallen, Ibn Rawāḥa seized the standard. In this instance there was no need for Satan to arouse his will to live, for a reason that immediately will become apparent. Like Zayd and Jaʿfar, Ibn Rawāḥa was slain. But whereas Zayd entered the Garden running and Jaʿfar entered the Garden flying, Ibn Rawāḥa crawled into the Garden. Upon receiving this news, the Helpers in Medina were sorely distressed. What had prevented their comrade, they no doubt asked the Prophet, from running or flying into the Garden? Muḥammad explained that when Ibn Rawāḥa was wounded, he could not at first relinquish his will to live. Before he could become a martyr, he had to chastise his soul and recover his courage ("I swear, my soul, you shall come to the battle // You shall fight or be made to fight"). Eventually, he too entered the Garden, albeit neither running nor flying but crawling on all fours.[25]

Thus it was that all three of the commanders appointed by Muḥammad fell in battle precisely in the order specified by the Prophet, all three of them became martyrs, and all three of them entered the Garden—as confirmed by the Prophet himself on the basis of a miraculous vision.[26]

3.6 CHOOSING A NEW COMMANDER

In the event that all three commanders were killed, it will be recalled, the Prophet had instructed the believers to select one of their comrades and to make him their commander. The focus of the narrative now shifts to Khālid b. al-Walīd al-Makhzūmī (d. 21/642), a man who until recently had been one of the Prophet's inveterate enemies. Only five years earlier, in 3/625, Khālid had fought against the believers at the Battle of Uḥud, and it was not until Ṣafar 8/June 629, just three months prior to the Battle of Muʾtah, that he became a believer (which is why many sources date the battle to the year 8 rather than 7 A.H.).[27] The exact timing of Khālid's conversion was an important narrative detail.

Khālid's performance as a soldier at the Battle of Muʾtah is the subject of widely varying assessments. Some sources are highly critical of him. According to one ostensible eyewitness, after the three commanders appointed by the Prophet had been slain, Khālid grabbed the standard and led the retreat, with the polytheists in hot pursuit. An unspecified number of believers were killed, and the Army of Muʾtah was routed. As the believers fled, Quṭba b. ʿĀmir yelled out, "O soldiers! It is better to be killed facing the enemy than to be killed with your backs turned to them." His words had no effect, however, and the enemy pursued Khālid and his comrades as they fled from the battlefield.[28] Another source confirms Khālid's flight from the battlefield, as a result of which the commander and his soldiers were accused of being runaways—an evil omen.[29]

Other sources portray Khālid in a better light. One unidentified soldier who reportedly participated in the battle refuted the charge that Khālid fled from the polytheists. This soldier explained that after Ibn Rawāḥa had been slain, chaos prevailed on the battlefield: believers and polytheists were side-by-side, the standard was lying on the ground, and the believers were without a commander. It was at this critical moment that Khālid seized the standard and led the survivors to safety. The point of this report is that even if the believers did suffer—inexplicably—a humiliating defeat, many more men would have been killed that day had it not been for Khālid.[30] According to another source, after Ibn Rawāḥa had been slain, the Army of Muʾtah regrouped, whereupon a Helper named Thābit b. Arqam came forward and grabbed the standard. "Gather round me, soldiers," he cried out, whereupon the believers came running to him from every direction. When Thābit saw Khālid b. al-Walīd, he ordered him to take hold of the standard. Khālid refused on the grounds that Thābit was older than him and had fought at Badr in 2 A.H. However, Thābit explained that the only reason he had taken the standard was to give it to Khālid, and he insisted that the son of al-Walīd b. al-Mughīra take his place as the commander of the army. Reluctantly, Khālid agreed. After he had taken hold of the standard, the polytheists attacked. Khālid held his ground. Indeed, when the polytheists turned around to prepare for a second attack, Khālid and his men managed to destroy one of the enemy's units. Eventually, however, the enemy prevailed over the believers by virtue of superior numbers. The believers lost courage and fled from the battlefield, making their way back to Medina. This was the worst defeat that the community of believers had suffered to this point in its short history.[31]

In fact, Muslim historians are divided about the outcome of the Battle of Muʾtah. In the earliest sources, the battle is portrayed as a resounding and humiliating defeat. This characterization is inconsistent with God's promise to the believers in the Qurʾān that they would be victorious on the battlefield. The early source material was reworked by later generations of historians who revised the narrative account of the battle in order to bring it into line with *sunnat Allāh* or God's practice.[32] In these later sources, we read that God caused the believers to be victorious over the enemy—presumably by saving the lives of most of the soldiers.[33] The changing perception of the outcome of the battle is related to differing assessments of Khālid b. al-Walīd's conduct at Muʾtah. Khālid is remembered by posterity as Sayf Allāh or "the Sword of God." There is considerable variation in the sources, however, as to where and when he acquired his *nom de guerre*. Muslim historians active in the second century A.H. indicate that it was the first caliph Abū Bakr who conferred the title upon Khālid as a reward for his conduct during the so-called War of Apostasy (*ridda*). It was only in the third century A.H., when Muslim historians began to portray the Battle of Muʾtah as a victory, that reports were circulated in which it was Muḥammad (not Abū Bakr) who rewarded Khālid for his efforts at Muʾtah (not during the *Ridda* wars) by dubbing him the Sword of God (not a runaway).[34]

3.7 THE DEAD

It is curious that almost all of the 3,000 believers who participated in the Battle of Muʾtah are said to have survived. In fact, Wāqidī and Ibn Isḥāq mention the names of only eight believers, including the three commanders, who died at the battle. To these eight names, Ibn Hishām added four, bringing the total to twelve.[35] The fact that at most twelve believers were killed in the battle was subsequently characterized by Ibn Kathīr as "very serious" (*ʿaẓīm*^{un} *jidd*^{an}).[36]

Wāqidī and Ibn Isḥāq classify the fallen soldiers according to their tribal and clan affiliations. The dead included two men from the Banū Hāshim—Jaʿfar b. Abī Ṭālib and Zayd b. Ḥāritha; one from ʿAdī b. Kaʿb—Masʿūd b. al-Aswad b. Ḥāritha b. Naḍla; and one from Banū ʿĀmir b. Luwayy—Wahb b. Saʿd b. Abī Sarḥ. The dead also included four Helpers, one from the Banū Māzin—Surāqa b. ʿAmr b. ʿAṭiyya b. Khansāʾ; one from the Banū al-Najjār—al-Ḥārith b. al-Nuʿmān b. Yusāf b. Naḍla b. ʿAmr b. ʿAwf b. Ghanm b. Mālik; and two from the Banū al-Ḥārith b. al-Khazraj—ʿAbdallāh b. Rawāḥa and ʿUbāda b. Qays.[37] The identification of Zayd as a member of the Banū Hāshim confirms our contention that Zayd continued to be regarded as a member of this noble clan even after his repudiation by Muḥammad.

3.8 DEFEAT

If there were at most twelve fatalities at Muʾtah, then there would have been approximately 2,990 survivors who made their way back to the Hijaz. Just as the noncombatants had bid farewell to the Army of Muʾtah when the soldiers had set off on their mission, so too they were waiting at al-Jurf, the initial staging ground, to greet them upon their return. Now, however, the same people who had prayed for the safe return of the army began to throw dirt in the soldiers' faces and to taunt them: "O runaways, have you fled while fighting in the path of God?" In an effort to restore order, the Prophet intervened, explaining that these men were not runaways (*furrār*) but rather men who soon would return to the battlefield (*kurrār*)—a play on words.[38] The intervention of the Prophet himself, however, could not at first remove the stigma of cowardice, flight, and defeat. Members of the defeated soldiers' families refused to open the door of their houses to them. The shame was so great that the Companion Abū Hurayra is said to have shut himself indoors. "When we would emerge from our houses," he later explained, "we would hear the denunciations of the people. [One day,] as I was speaking with one of my paternal cousins, he asked, 'Did you not flee on the day of Muʾtah?' I was at a loss as to how to respond to him."[39] When the Prophet became aware of the situation, he sent the following message to each of the soldiers: "You are the ones who will return to the path of God."[40]

Another survivor of the battle was Salama b. Hishām b. al-Mughīra. Sometime after the battle, Salama's wife paid a visit to Umm Salama, one of the Prophet's wives. The Prophet's wife asked the Companion's wife, "Why have I not seen Salama b. Hishām recently? Is something the matter?" To which the Companion's wife responded, "No, nothing is the matter, but he cannot come out of the house, for when he does, the people reproach him and his comrades, saying, 'O runaways, have you fled in the path of God!' This is why he sits in the house." When Umm Salama conveyed this information to the Prophet, he said, "No, they are the ones who will return to the path of God, so let him come out!" Only then did Salama emerge from his residence.[41]

3.9 MOURNING THE DEAD

The defeat of his army at Muʾtah dealt a major blow to the Prophet, who lost three of his closest Companions. As the leader of the community, it was Muḥammad's duty to convey news of the deaths to the widows and orphans.

The Prophet began the round of condolence calls by paying a visit to Zayd's wife Umm Ayman, her son Usāma, and the rest of Zayd's family. Later the same day, Muḥammad returned to the House of Zayd, where the martyr's young daughter—another Zaynab—jumped into his arms. Muḥammad began to weep uncontrollably to the point that his body was shaking. This spectacle—the Prophet weeping for Zayd—was witnessed by the Companion Saʿd b. ʿUbāda. "O Messenger of God," Saʿd asked, "what is the meaning of this?" To which Muḥammad responded, "This is the beloved yearning for his beloved (*shawq al-ḥabīb ilā ḥabībihi*)."[42] Although Zayd was no longer the Prophet's son and heir, he was still the Beloved of the Messenger of God.

It was only after Muḥammad had paid his respects to the House of Zayd that he made the rounds of the other war widows and orphans. The sources devote considerable attention to the Prophet's visit to the House of Jaʿfar. The details are related on the authority of different members of Jaʿfar's family who are said to have been present during the condolence call. It is related on the authority of Jaʿfar's wife Asmāʾ bt. ʿUmays, for example, that Muḥammad informed her of her husband's death at Muʾtah on the very day on which he died. Since it would have taken several days for messengers to traverse the five hundred miles that separated Muʾtah from Medina, this information could only have been based upon the Prophet's above-mentioned vision.[43] Asmāʾ was a model wife and caring mother who worked herself to exhaustion for the sake of her family. She reports that the Prophet arrived at her residence just after she had finished preparing forty *mann* (a unit of weight equivalent to 2 *raṭl*s or one and a half pounds) of condiments and kneading dough for bread; she also had found the time to wash the faces of her sons and to anoint them with oil. After entering the apartment, the Prophet ordered Asmāʾ to summon her sons. When the boys appeared, the Prophet hugged them and put his nose next to their bodies so that he could smell them. Overcome with grief, his eyes welled up with tears and he began to cry. Asmāʾ asked Muḥammad if he had perhaps received news about Jaʿfar. "Yes," the Prophet replied. "He was killed today." The widow immediately stood up and began to wail, whereupon the other women in the apartment gathered around her. After instructing Asmāʾ not to use unseemly language or to beat her chest, the Prophet departed.[44]

Another version of the Prophet's visit to the House of Jaʿfar is related on the authority of one of the slain man's young sons, ʿAbdallāh. The visit made a deep impression on the boy, who would later recall the event in vivid detail. ʿAbdallāh reports that Muḥammad entered their apartment and then began gently to stroke his head and that of his brother and to cry so hard that the tears were dripping off his beard. The spectacle was gripping, and ʿAbdallāh could not take his eyes off the Prophet. Muḥammad now made the announcement: "Jaʿfar has received the best reward and, as a result, God has replaced him with the best descendant (*dhurriyya*, viz., of Abū Ṭālib) who could have replaced him out of all His servants"—referring to ʿAlī b. Abī Ṭālib, who was now the Prophet's closest male relative within the community of believers (Muḥammad's paternal uncle al-ʿAbbās did not become a believer until the conquest of Mecca later in the year 8 A.H.).[45] Turning to Asmāʾ, he asked her, "Have I not given you the good tidings [*sic*]?" When she responded that he had not, he said, "Verily, God gave Jaʿfar two wings so that he might fly in the Garden." Asmāʾ suggested to the Prophet that he convey the "good tidings" to the rest of the community. Taking ʿAbdallāh b. Jaʿfar by the hand, Muḥammad made his way to the mosque, gently stroking the boy's head. When they reached the mosque, the Prophet took care to seat ʿAbdallāh in front of him on the lowest step of the pulpit and then climbed to the top. The grief was visible on his face. The Prophet declared, "Verily, a man's reputation is tied to the merits of his siblings and cousins. Verily, Jaʿfar has been martyred. God has given him two wings so that he might use them to fly in the Garden." After making this public announcement, the Prophet climbed down from the pulpit, once again took ʿAbdallāh b. Jaʿfar by the hand, and walked to his apartment. Upon his arrival, Muḥammad instructed the women of his house to prepare a meal for the House of Jaʿfar. He then summoned ʿAbdallāh's siblings. "We had a delicious, blessed dinner with him," ʿAbdallāh reports.[46]

The Prophet also paid a condolence call to his daughter, Fāṭima, the wife of ʿAlī b. Abī Ṭālib, who, as a result of Jaʿfar's untimely death, had just received a tremendous boost in his political capital. Upon hearing the news, Fāṭima cried out, "Woe for his [viz., her father's] paternal cousin!" To which the Prophet responded, "Let the weepers mourn for the likes of Jaʿfar." As in the previous narrative, the Prophet instructs a woman—here his daughter—to prepare food for Jaʿfar's family because they would have no time to devote to this task during their period of mourning.[47]

Thus it was that Zayd b. Ḥāritha, Jaʿfar b. Abī Ṭālib, and ʿAbdallāh b. Rawāḥa were all martyred at Muʾtah. One wonders how the course of Islamic history would have unfolded had either Zayd or Jaʿfar—or both—survived the battle and outlived the Prophet. Be that as it may, the deaths of these two key figures was no doubt regarded by the early community of believers as yet another manifestation of *sunnat allāh* or divine providence.

The Islamic narratives about the Battle of Muʾtah draw on biblical and postbiblical themes and motifs relating to the military campaigns of King

David and his general Joab, to the *aqedah*—Abraham's willingness to sacrifice Isaac, and to the notion of martyrdom. Let us first examine the relevant biblical and postbiblical models and then analyze the textual encounters.

Biblical and Postbiblical Models

3.1 A PROVOCATION

King Nahash of Ammon had been on peaceful terms with King David. When the Ammonite king died, he was succeeded by his son Hanun. David sent messengers to convey his condolences to the new king. Ammonite officials, however, advised Hanun that David's men were spies seeking intelligence about how to overthrow the kingdom. The new king humiliated the Israelites by clipping their beards, cutting their garments, and sending them back to Jerusalem in disgrace. Thus did the Ammonites incur the wrath of King David. This provocation resulted in the battle in which Uriah the Hittite was killed (II Sam. 10:1–5).

3.2 SACRIFICE: A FATHER AND HIS SON

Shortly after Abraham had sent his older son Ishmael off into the wilderness, God tested the patriarch by ordering him to take his younger son Isaac to the land of Moriah, where he was to sacrifice him on a mountaintop. When they reached the site of the sacrifice, Isaac and Abraham spoke to one another: "Then Isaac said to his father Abraham, 'Father!' And he answered, 'Yes, my son'" (Gen. 22:7).

In a midrashic expansion upon this episode, Samael or the Angel of Death first attempts to dissuade Abraham from carrying out the sacrifice, and, when he is unsuccessful, turns his attention to Isaac:

> Samael went to the Patriarch Abraham and reproached him, saying: What means this, old man? Have you lost your mind? Are you going to slay a son granted to you at the age of one hundred?
>
> Abraham replied: Even this I do.
>
> Samael asked: And if He sets you an even greater test, can you stand it, as it is written, If a thing be put to you as a trial, will you be wearied (Job 4:2)?
>
> Abraham replied: Even more than this.

> Samael said to Abraham: Tomorrow He will say to you, "You are a murderer and you are guilty."
>
> Abraham replied: Still I am content.
>
> When Samael saw that he could accomplish nothing with him, he approached Isaac and said: O son of an unhappy mother! He is going to slay you!
>
> Isaac replied: I accept my fate.
>
> Samael said to Isaac: If so, shall all those fine tunics which your mother made be a legacy for Ishmael, the hated one of her house?
>
> If a word is not wholly effective, it may nevertheless avail in part; hence it is written, And Isaac said to his father Abraham, "My father." (*Midrash Rabbah*, trans. Freedman and Simon, 1:493–44)

According to the standard interpretation of Genesis 22, Abraham did not sacrifice Isaac. In some midrashic sources, however, it is suggested that Abraham did fulfill God's command to sacrifice his beloved son.[48] That Abraham did in fact sacrifice Isaac is stated explicitly in *Pirkei de Rabbi Eliezer*:

> When the sword touched Isaac's throat his soul flew clean out of him. And when He let His voice be heard from between the two cherubim, "Lay not thy hand upon the lad," his soul returned to his body. Then he [viz. Abraham] unbound him, and he [viz. Isaac] rose. Thus did Isaac come to know the Resurrection of the dead as taught by the Torah: all of the dead will come back to life in the future; whereupon he began to recite, "Blessed art Thou, O Lord, who revives the dead."[49]

The text suggests that the sacrifice was completed ("the sword touched Isaac's throat"), as a result of which Isaac died ("his soul flew clean out of him"), but no sooner had his soul departed from his body than he was given a new life ("his soul returned to his body"). Abraham now loosened the ropes that he had used to bind his son to the altar, whereupon the newly reborn Isaac ascended to Heaven ("rose"), where, as we learn from other texts, he remained for three years, recovering from the wound inflicted by his father.[50] It was only after the wound had healed that he returned to earth, as it is written, "Isaac had just come back" (Gen. 24:62).

3.3. RULES OF ENGAGEMENT—AND THE STANDARD

No biblical or postbiblical model.

3.4 A MOTIVATIONAL SPEECH

After the Ammonites had incurred David's wrath (II Sam. 10:1–5), the Israelite king appointed his nephew Joab as the commander of his army and instructed him to attack the kingdom of Ammon. Anticipating the arrival of the Israelites, the Ammonites hired 33,000 Aramean mercenaries who took up positions on the battlefield, while the Ammonites themselves took up position at the entrance to the gate of Rabbah. When the Israelites found themselves surrounded by their enemies, Joab divided his army into two divisions, one led by him, to engage the Arameans, and the other led by his brother Abishai, to engage the Ammonites. First, however, Joab addressed his brother as follows: "If the Arameans prove too strong for me, you come to my aid; and if the Ammonites prove too strong for you, I will come to your aid. Let us be strong and resolute for the sake of our people and the land of our God; and the Lord will do what He deems right" (II Sam. 10:11–12). In the ensuing battle, the Arameans fled and the Ammonites withdrew into the city of Rabbah.

3.5 MARTYRDOM

After torturing an old Jew for refusing to comply with a royal decree requiring the consumption of defiling food, Antiochus IV Epiphanes (r. 175–164 B.C.E.) attempted to persuade seven Jewish brothers to choose life over death by dangling before them the allure of power and the trappings of this world:

> Young men, with favorable feelings I admire each and every one of you, and greatly respect the beauty and the number of such brothers. Not only do I advise you not to display the same madness as that of the old man who has just been tortured, but I also exhort you to yield to me and enjoy my friendship. Just as I am able to punish those who disobey my orders, so I can be a benefactor to those who obey me. Trust me, then, and you will have positions of authority in my government if you will renounce the ancestral tradition of your national life. Enjoy your youth by adopting the Greek way of life and by changing your manner of living. (4 Macc. 8:5–8).

The seven brothers ignored the tyrant's entreaty and each one suffered a gruesome death. Their mother made no attempt to dissuade her sons from choosing death. To the contrary, she "urged each child separately and all of them together . . . on to death for religion's sake" (4 Macc. 14:12). As she herself was about to be seized and tortured, "she threw herself into the flames so that no one might touch her body" (4 Macc. 17:1). By refusing to violate Jewish law and choosing death over life, the seven children and their mother were engaging in the practice that would come to be known as martyrdom.

Textual Encounters

3.1 A PROVOCATION

In 7 or 8 A.H., a messenger dispatched by the Prophet Muḥammad on a diplomatic mission to the Governor of Provincia Arabia was captured and slain by a Ghassanid Arab tribesman. The Islamic narrative echoes II Samuel 10:1–5, where messengers dispatched by King David on a diplomatic mission to the newly anointed King Hanun of Ammon were mistreated by the king. In each case, one or more messengers sent to a foreign power on a peaceful mission was treated as a spy. Whereas the Israelite messengers were humiliated by the clipping of their beards and the rending of their garments, Muḥammad's messenger was slain. In each case the provocation served as a *casus belli*. The Ammonite provocation would lead to the death of Uriah the Hittite outside the walls of Rabbah; the Ghassanid provocation would lead to the death of Zayd b. Ḥāritha in the village of Muʾtah—not far from Rabbah.

3.2 SACRIFICE: A FATHER AND HIS SON

No sooner did Muḥammad appoint Zayd b. Ḥāritha al-Kalbī—his erstwhile son and heir—as the commander of a military expedition to southern Jordan, than a Jew by the name of al-Nuʿmān b. Funḥuṣ attempted to dissuade the Prophet from sending Zayd to certain death on the battlefield. The Islamic narrative is modeled on *Genesis Rabbah* 22:7, a midrashic text in which Samael or the Angel of Death attempts to dissuade Abraham from carrying out the sacrifice of his son and heir Isaac.

In both the biblical and the Islamic narratives, a father and his son are tested. In both cases, father and son worship or pray before attending to the sacrifice, the intended sacrifice is an adult male who is a willing participant in the ritual, the intended sacrifice is eager for death, and he fails to return from the site of the sacrifice. In at least one postbiblical midrash, Isaac is reported to have ascended to Heaven (albeit for only three years); similarly, Zayd is said to have ascended to the Garden following his martyrdom at Muʾtah. In both narratives, the motif of vision is prominent: In the biblical narrative Abraham calls the site of the sacrifice *Adonai-yireh*, which gave rise to the expression, "On the mount of the Lord there is vision" (Gen. 22:14); in the Islamic narrative Muḥammad has a vision in which he is shown the events of a battle taking place more than five hundred miles away in southern Jordan.

3.3 RULES OF ENGAGEMENT—AND THE STANDARD

No textual encounter.

3.4 A MOTIVATIONAL SPEECH

As Zayd led his men toward southern Jordan, the believers learned that they were badly outnumbered by enemy forces, and some wanted to return to the Hijaz. At this key moment, ʿAbdallāh b. Rawāḥa stood up and delivered a stirring speech that echoes a speech delivered by Joab under similar circumstances, as recorded in II Sam. 10:11–12.

In both cases, a treacherous provocation was followed by a military expedition whose goal was revenge; and in both cases the leader of the community chose a commander who was a close relative: Joab was David's nephew and Zayd was Muḥammad's (erstwhile) son. Whereas the Israelite forces found themselves surrounded by an army composed of Ammonites and Aramaens, the believers found themselves badly outnumbered by an army composed of Byzantines and Arabs. In both cases, a stirring speech played an instrumental role in motivating the soldiers to fight despite a strategic or numerical disadvantage. In the biblical narrative, Joab proposes a pact of mutual support between his forces and those of his brother Abishai, urges the Israelites to "be strong and resolute for the sake of our people and the land of our God," and places his trust in God ("the Lord will do what He deems right"). Similarly, Ibn Rawāḥa urges his comrades to fight for the sake "of this religion by means of which God has honored us," downplays the numerical disadvantage, and explains that there were only two possible outcomes, both of them good—victory or martyrdom.

3.5 MARTYRDOM

Just before the battle was engaged at Muʾtah, Satan attempted to dissuade first Zayd and then Jaʿfar from sacrificing themselves on the battlefield by dangling before them the trappings of this world. The Islamic narrative brings to mind the postbiblical midrash in which Samael attempts to dissuade Abraham from carrying out the sacrifice of his son Isaac. It also brings to mind the attempt by Antiochus IV Epiphanes to dissuade seven Jewish brothers from sacrificing themselves by dangling before them the allure of power and the trappings of this world (4 Macc. 8:5–8). Like Isaac and like the seven brothers (and their mother), all of whom were willing to die for the sake of their God, so too Zayd and Jaʿfar were willing to die for the sake of theirs.

3.6 CHOOSING A NEW COMMANDER

3.7 THE DEAD

No textual encounter.

3.8 DEFEAT

Unlike the Israelites, who were victorious over the combined Ammonite and Aramaen army at Rabbah (II Sam. 10:13ff.), the believers suffered a humiliating defeat at the hands of the combined Byzantine and Arab army at Muʾtah. Was this defeat a manifestation of *sunnat allāh*? If so, one wonders why God's plan made it necessary for the believers to lose this particular battle and why His plan demanded the premature deaths of both Zayd and Jaʿfar on a battlefield in southern Jordan.

Chapter 4

Usāma

O you who believe, obey God and obey His Messenger
and those of you who have authority.—Q. 4:59

Those who believe and do righteous deeds—
those are the best of creation.—Q. 98:7

Islamic Narratives

INTRODUCTION

In 610 C.E., shortly after receiving his first revelation, the Prophet arranged for his son Zayd b. Muḥammad to marry Umm Ayman, a dark-skinned Ethiopian woman. Circa 613, Umm Ayman gave birth to a son whose name would have been Usāma b. Zayd b. Muḥammad al-Hāshimī—although he is never identified in this manner in any source known to me. Usāma was Muḥammad's grandson and, in the event that his father Zayd were to predecease the Prophet, his heir (Zayd, it will be recalled, is said to have died in either 7 or 8 A.H.). Usāma grew up in close proximity to the Prophet, who played an active role in the boy's upbringing, attending to him when he was sick or injured.

Usāma had the merit of being born into Islam and knowing no other religion. Like his father, he was a member of the clan of Hāshim and he grew up in the Prophet's House. He was known as "The Beloved of the Messenger of God" (Ḥibb Rasūl Allāh)[1] or, to distinguish him from his father, as "The Beloved Son of the Beloved of the Messenger of God" (Ḥibb b. Ḥibb Rasūl Allāh). Muḥammad is reported to have loved Usāma very much.[2] Like his father, Zayd, Usāma was the "the person most beloved to me [viz., the Prophet]" (*aḥabbu 'l-nās ilayya*).[3] On one occasion, the Prophet is said to have commanded his wife ʿĀʾisha to love Usāma because "I love him."[4] On another occasion, he is reported to have said, "Whoever loves God and His Messenger, let him love Usāma!"[5]

Muḥammad's love for Usāma is said to have been as great as his love for another of his grandchildren, al-Ḥasan b. ʿAlī. When Usāma was a child, the Prophet would place him on one knee and al-Ḥasan on the other. Once the two children were seated in position, the Prophet would draw them close and exclaim, "By God, have compassion for the two of them, for indeed I have compassion for the two of them"[6] or "By God, I love both of them. Indeed, I love both of them."[7]

Muḥammad was solicitous of Usāma's health and welfare. Shortly after the hijra to Medina in 1/622, when Usāma would have been between eight and ten years old, he contracted smallpox. The illness occurred after the Prophet had consummated his marriage with ʿĀʾisha, who would have been about the same age as Usāma. The two youngsters no doubt lived in close proximity to one another and spent a considerable amount of time together. When ʿĀʾisha saw mucus running down the nose and into the mouth of her ailing step-grandson, she experienced a feeling of disgust and repulsion. At that very moment, the Prophet entered the room, washed Usāma's face, and kissed him. After that, ʿĀʾisha reports, she never again kept Usāma at a distance.[8] In a variant narrative, it is related that Usāma tripped over the threshold of a door and the resulting bruise on his face became infected. When the Prophet instructed ʿĀʾisha to remove the pus, once again, she experienced a feeling of disgust and repulsion. Again, Muḥammad intervened, this time by sucking the pus—or blood—out of the wound and spitting it out.[9] These two gestures, the kiss in the first narrative and the exchange of bodily fluids in the second, highlight the closeness (*qarāba*) between Muḥammad and Usāma—a closeness that verges on kinship. In addition, the exchange of bodily fluids may signal a transfer of authority.[10]

Like his father, Usāma had a flat nose. Unlike his father, who was light-skinned, Usāma—whose mother, it will be recalled, was Ethiopian—was dark-skinned.[11] The difference in skin color appears to have raised suspicions in the minds of hypocrites and infidels about Usāma's paternity. Muḥammad's opponents are said to have questioned the identity of Usāma's biological father. To address this concern, a physiognomist by the name of Mujazziz al-Mudlijī was summoned. Upon his arrival, Zayd and Usāma were lying side by side underneath a blanket that covered their heads, torsos, and legs, leaving only their lower extremities visible. After examining their feet, the physiognomist announced, "Indeed these two sets of feet resemble one another"—that is to say, the two individuals under the blanket were father and son. The Prophet was delighted with the outcome of the examination.[12]

In 5 A.H., it will be recalled, Muḥammad repudiated Zayd by declaring, "I am not your father." The repudiation was followed by the abolition of the institution of adoption (Q. 33:4–5). As a result, Zayd was no longer the Prophet's son and heir. Muḥammad's repudiation of Zayd had important consequences for Usāma, who would have been approximately twelve years old at the time: The Beloved Son of the Beloved of the Messenger of God relinquished his status as the Prophet's grandson and potential heir. Like his father, he underwent a name change: He was no longer Usāma b. Zayd b. Muḥammad al-Hāshimī but rather Usāma b. Zayd b. Ḥāritha al-Kalbī.

Although Usāma was no longer the Prophet's grandson, Muḥammad continued to take a special interest in the boy as he grew to manhood. It is reported that Usāma attained puberty circa 7 A.H., when he was either fourteen or fifteen years old. He was now a man who was old enough to marry and fight. The Prophet attended to both matters. First, he arranged for Usāma to marry Zaynab bt. Ḥanzala b. Qusāma from the tribe of Ṭayy. This marriage—like that of his father, Zayd, to another Zaynab, the daughter of Jaḥsh—was unsuccessful and ended in divorce. It was not long before Muḥammad arranged for Usāma to marry a woman who bore him a son "during the lifetime of the Messenger of God."[13] Had it not been for the Prophet's repudiation of Zayd in 5/626–27 and the abolition of adoption, this son of Usāma's would have been the Prophet's first great-grandson.

Also in 7 A.H., Muḥammad sent Usāma on a raid against unidentified polytheists. This was the young man's first experience in combat. During the raid, Usāma came face to face with Nuhayk b. Mirdās al-Juhanī. As Usāma raised his spear to strike the polytheist, Nuhayk uttered the first words of the testimony of faith: "There is no God but God"—thereby signaling his intention to join the community of believers. Usāma had to make a decision—and quickly. Sensing that the polytheist's profession of faith was insincere and that he was only trying to save his life, Usāma struck Nuhayk dead and seized his flocks as booty. When the believers returned to Medina, Usāma met with the Prophet, who was pleased to learn the outcome of the encounter with the polytheists. "Give me details," he instructed, whereupon Usāma related how he had slain Nuhayk. The Prophet's demeanor changed. "Woe to you, Usāma! Did you kill someone who said 'there is no God but God'? Woe to you, Usāma! Did you kill someone who said 'there is no God but God'?" Muḥammad kept repeating this statement until Usāma wanted to wipe his slate of actions clean so that he might rejoin the community of believers without any sins. As a result of this experience, Usāma vowed never again to raise his spear against a man who said "there is no God but God."[14]

Unlike other stories related about Usāma, this one casts him in a decidedly negative light. In fact, the story is polemical and it was no doubt an invention of storytellers who needed it to explain a dilemma faced by Usāma twenty-eight years later in 35/655 (see Postscript).

4.1 ROYAL CLOTHING, JEWELRY, AND RIDING BEHIND THE RULER

Muḥammad is said to have paid careful attention to the clothes that Usāma wore. On one occasion, Ḥakīm b. Ḥizām b. Khuwaylid purchased a fine garment (*ḥulla*) that had once belonged to Dhū Yazan, King of the Yemen. When Ḥakīm offered the garment to Muḥammad, the Prophet objected that he could not accept a gift from a polytheist, although he had no qualms about purchasing the garment. "How much did you pay for it?" the Prophet asked Ḥakīm. "Fifty *dīnārs*," he replied. After the money had changed hands, the Prophet put on the garment, walked to the mosque, climbed to the top of the pulpit, and performed the Friday prayer. After completing the prayer, he descended and put the garment on Usāma b. Zayd.[15] On another occasion—or in a variant—Diḥya al-Kalbī gave the Prophet a white garment made of fine Egyptian linen. Muḥammad gave the garment to Usāma, who gave it to his wife. When the Prophet noticed that Usāma was not wearing the garment, he asked, "Why aren't you wearing the linen garment?" Usāma replied, "O Messenger of God, I have given it to my wife to wear." Muḥammad ordered Usāma to instruct his wife to wear a shift (*ghilāfa*) underneath the linen garment, lest her body be exposed.[16] Like the transfer of bodily fluids, the act of clothing a subordinate in fine garments is a sign of the transfer of power and authority.[17]

Muḥammad also chose the jewelry—another symbol of power and authority—worn by Usāma. A curious narrative relates that on one occasion, when the Prophet was sitting with both ʿĀʾisha and Usāma, Muḥammad looked at Usāma's face and laughed. "Were Usāma a slave girl (*jāriya*)," he said, jokingly, "I would bedeck her [*sic*] with ornaments and beautify her so that I might give her away as a gift."[18] (The sources do not specify the type of ornament that the Prophet would have had Usāma wear.)

On important occasions Usāma—like his father before him—rode directly behind the Prophet's horse—yet another manifestation of his closeness to Muḥammad. As a result, Usāma came to be known as *al-ridf* or *al-radīf*, literally, "the man who rides behind another man on the back of the same [or another] mount."[19] On the day of the *fatḥ* or conquest of Mecca in 8/630, the Prophet entered the city and made his way to the Kaʿba, followed immediately by Usāma—his *radīf*.[20] Two years later, when the Prophet performed the Farewell Pilgrimage, Usāma was again his *radīf*.[21] On 9 Dhū al-Ḥijja, the Prophet completed the day-long ritual at ʿArafāt and then prepared for the "pouring out" (*ifāḍa*) from ʿArafāt to Muzdalifa. Realizing that Usāma had fallen behind, Muḥammad pulled hard on the reins of his camel, causing the pilgrims behind him to stop in their tracks.[22] The pilgrims waited until Usāma had caught up with the Prophet and resumed his position as the *radīf*. Upon learning that they had been delayed by a black-skinned, flat-nosed youth, a group of Yemeni pilgrims exclaimed: "Have we been held back on account of that one?" This incident is said to have been the cause of the subsequent decision by the Yemenis to apostatize during the caliphate of Abū Bakr.[23]

The term *al-radīf* is commonly used by Muslim scholars to signify a "successor." Writing about the Christian kings of al-Ḥīrah, for example, Ibn Qutayba uses the term to refer to the man who takes the place of the king while he is on military campaign.[24] When writing about the Persians, the lexicographer Ibn Manẓūr reports, some authors use the term *al-radīf* to signify the "successor to the throne."[25] It is also reported that in the language of the Bedouin, *al-radīf* signifies "the person who they want to rule them after their ruler dies."[26] The association between *al-radīf* and succession was also applied to caliphs. The historian Sayf b. ʿUmar (d. 180/796), for example, refers to ʿUthmān b. ʿAffān as the *radīf* of the second caliph ʿUmar, that is to say, ʿUthmān was the man whom the Muslims expected to succeed ʿUmar.[27] The identification of Usāma as the Prophet's *radīf* suggests that whoever circulated the above-mentioned narratives regarded him as a candidate to succeed Muḥammad as leader of the Muslim community.

4.2 REVENGE

In the three years or so following the defeat of the Muslim army at Muʾtah (see Chapter 3), the Prophet was stricken with grief for Zayd b. Ḥāritha, Jaʿfar b. Abī Ṭālib, and the other men said to have been killed during the battle. The names of the dead martyrs are said to have been constantly on his lips. On Monday 26 Ṣafar 11 A.H. Muḥammad instructed his Companions to prepare for a military expedition against the Byzantines. The goal of this mission was to exact revenge for the slaying of Zayd.

4.3 APPOINTMENT OF THE COMMANDER AND BATTLE INSTRUCTIONS

On Wednesday 28 Ṣafar 11 A.H., the Prophet summoned Usāma and appointed him as the commander of the upcoming military expedition. The Prophet's instructions to Usāma were as follows:

> O Usāma, go in the name of God and with His blessing, until you reach the place where your father was killed, where you are to trample them with your horses, for I have appointed you as the commander (*wallaytuka*) of this army. Carry out a morning raid against the people of Ubna and burn them. Travel fast so that you will arrive before reports [of your approach]. If God makes you victorious, limit [the amount of time] that you remain among them. Take guides with you, and send spies and scouts ahead of you.[28]

Two points merit attention: First, the objective of the military expedition was Ubna, the Arabic equivalent of Yavneh, a town near the Mediterranean coast, between Ashkelon and Ramla, and the home of many Samaritans. In the seventh century C.E., Ubna/Yavneh would not have been an obvious military target.[29] Second, the Prophet's instructions to trample the enemy and to scorch the settlement were inconsistent with what was—or would become—standard practice, namely, to invite pagans and polytheists to accept Islam before attacking them; and to desist from fighting non-Muslim monotheists after they had agreed to pay the poll tax.

It was later the same day—Wednesday—that the Prophet began to manifest signs of the illness from which he would soon expire. On Thursday, suffering from a headache and fever but still lucid, Muḥammad placed in Usāma's hand the community flag or banner, another important symbol of authority. He also is said to have issued a second version of the battle orders—or a variant of the first—in which he instructed Usāma to spare the lives of women and children:

> O Usāma, carry out a raid in the name of God, in the path of God, and fight (pl.) those who deny God. Carry out the raid, and do not be unfaithful. However, do not kill a child or a woman. Do not desire to meet the enemy, for you do not know, perhaps you will be tested by them. Rather, say: "O God, protect us against them and avert their evil from us." And if, when they encounter you, they are making noise and shouting, [you are to] maintain repose (*al-sakīna*; cf. Q. 2:248) and silence. "Do not quarrel lest you falter and your strength depart" (Q. 8:46). Say: "O God, we are your servants, and they are your servants; our forelocks and their forelocks are in your hands. It is only You who prevails over them." Know that Paradise is under the swords (*al-bāriqa*).[30]

After receiving the banner from Muḥammad, Usāma tied it to his spear and gave it to Burayda b. al-Ḥuṣayb al-Aslamī, who planted the spear in the ground in front of Usāma's house. The presence of the standard in front of Usāma's house was a visible sign of his authority and his status as the *amīr* or military commander of the believers.[31]

STAGE NOTE: WHO WILL ENTER THE PROMISED LAND?

Usāma traveled to al-Jurf, where he set up camp at Solomon's Well—a textual allusion to the biblical king and Qurʾānic prophet who was David's son and successor.

The sources are keen to note that *all* of the first Emigrants (*muhājir*s) who were still alive volunteered for the expedition to Palestine, including ʿUmar b. al-Khaṭṭāb, Abū ʿUbayda b. al-Jarrāḥ, Saʿd b. Abī Waqqāṣ, and Abū al-Aʿwar Saʿīd b. Zayd b. ʿAmr b. Nufayl; in addition, the volunteers included several later Emigrants and Helpers such as Qatāda b. al-Nuʿmān and Salama b. Aslam b. Ḥarīsh.[32]

4.4 DISSENSION IN THE RANKS ELICITS ANGER FROM A PROPHET

Over the course of the next fortnight, Usāma made preparations for the upcoming military expedition. There was considerable grumbling in the ranks, however, and senior Emigrants began to express their dissatisfaction with the Prophet's choice of an inexperienced youth as their commander—according to different estimates, Usāma would have been between eighteen and twenty-one years old at the time. It will be recalled that two of the senior Emigrants, ʿAyyāsh b. Abī Rabīʿa and ʿUmar b. al-Khaṭṭāb, had arrived in Yathrib/Medina together (see Introduction). Upon learning of Usāma's appointment as commander of the military expedition, ʿAyyāsh protested, "Has the Prophet put this youth (*ghulām*) in charge of the first Emigrants?"[33] When ʿUmar learned about the dissatisfaction of ʿAyyāsh and the other senior Emigrants, he tried to defend the Prophet's selection of Usāma as commander, albeit without success.

ʿUmar now approached the Prophet and informed him about the dissension in the ranks. Muḥammad became very angry. On Saturday 10 Rabīʿ I he emerged from his residence draped in a cloak and with a turban wrapped around his head. He climbed to the top of the pulpit where, after invoking the name of God, he rebuked the senior Emigrants, as follows:

> Now to the heart of the matter: O people! What is the statement that has been brought to my attention about some of you regarding my appointment of Usāma b. Zayd as commander? By God, if you criticize my appointment of Usāma as commander, previously you criticized my appointment of his father. By God, if Zayd was qualified to serve as commander, verily his son, after him, is qualified to serve as commander. Just as [Zayd] was one of those most beloved to me, so too that one [viz., Usāma] is one of those most beloved to me. Verily, the two of them are, by their [very] nature, disposed to goodness. So I command you to treat him [viz., Usāma] well (*fa-'stawṣū bihi khayr*^{an}), for he is one of your best (*min khiyārikum*).[34]

After finishing his speech, the Prophet descended from the pulpit and entered his residence.

This carefully constructed speech merits attention: First, the senior Emigrants appear to have been unaware of, or had chosen to ignore, Q. 4:59, which commands believers to obey God, His Messenger, and "those who have authority among you" (*ūlū 'l-amr minkum*). Second, to the best of my knowledge, no one ever criticized (*ṭaʿana*) the Prophet's appointment of Zayd as the commander of any military expedition (although, as noted, unidentified persons did challenge [*ṭaʿana*] Zayd's paternity of Usāma on the grounds of the difference in the color of their skins).[35] Third, the Prophet's statement that Zayd and Usāma were both qualified to serve as military commanders (*khalīq*[un] *li'l-imāra*) echoes a statement attributed to ʿAlī in which he states that the Muslims appointed Abū Bakr as their leader because he was the one with whom the Messenger of God had been pleased, "and by God he was qualified for that" (*wa-kāna wallāhi ahl*[an] *lahā*).[36] Fourth, the Prophet's pronouncement that Zayd and Usāma were each "one of those most beloved to me" (*min aḥabb al-nās ilayya*) echoes his expressions of love for *inter alia* Abū Bakr and ʿAlī.[37] Fifth, the Prophet's statement that the senior Emigrants should "treat Usāma well" brings to mind al-ʿAbbās' proposal to ʿAlī that the two of them should approach the dying Prophet and ask him, in the event that neither would be chosen as leader of the community, to "enjoin the people to treat us well."[38] Sixth, and finally, the Prophet's closing statement that Usāma "is one of your best" (*min khiyārikum*) is a standard topic in sectarian discourse. It responds to the question: Who, after the Prophet, is the best of creation or the best of mankind (in Arabic, alternatively, *khayr al-arḍ*, *khayr al-bariyya*, *khayr al-bashar*, *khayr al-khāliqa*, *khayr al-nās*). The standard Sunni response to this question is that Abū Bakr was the best, while the standard Shiʿi response is that ʿAlī was the best. Viewed in this context, the Prophet's assertion that Usāma was "one of your best" suggests that the young commander was a candidate for the "best man" rubric and that his qualifications arguably were as strong as those of Abū Bakr and ʿAlī.

4.5 A FINAL BLESSING AND THE LAYING ON OF HANDS

The Prophet's illness, which began just before the departure of an important military expedition, was a matter of great concern. Before the soldiers set off for Palestine, some of them, including ʿUmar b. al-Khaṭṭāb, returned to Medina in order to visit their ailing leader. The visitors advised the Prophet to cancel the military expedition. In response, Muḥammad exclaimed, "Carry out Usāma's mission!"[39]

The elderly Umm Ayman now appealed to Muḥammad on behalf of her son. "O Messenger of God! Will you not instruct Usāma to remain in his military camp until you have recovered? Indeed, if Usāma leaves under the present circumstances, it will not be to his advantage [as the *amīr*]."[40] The Prophet repeated his exhortation, "Carry out Usāma's mission!" As believers, the soldiers had no choice but to obey the Prophet's explicit command, as required by Q. 4:59: "O you who believe, obey God and obey His Messenger and those of you who have authority." On Saturday night, the soldiers returned to al-Jurf.[41]

On Sunday, the Prophet's health took a turn for the worse and the members of his House began to administer medicine that made him drowsy and unresponsive. Usāma postponed the army's departure so that he might pay a sick visit to the man who had played such an important role in his upbringing (and who, for much of his life, had been his grandfather). As he entered the Prophet's room, tears were streaming down his face. In a poignant scene, the young man known as the Beloved Son of the Beloved of the Messenger of God bent down next to the Prophet and kissed him. Although Muḥammad was unable to speak, he did manage to make a physical gesture: He lifted one of his hands high in the air and brought it down on Usāma's head.[42]

After receiving the Prophet's blessing, Usāma returned to al-Jurf. Although it was late in the day, he ordered the soldiers to prepare for departure. Just as the expedition was about to leave, however, Usāma received a message from Umm Ayman—the timing of his mother's intervention was exquisite—informing him that the Prophet had taken a turn for the worse and was on the point of death. Usāma hurried back to Medina, accompanied by ʿUmar b. al-Khaṭṭāb and Abū ʿUbayda b. al-Jarrāḥ. The trio reached the Prophet "as he was dying," just as the sun was about to set on Monday 12 Rabīʿ I 11 A.H.[43] Usāma was one of the select few who prepared the Prophet's body for burial and lowered the corpse into the grave.[44]

4.6 EXEMPTION FROM MILITARY SERVICE

The Prophet's death must have taken the community of believers by surprise. In fact, on the very morning of the day on which he died, Muḥammad had awoken feeling better than the day before and is said to have been in good spirits. At that time, he received a second visit from Usāma. As his former grandson departed, the Prophet bid him farewell and said, "Depart, with the blessing of God."

Shortly thereafter, the Prophet received a visit from Abū Bakr, the man who, in less than twenty-four hours, would succeed him as leader of the community. After acknowledging the improvement in Muḥammad's health, Abū Bakr made a curious request. On this particular Monday, it was the "turn" of one of his wives, Ḥabība bt. Khārija b. Zayd, to receive a conjugal visit from her husband. If Abū Bakr were to participate in the military expedition, he would be unable to "visit" Bint Khārija. For this reason, he asked the Prophet to exempt him from the obligation to participate in the upcoming military campaign. The Prophet agreed, and Abū Bakr set off for his house in the area of Medina known as al-Ṣunḥ. The exemption from military duty was important—from a narrative perspective—because it insured that Abū Bakr would be in Medina, rather than in al-Jurf or on his way to Palestine, at the moment when the Prophet died.[45]

4.7 THE BANNER—AND DIVISION OF AUTHORITY

Following the Prophet's death, the soldiers who had gathered in al-Jurf returned to Medina in order to attend his funeral. Burayda b. al-Ḥuṣayb al-Aslamī entered the town carrying the banner of the community, which, it will be recalled, was attached to Usāma's spear. Burayda carried the spear to the door of the Prophet's apartment, where he planted it in the ground.

There were now two *amīr*s or commanders: Abū Bakr was the *Amīr al-Mu'minīn* or Commander of the Believers, while Usāma was the *Amīr al-Jaysh* or Commander of the Army. Abū Bakr instructed Burayda to take the banner to the house of Usāma, the military commander, adding that under no circumstance was he to untie the banner from the spear before Usāma had completed the expedition against Ubna. Even after the expedition had been successfully completed, however, the banner remained with Usāma. As Burayda himself would later explain, "I went out with the banner and brought it to Usāma's house. Then I took it to Syria, tied [to the spear,] with Usāma. Then I returned it to Usāma's house. [The banner] remained in Usāma's house until he died."[46] If so, the banner would have remained in Usāma's possession for more than forty years, from 11/632 until his death circa 54/674—a powerful reminder of his status as military commander at the moment when the Prophet died and of his successful execution of the Prophet's final instruction to his community.

4.8 OBEDIENCE TO AUTHORITY

In the year 9 A.H., numerous Arab tribes had joined the community of believers during the "year of the deputations." Shortly before the Prophet's death in 11 A.H., several of these Arab tribes began to withdraw their support for the new community and to threaten the inhabitants of Medina. Immediately following the Prophet's death, Abū Bakr, who only recently had received permission from Muḥammad *not* to participate in a dangerous military expedition so that he might visit one of his wives, was now confronted with a dilemma. Should the new Commander of the Believers dispatch the soldiers to Palestine, in accordance with the Prophet's instruction to Usāma on Wednesday 28 Ṣafar, or should he hold them back to defend Medina against a possible attack by apostate Arab tribes? Without hesitation, Abū Bakr issued the following instruction to Usāma: "Set out (*unfudh*) in the direction [of the target] toward which the Messenger of God sent you." In response to this instruction, the soldiers made their way, once again, to al-Jurf, albeit not before Burayda had pulled the standard out of the ground in front of Usāma's house so that he might carry it to al-Jurf.[47]

Dissension within the ranks now resurfaced among the first Emigrants. At this critical juncture, Abū Bakr received a delegation composed of several distinguished Companions: ʿUmar, ʿUthmān, Saʿd b. Abī Waqqāṣ, Abū ʿUbayda b. al-Jarrāḥ, and Saʿīd b. Zayd—five of the ten believers who are said to have been promised Paradise by the Prophet before he died. This illustrious group advised Abū Bakr as follows:

> O Successor (*khalīfa*) of the Messenger of God, the Bedouin Arabs have reneged on the agreement with you on every front, so you should not dispatch the army that has been assembled. Use them as a weapon against the apostates. Send them [to smite] their throats. And one more thing. We fear that a raid will be carried out against the people of Medina, including women and children. Will you not postpone the raid against the Byzantines until Islam has become established and until the apostates have [either] been sent back to where they came from or destroyed by the sword? Only then should you send Usāma, for we are confident that the Byzantines will not attack us [in the Hijaz].[48]

When the Companions had finished speaking, Abū Bakr asked, "Is there anyone among you who wants to say something [else]?" "No," they replied. "You have heard what we have to say." The caliph now delivered a stirring speech:

> In the name of the One who holds my soul in His hand. Even if I suspected that wild animals were to consume me in Medina, I would execute that mission; and I would not take any action before it. While inspiration was [still] descending upon the Messenger of God from the sky, he said, "Dispatch (*anfidhū*) Usāma's

> army." However, [I have] an idea. I will speak to Usāma about ʿUmar, [and I will ask him] to leave him behind, so that he can remain with us, for he is indispensable to us. By God, I don't know whether or not Usāma will agree. By God, it is an idea, [but] I will not force him [to do it].[49]

Abū Bakr may have been the commander (*amīr*) but he was nevertheless subject to Usāma's command (*maʾmūr*).[50] The caliph now approached Usāma at his house and asked him to excuse ʿUmar from the expedition so that he might remain in Medina. Usāma agreed. Abū Bakr, however, would not take "yes" for an answer until he had established that Usāma had given permission of his own free will. Only after Usāma had confirmed that he was in fact acting of his own free will did Abū Bakr emerge from the house and instruct his herald to call out: "I [viz. Abū Bakr] have determined that no one who volunteered to participate in this mission with him [viz., Usāma] during the lifetime of the Messenger of God should absent himself from Usāma. Indeed, [if I am informed] that anyone drags his feet so as not to leave with him, I [myself] will present him with his marching orders."[51] In addition, Abū Bakr sent a harsh message to the Emigrants who previously had criticized the appointment of Usāma as commander of the army, ordering them to participate in the military expedition. Thus it was that not a single Emigrant who initially had volunteered for the expedition failed to participate—with two notable exceptions, Abū Bakr and ʿUmar.[52]

Just as the Prophet had traveled to al-Jurf and then accompanied the Army of Muʾtah to the Farewell Pass (see Chapter 3, section 3.3), so too Abū Bakr traveled to al-Jurf and then accompanied the Army of Ubna—three thousand men and one thousand horses—for the first hour or so of the march to Palestine. Before halting his advance and peeling off from the expedition, Abū Bakr turned to Usāma and addressed him as follows: "I entrust to God your religion, your safety, and the outcome of your actions. Verily, I heard the Messenger of God give you a [final] instruction (*yūṣīka*), so execute (*faʾnfudh*) the order of the Messenger of God. Verily it is not I who has given you the order and I will not prevent you from [executing] it. Rather, I am merely carrying out an order that was issued by the Messenger of God."[53] The expedition to Ubna was important because it had been the final instruction issued by the Prophet. This was his *waṣiyya* or final command to Usāma, and, by extension, to the community of believers.[54]

4.9 SCOUTS—AND A CLOUD

The area between the Hijaz and southern Palestine was the home of several tribes that had apostatized. Usāma chose his route carefully, leading his men through the territory of Juhayna and Quḍāʾa, two tribes that had remained loyal to the believers.

Upon reaching Wādī al-Qurā, Usāma dispatched a scout from the Banū ʿUdhra by the name of Ḥurayth. The scout galloped ahead toward Ubna at top speed. Upon his arrival, he engaged in reconnaissance and then returned to his comrades, rejoining Usāma and his men at a distance of approximately two days' march from the target. The scout reported that the inhabitants of Ubna were unprepared for an attack and had no military forces to defend them. He advised Usāma to act quickly and to carry out a surprise attack before the inhabitants of the town had time to make preparations to defend themselves.[55]

As the three-thousand-man army entered Palestine, it is reported, the countryside was covered with a thick fog—an act of God that made it possible for the believers to traverse enemy territory undetected and unmolested. No army, it is said, was ever as safe or as secure as this one.[56]

4.10 EXTERMINATION OF THE ENEMY

Before Usāma could act on the advice of his scout, he was confronted by his standard-bearer, Burayda b. al-Ḥuṣayb, who drew his attention to a disturbing discrepancy between the battle instructions issued by the Prophet to Zayd b. Ḥāritha immediately before the Muʾtah expedition in 7 or 8 A.H. (Chapter 3, section 3.3) and the instructions issued to Usāma immediately before the Ubna expedition in 11 A.H. (section 4.2, above).

It just so happened—as required by the logic of the narrative—that Burayda had been present at al-Jurf when Muḥammad issued the battle instructions to Zayd. On the earlier occasion, the standard-bearer now explained to Usāma, the Prophet had instructed his father "to invite the enemy to accept Islam." And he reiterated the content of the Prophet's instructions: If the enemy accepted Islam, they were to be given a choice of either (1) remaining in their homes without participating in *jihād*, in which case they would not receive any booty or spoils, or (2) moving to the Abode of Islam and participating in *jihād*, in which case they would have the same rights and obligations as any Emigrant.[57]

One wonders why Muḥammad would have instructed Usāma to carry out a surprise attack against the people of Ubna and to scorch the settlement. Had not God Himself delivered the following revelation to the Prophet: "Your Lord would not destroy the settlements wrongfully, when their people are unaware" (Q. 6:131)? Would it not have been proper for the believers to invite the enemy to join their community before attacking them? To this question, Usāma responded as follows: "That was the command (*waṣiyya*) of the Messenger of God to my father. However, the Messenger of God commanded me—and this was his final instruction (*ʿahd*) to me—that I should travel fast and precede reports [about our approach], that I should carry out a surprise attack against them, without an invitation [to join the community of believers], and that I should set fire [to the settlement] and lay waste [to it]."[58] In response to this statement, there was nothing that Burayda could say but, "[We] hear and obey the command of the Messenger of God."[59] The fate of the inhabitants of Ubna had been sealed. They had been doomed to destruction by the Prophet and, perhaps, by God Himself.

Usāma now issued the battle instructions. Looking down on Ubna from a hilltop high above the settlement, the commander instructed his men as follows: "Carry out a raid, but do not penetrate deeply and do not split up. Stay together and lower your voices. Mention God to yourselves [viz., silently, not out loud]. Draw your swords and thrust them into whomever comes within your sight."[60]

It was early in the morning and the inhabitants of Ubna were asleep in their dwellings when Usāma gave the signal to initiate the raid. Within the settlement, not a soul moved "and not a dog barked." The soldiers issued their battle cry: "O you to whom victory has been granted. Kill." The believers killed or captured every inhabitant of the settlement who came into sight. They set fire to their homes, fields, and date-palm trees. Smoke rose "like a whirlwind" in the air. The Muslims seized as booty whatever was at hand and spent the rest of the day preparing the spoils of victory.[61]

The stated purpose of the expedition, it will be recalled, was to exact revenge for the slaying of Zayd at Muʾtah. We now learn that on the day on which Zayd had been slain he was riding a horse named Sabḥa or "Majesty [of God]." Appropriately, Usāma was riding this very horse on the day of the attack on Ubna. And it just so happened—again as required by the logic of the narrative—that one of the prisoners captured at Ubna possessed information regarding the whereabouts of the man who had slain Zayd at Muʾtah—in Transjordan. After this information had been extracted from the prisoner, Usāma proceeded to track down the unbeliever who had killed his father—the man just happened to be in the vicinity of Ubna—and to slay him on the spot. Mission accomplished.[62]

Before departing, Usāma divided the booty among his men, allocating two shares to every horse and one share to its owner. His share was exactly the same as that of the other soldiers.[63]

4.11 HOMECOMING

As evening fell, Usāma ordered his men to prepare their mounts. Once again, he dispatched Ḥurayth al-ʿUdhrī, this time to scout out the return route to the Hijaz. The soldiers returned to the Hijaz along the same route that they had taken to Ubna. By the first nightfall, they had traveled a considerable distance.[64] It took nine more days to reach Wādī al-Qurā, from where Usāma dispatched a messenger to Medina with the good news that the army was safe and sound and that the expedition had accomplished its mission. As the soldiers approached Medina, they were met at al-ʿAwātiq by Abū Bakr and others who had remained in Medina. The noncombatants were relieved to learn that their loved ones were safe. And they rejoiced. Usāma entered the city riding Sabḥa (the horse is said to have been lean and emaciated) and wearing a coat of mail, preceded only by the standard-bearer, Burayda, who carried the banner to the mosque, where Usāma prayed the pre-dawn prayer—two *rakʿa*s or prayer units—and then made his way home, taking the banner with him. As noted, the banner remained in his possession for more than forty years, until his death circa 54/674.[65]

The length of the mission is disputed: Some sources specify that Usāma was gone for forty nights, a common biblical topos: Forty was the number of years that the Israelites wandered in the desert and also the number of days that it took for scouts sent by Moses to complete their reconnaissance of the land (Num. 13:1–2, 25).[66] Other sources say seventy nights;[67] still others say thirty-five nights (twenty nights out and fifteen nights in).[68]

Miraculously, not a single member of the expedition had been killed in the campaign.

POSTSCRIPT: USĀMA'S CAREER FOLLOWING THE DEATH OF THE PROPHET

The spectacularly successful Ubna campaign marked the high point of Usāma's military career. According to the testimony of our sources, he played little or no role in subsequent events. Never again did he serve as the *amīr* or commander of a military expedition nor did he participate in the *ridda* campaigns or in the battles that resulted in the conquest of Syria, Egypt, and Iraq. Like al-Ḥasan b. ʿAlī, Usāma withdrew from public life, reportedly settling down in Wādī al-Qurā, where he tended to his property.[69] Subsequently, he "went down" to Medina.[70]

The sources identify Usāma as one of those who withheld their support from ʿAlī after he became caliph in 35/655.[71] In that year, ʿAlī led his forces toward Basra, where he would confront ʿĀʾisha, the Prophet's widow, at the Battle of the Camel. (It will be recalled that ʿĀʾisha had been Usāma's step-grandmother for over a decade and that the two lived in close proximity when they were young). As ʿAlī was leaving the Hijaz, he sent a message to Usāma asking for his support. Usāma sent one of his clients, a certain Ḥarmala, to ʿAlī and instructed him to make the following statement: "Say 'May peace be upon you' and then say to him, 'If you were in the jaws of a lion, I would be there with you—but this matter is something that I cannot do.'" ʿAlī was not pleased and he expressed his displeasure by not bestowing a gift on the messenger. By contrast, when Ḥarmala approached ʿAlī's son al-Ḥasan and his nephew Ibn Jaʿfar, the two are said to have showered him with gifts.[72] In this report Usāma expresses sympathy for ʿAlī but nevertheless withholds his support. One wonders why? The answer to this question is found in the Prophet's rebuke of Usāma in 7 A.H. after he had killed a polytheist who had just said "there is no God but God." Had Usāma participated in ʿAlī's military campaign against ʿĀʾisha, he no doubt would have been compelled to break his vow not to fight against a believer.

The sources portray Usāma as a pious man who, like the Prophet, fasted on Mondays and Thursdays—even if he was traveling to Wādī al-Qurā.[73] However, he apparently made up for the lost meals by doubling up on food during the other days of the week, with the result that he gained so much weight that his belt (*izār*) would slip below his waist. For this reason, he was called "a portly man" (*dhū baṭan*) by one of the Prophet's widows, Maymūna.[74]

As noted, Usāma married and divorced Zaynab bt. Ḥanzala while the Prophet was still alive. Subsequently, he married six additional women: Hind bt. al-Fākih b. al-Mughīra, Durra bt. ʿAdī b. Qays, Fāṭima bt. Qays (sister of al-Ḍaḥḥāq b. Qays al-Fihrī), Umm al-Ḥakam bt. ʿUtba b. Abī Waqqāṣ, Bint Abū Ḥamdān al-Sahmī, and Barza bt. al-Ribʿī. His wives bore him as many as twenty children, including Muḥammad and Hind (their mother was

Durra); Jubayr, Zayd, and ʿĀʾisha (their mother was Fāṭima), and Ḥasan and Ḥusayn (their mother was Barza).[75] It is curious that Usāma should have had sons named Muḥammad, Zayd, Ḥasan, and Ḥusayn; wives named Zaynab and Fāṭima; and a daughter named ʿĀʾisha. As a group, Usāma's children were known as the Banū al-Ḥibb or "the sons of the Beloved."[76]

The special relationship between the Prophet and Usāma is reflected in the size of the stipend that Usāma received from the *dīwān*. The sources indicate that Usāma's stipend was as large as, or larger than, the stipend of other distinguished Companions. He reportedly received a stipend of 4,000 coins per year from the second caliph ʿUmar b. al-Khaṭṭāb. This was the same amount received by Companions who had participated in the Battle of Badr in 2 A.H. When the caliph's son, Ibn ʿUmar (whose stipend was only 3,500 coins), learned about the size of Usāma's stipend, he protested to his father: "Why have you awarded Usāma a larger stipend than you have awarded me, when I participated in every battle in which he participated?" The caliph responded to his son as follows: "The Messenger of God loved Usāma more than he loved you, and he loved his father [Zayd] more than he loved your father [viz., me!]."[77]

Just as Muḥammad was solicitous of Usāma's welfare as a child, so too Usāma was solicitous of the welfare of his mother Umm Ayman as she approached the end of her life. Umm Ayman, it will be recalled, had been Muḥammad's caretaker and surrogate mother, and she reportedly was ten years older than the Prophet. If so, she would have been at least eighty years old when ʿUthmān b. ʿAffān became caliph in 23/644. At an unspecified date during ʿUthmān's caliphate, Usāma took a knife, removed the pith from a date-palm tree, and used this valuable commodity to purchase food for his elderly mother. Someone asked Usāma, "Why did you do that, when you know that a single date-palm tree is worth 1,000 dirhams?" "My mother asked me to do that," Usāma explained, "and I will do anything that she asks me to do—if I am able to do so."[78]

Usāma died in al-Jurf circa 54/674 during the caliphate of Muʿāwiya b. Abī Sufyān (r. 661–680) and was buried in Medina.[79]

The Islamic narratives about the relationship between Usāma and Muḥammad and the military campaign against Ubna draw on a wide range of biblical themes and motifs associated primarily—albeit not exclusively—with the relationship between Joshua and Moses and the conquest of Canaan. Let us first consider the relevant biblical models and then analyze the textual encounters.

Biblical Models

4.1 ROYAL CLOTHING, JEWELRY, AND RIDING BEHIND THE RULER

4.1.1 Joseph

After Joseph had interpreted Pharaoh's dreams, the ruler of Egypt put the former slave in charge of his court and announced that the Egyptians would be subject to his command. Joseph was now "in charge of all the land of Egypt." To formalize the appointment, Pharaoh removed his signet ring from his hand and put it on Joseph's hand, dressed Joseph "in robes of fine linen," and "put a gold chain about his neck." In addition Pharaoh placed Joseph "in the chariot of his second-in-command." When the Egyptians saw Joseph riding in the chariot, they would cry out "Abrek!" or "bow down" (Gen. 41:40–43).

4.1.2 Solomon

Before he died, King David instructed his men to place Solomon on his mule and have him ride to Gihon, where Zadok the priest and Nathan the prophet would anoint him as king over Israel. "For he shall succeed me as king; him I designate to be ruler of Israel and Judah" (I Kings 1:32–35).

4.1.3 Mordechai

When King Ahasuerus asked Haman, "What should be done for a man the king wishes to honor?" the minister replied that the man should be paraded in the city square, riding the king's horse and wearing his royal garb and royal diadem (Esther 6:6–9).

4.2 REVENGE

Before Moses died, God ordered him to "avenge the Israelite people on the Midianites"—no doubt for the evil that they had perpetrated. Moses instructed the Israelites as follows: "Let men be picked out from among you for a campaign, and let them fall upon Midian to wreak the Lord's vengeance on Midian" (Num. 31:1–3).

4.3 BATTLE INSTRUCTIONS

Before entering the Promised Land, the Israelites were instructed by God to eradicate the Canaanites and all manifestations of local idolatry. The Israelites destroyed a series of Canaanite towns and slew their inhabitants. In some narratives, the attack is said to have been an ambush. An essential element of the narratives is destruction by fire (e.g. Deut. 13:16–17, Josh. 6:24, 8:8, 28).

STAGE NOTE: WHO WILL ENTER THE PROMISED LAND?

No Israelite who was twenty years old or above at the time of the Exodus from Egypt was allowed to enter the Promised Land. Moses himself pleaded with God for permission to enter, but was not allowed to lead this "evil generation" across the Jordan River because of their unfaithfulness and acts of disobedience—and his own (Num. 20:12). Two exceptions were made, one for Caleb son of Jephunneh and the other for Joshua son of Nun, in both instances as a reward for continuous loyalty to God (Num. 32:12; Deut. 1:36). The conquest of Canaan did not commence until the entire generation of Israelites who participated in the Exodus had died.

4.4 DISSENSION IN THE RANKS ELICITS ANGER FROM A PROPHET

During the forty-year period of wandering in the desert, the Israelites bickered among themselves and annoyed Moses, who bemoaned his people's flouting of the divine command, their sulking in their tents, and their claim that God had brought them out of Egypt only to hand them over for destruction to the Amorites (Deut. 1:12, 26–27, 34–36).

4.5 A FINAL BLESSING AND THE LAYING ON OF HANDS

Upon learning that he would not enter the Promised Land, Moses asked God to appoint his successor as leader of the Israelites. God instructed Moses to "single out Joshua son of Nun, an inspired man, and lay your hand upon him. Have him stand before Eleazar the priest and before the whole community, and commission him in their sight. Invest him with some of your authority, so that the whole Israelite community may obey." Moses took

Joshua and, in the presence of Eleazar the priest and the entire community, "he laid hands upon him and commissioned him" (Num. 27:18–23). The Israelites heeded Joshua, doing as the Lord had commanded Moses (Deut. 34:1–7, 9).

4.6 EXEMPTION FROM MILITARY SERVICE

Before the Israelites invaded the Promised Land, God declared that any man who had built a new house but not yet dedicated it, planted a vineyard but not yet harvested it, or paid the bride-price for a wife but not yet consummated the marriage, would be excused from the obligation to fight. The purpose of the exemption was to insure that no third party would dedicate the man's house, harvest his field, or marry his wife in his absence (Deut. 20: 5–7).

4.7 THE BANNER—AND DIVISION OF AUTHORITY

No biblical model.

4.8 OBEDIENCE TO AUTHORITY

Immediately prior to the Battle of Ai, Joshua instructed his troops as follows: "Mind, you are to lie in ambush behind the city; don't stray too far from the city, and all of you be on the alert. . . . And when you take the city, set it on fire. Do as the Lord has commanded. Mind, I have given you your orders" (Josh. 8:3–8).

INTERLUDE: A REFRAIN

The narrative account of the conquest of Canaan is punctuated by a series of commands that recur in the manner of a refrain: "Go up, take possession" (Deut. 1:21), "Up now! Cross the wadi Zered!" (Deut. 2:13), and "Up! Set across the wadi Arnon!" (Deut. 2:24).

4.9 SCOUTS—AND A CLOUD

As the Israelites were preparing to enter Canaan, they demanded that Moses send ahead scouts "to reconnoiter the land for us and bring back word on the route we shall follow and the cities we shall come to." Moses complied (Deut. 1:22). In fact, there was no need for scouts, as God Himself was traveling by fire at night and in cloud by day so as to guide the Israelites to their destination (Deut. 1:32–33).

4.10 EXTERMINATION OF THE ENEMY

The Israelites entered the Promised Land as shock troops (Deut. 3:18). They doomed every town (Deut. 2:34, 3:6, 7:2, 13:16), granting the inhabitants no terms and giving them no quarter (Deut. 7:2). They killed men, women, and children, leaving no survivors (Deut. 2:34; 13:16–17). They slew the cattle (Deut. 13:16–17) or seized them as booty (Deut. 2:34, 3:6–7, 13:16). They tore down altars, smashed pillars, cut down sacred posts, and set fire to images (Deut. 7:5). They gathered all the spoils and set fire to them in the town square as a "holocaust" to the Lord (Deut. 13:17).

4.11 HOMECOMING

After successfully exacting revenge on the Midianites, the Israelites—twelve thousand strong—made their way back to their home base near the Jordan River. Just outside the camp, they were met by Moses, Eleazar the priest, and all the chieftains, who came out to greet them (Num. 31:13). The booty was inventoried and divided equally between the combatants who had engaged in the campaign and the rest of the community—after the removal of a levy for the Lord (Num. 31:31–47). Miraculously, not a single Israelite warrior had died in the campaign (Num. 31:48–49).

Textual Encounters

4.1 ROYAL CLOTHING, JEWELRY, AND RIDING BEHIND THE RULER

Muḥammad took a special interest in Usāma, dressing him in royal garments and adorning him with bracelets and earrings. He also made sure that on important public occasions, such as the conquest of Mecca and the pilgrimage, it was Usāma who was riding directly behind him as his *radīf*. An audience familiar with the Hebrew Bible would have understood these gestures as signs of the transfer of power and authority from a leader to his trusted agent or successor.

In the Hebrew Bible, Pharaoh dressed Joseph in robes of fine linen, placed a gold chain around his neck, and made sure that it was Joseph who rode directly behind him on important public occasions (Gen. 41:40–43). Similarly, King David instructed his men to place Solomon on the king's horse prior to his anointment as king of Israel (I Kings 1:32–35). And Haman advised King Ahasuerus that if he wished to honor Mordechai, he should give him the king's horse, dress him in royal garb, and parade him through the city (Esther 6:6–9).

4.2 REVENGE

Just before Muḥammad died, he commissioned Usāma b. Zayd to lead a military expedition into Palestine. The goal of the expedition was to exact revenge for the slaying of Zayd b. Ḥāritha at Muʾtah. Just before he died, Moses commissioned Joshua to lead a military expedition into Canaan to exact revenge upon the Midianites for the evil they had perpetrated against the Israelites (Num. 31:1–3).

4.3 BATTLE INSTRUCTIONS

Just as Muḥammad ordered Usāma to "trample them [viz. the inhabitants of Ubna] with your horses" and "set fire to them," God ordered the Israelites to set fire to a series of Canaanite towns and slay their inhabitants (Deut. 13:16–17, Josh. 6:24, 8:8, 28) (see further section 4.4, below).

STAGE NOTE: WHO WILL ENTER THE PROMISED LAND?

Islamic sources emphasize the fact that *all* of the first Emigrants (*muhājirūn*) participated in the military expedition to Palestine—with only two exceptions, Abū Bakr and ʿUmar (see further section 4.6 below).

The Islamic narrative inverts the biblical narrative, in which *none* of the Israelites who participated in the Exodus—including Moses—was allowed to enter the Promised Land; the prohibition was a punishment for lack of faith and disobedience (Num. 20:12). Two exceptions were made, one for Caleb son of Jephunneh and the other for Joshua son of Nun, in both instances as a reward for continuous loyalty to God (Deut. 1:36).

4.4 DISSENSION IN THE RANKS ELICITS ANGER FROM A PROPHET

Several Emigrants criticized Muḥammad's appointment of Usāma b. Zayd as the commander of the military expedition to Palestine on the grounds of his youth and lack of military experience. When the Prophet learned of their insubordination, he became very angry: "O people," he exclaimed, "what is this statement that has been brought to my attention about some of you regarding my appointment of Usāma b. Zayd as commander!?"

As the Israelites were wandering in the desert for forty years, they bickered among themselves, sulked in their tents, and concluded that God intended to hand them over for destruction to the Amorites. Moses became very angry: "How can I bear unaided the trouble of you," he exclaimed, "and the burden, and the bickering!" (Deut. 1:12).

4.5 A FINAL BLESSING AND THE LAYING ON OF HANDS

Arguably the last act performed by the Prophet before he died was to bless Usāma by lifting one of his hands high in the air and bringing it down upon the young man's head. This act was performed in the presence of members of Muḥammad's House.

One of the last acts performed by Moses before he died was to ask God to appoint his successor. God responded by instructing Moses to "single out Joshua son of Nun, an inspired man, and lay your hand upon him. . . . Invest him with some of your authority" (Num. 27:12–21). Moses "took Joshua . . . and laid his hands upon him and commissioned him—as the Lord had spoken through Moses" (Num. 27:22–23). This act was performed in the presence of Eleazar the priest and the entire community (Num. 27:19, 22).

4.6 EXEMPTION FROM MILITARY SERVICE

Shortly before Muḥammad died, he exempted Abū Bakr from his obligation to participate in the military expedition to Ubna so that the Companion might pay a conjugal visit to one of his wives. Shortly after the Prophet died, Abū Bakr exempted ʿUmar b. al-Khaṭṭāb from his obligation to participate in the same military expedition so that he might assist the new caliph in Medina.

Similarly, prior to the conquest of Canaan, a military exemption was granted to any Israelite who had an important excuse, such as a house that had not yet been dedicated, a vineyard that had not yet been harvested, or a bride whose marriage had not yet been consummated (Deut. 20:5–7).

4.7 THE BANNER—AND DIVISION OF AUTHORITY

No textual encounter.

4.8 OBEDIENCE TO AUTHORITY

The last command or order issued by the Prophet was to dispatch Usāma's army to Palestine. This instruction was ignored, first by senior Emigrants who complained of Usāma's youth and lack of military experience and, after the Prophet's death, by senior Emigrants who advised the new leader of the community, Abū Bakr, to delay the expedition until the turbulent and unstable situation in the Hijaz had returned to normal.

The Islamic narrative inverts the biblical narrative in which the Israelites carried out the battle instructions issued by Joshua immediately before the Battle of Ai. Joshua began by saying, "Mind, you are to lie in ambush behind the city." And he concluded by saying, "Do as the Lord has commanded. Mind, I have given you my orders" (Joshua 8:3–8).

INTERLUDE: A REFRAIN

The Islamic narrative about the military expedition to Ubna is punctuated several times by the Prophet's instruction to "dispatch Usāma's army" (*anfidhū baʿth Usāma*). After the Prophet's death, this instruction was repeated several times by Abū Bakr.

The repetition of this instruction in the manner of a refrain brings to mind Joshua's instruction to the Israelites as they were entering Canaan: "Go up, take possession," "Up now! Cross the wadi Zered!" and "Up! Set across the wadi Arnon!" (Deut. 1:21, 2:13, 2:24).

4.9 SCOUTS—AND A CLOUD

Usāma dispatched a scout who raced ahead to Ubna, where he engaged in reconnaissance. The scout then rejoined the expeditionary force and informed them that the inhabitants of Ubna were defenseless and unprepared for any attack. As the believers approached Ubna, a thick fog allowed them to traverse the land undetected.

In the biblical account of the conquest of Canaan, Moses sent scouts into the land to reconnoiter, select the best route, and identify military targets. Upon entering the Promised Land, the Israelites were guided by God, who traveled by fire at night and in a cloud by day (Deut. 1:22, 32–33).

4.10 EXTERMINATION OF THE ENEMY

Just as Joshua instructed the Israelites to carry out an ambush against Ai and ordered his men not to stray too far from the town, so too Usāma instructed his men to carry out a surprise attack against Ubna and ordered them to focus their attention on this town and to remain united. The believers killed or captured every inhabitant of the settlement who came into sight and set fire to their homes, fields, and date-palms. Smoke rose like a "whirlwind" in the air. They also seized booty and prepared the spoils of victory, which were divided among the soldiers: two shares for every horse and one share for its owner.

The Islamic narrative is informed by the biblical notion of *ḥerem* (literally, "to dedicate to destruction"),[80] in accordance with which the Israelites demonstrated their commitment to God's law and asserted their right to occupy the land by eradicating the Canaanites and all manifestations of idolatry. The Israelites entered the Promised Land as shock troops (in some cases the attack is said to have been an ambush). They doomed every town, granting the inhabitants no terms and giving them no quarter. They killed not only men but also women and children, leaving no survivors. They either destroyed the cattle or seized them as booty. They tore down altars, smashed pillars, cut down sacred posts, and set fire to images. They gathered all the spoils and set them afire in the town square as a "holocaust" to the Lord. Immolation served two purposes: It purified and protected the Israelites from contamination by the cultic items belonging to the Canaanites; and the cultic items that were destroyed were thereby removed from this world and transferred to the divine (see, e.g., Deut. 13:16–17, Josh. 6:24, 8:8, 28).

4.11 HOMECOMING

After successfully exacting revenge on the man who had slain his father, Usāma b. Zayd divided up the booty and then led his men—three thousand in number—back to the Hijaz. As the soldiers approached Medina, they were greeted by the Caliph Abū Bakr and other noncombatants. Miraculously, not a single believer was killed during the military campaign.

After successfully exacting revenge on the Midianites, Joshua led his men—twelve thousand in number—back to their military camp near the Jordan River. As the Israelites approached the camp, they were greeted by Moses, Eleazar the priest, and the chiefs of the tribes, and the booty was divided up among combatants and noncombatants. Miraculously, not a single Israelite was killed during the military campaign (Num. 31:13, 31–47, 48–49).

Conclusion

The Many Faces of Zayd and Usāma

In the standard version of the Islamic foundation narrative, Zayd and Usāma play only a marginal role in the events associated with the rise of Islam. Clearly, however, the appearance of marginality is not an accurate reflection of the status of these two men in the minds of the early community. The importance of Zayd and Usāma in early historical narratives becomes apparent only after one has gathered and attended to the many reports about these two men that currently are scattered across a wide range of sources. Once this task has been performed, what emerges is a rich and colorful portrait of two extraordinary figures.

As Zayd passes from youth to maturity to manhood and, finally, to death, his character takes the shape of one or another biblical figure. As a youth he is Joseph, albeit with a twist. Unlike the biblical figure who welcomed family reunification, Zayd rejected his birth family in favor of his slave master. Just as Dammesek Eliezer, Abram's trusted servant, became his master's surrogate son and heir, so too Zayd, after a demonstration of supreme loyalty and devotion, became Muḥammad's adopted son and heir. Like Abraham, Moses, and Solomon, Zayd was favored by God—indeed, not only by God but also by His prophet. Like Ishmael, he was eventually repudiated, albeit not rejected, by his father. Like Uriah the Hittite, he was sent to certain death on a battlefield in southern Jordan by the man who fell in love with his wife. And like Isaac in Gen. 22 (and Jesus in the New Testament), Zayd became the prototype of the martyr who gains immortality as a consequence of his willingness to lay down his life for the sake of his God, his prophet, and his religion. Thus, Zayd is a hybrid figure whose persona is modeled on that of at least six different biblical characters: Joseph, Dammesek Eliezer, Solomon, Ishmael, Uriah the Hittite, and Isaac. He is each one of these men individually and all of them combined. One examines his life as one peers through a kaleidoscope: With each turn of the dial, a new and different image comes into focus.

Usāma's figure was also shaped by biblical models. Just as Pharaoh dressed Joseph in royal garments, adorned him with jewelry, and made sure that he rode directly behind him on important public occasions, so too Muḥammad dressed Usāma in royal garments, adorned him with bracelets and earrings, and made sure that he rode directly behind him on important public occasions. Just as Moses chose Joshua to lead a military expedition into Canaan to exact revenge on the Midianites for their mistreatment of the Israelites, so too Muḥammad chose Usāma to lead a military expedition into Palestine to exact revenge for the slaying of Zayd at Muʾtah. Just as Moses laid his hand upon Joshua and commissioned him as his successor, so too Muḥammad laid his hand upon Usāma and—arguably—commissioned him as his successor. Just as Moses instructed Joshua to scorch a series of Canaanite towns and slay their inhabitants, so too Muḥammad commanded Usāma to scorch Ubna and to trample its inhabitants with horses. Just as the Israelites decimated the inhabitants of Canaan, so too Usāma and his men decimated the inhabitants of Ubna. And just as not a single Israelite was killed during the military expedition against Midian, so too not a single believer was killed during the military expedition against Ubna.

This remarkable accumulation of correspondences suggests that the historical memory of the early Muslim community was strongly influenced by biblical models and that the community constructed its foundation narrative, at least in part, on a biblical stage or platform. The *dramatis personae* in the Islamic sacred drama were modeled on earlier biblical figures. By establishing connections between Muslim figures and their biblical counterparts, the storytellers sought to convey moral, religious, and political lessons to their audiences. Let us now explore the lessons embedded in the stories about Zayd and Usāma by returning to the starting point of our story, v. 37 of *Sūrat al-Aḥzāb*.

Verse 37 of *Sūrat al-Aḥzāb*, Revisited

> [Recall] when you said to the one on whom God and you yourself have bestowed favor, "Keep your wife to yourself and fear God," and you hid within yourself what God would reveal, and you feared the people when God had better right to be feared by you. When Zayd had finished with her, We gave her to you in marriage, so that there should be no sin (*ḥaraj*) for the believers concerning the wives of their adopted sons, when they have finished with them. God's command was fulfilled.

I began the present investigation by attempting to explain the meaning of v. 37 of *Sūrat al-Aḥzāb* based solely on its contents. As noted in the Introduction, the precise circumstances of the episode to which this revelation refers would have been a matter of record and thus well-known to its immediate audience. It was no doubt the familiarity of this audience with the episode that accounts for the narrative gaps in the verse. In Chapters 1 and 2, I attempted to recover the context in which this episode would have unfolded. Although we will never be in a position of full knowledge, we arguably are now in a position similar to that of the believers to whom this revelation was first recited. Let us use this knowledge to reexamine v. 37 in an effort to shed light on its earliest meaning and function. We begin by focusing attention on the man identified as *Zayd* in the middle of the verse.

Zayd was born circa 580 C.E., the son of Ḥāritha b. Sharāḥīl and Suʿda bt. Thaʿlab. His father belonged to the tribe of Kalb. He was thus Zayd b. Ḥāritha al-Kalbī. When Zayd was approximately twenty years old, he was captured by Arabs and transported to the Hijaz, where he was purchased as a slave by a merchant named Muḥammad b. ʿAbdallāh al-Hāshimī with funds provided by the latter's wife Khadīja. At the time of the purchase, Muḥammad had not yet received his first revelation or emerged as a prophet.

Upon learning of Zayd's disappearance, Ḥāritha b. Sharāḥīl was inconsolable (the sources are silent about Suʿda's reaction to her son's disappearance). By a stroke of good fortune, Kalbī tribesmen just happened to come across Zayd in the Hijaz. They brought the good news to Ḥāritha, who then made his way to Mecca, accompanied by his brother. The two men sought out Muḥammad and implored him to accept a ransom offer. Curiously, Muḥammad rejected the offer, suggesting that he had a better idea. He informed Zayd that the choice was his to make: If he wished, he could return to his homeland as a free man and be reunited with his birth family; or he could remain in Mecca as Muḥammad's slave. The important point, for Muḥammad, was that Zayd should make the decision of his own free will. Apparently, a close bond had been established between master and slave: Muḥammad reminded Zayd of the "companionship" (*ṣuḥba*) between the two men; and Zayd declared that Muḥammad had the status of "both his father and his mother." In addition, Zayd's intuition told him that there was something special about Muḥammad. For these reasons, and to the astonishment of his father and his uncle, Zayd chose to remain a slave.

It was only after this demonstration of supreme loyalty that Muḥammad decided to adopt Zayd as his son. At the time of the adoption, Zayd would have been between twenty and twenty-five years old. The ceremony was performed in front of the Kaʿba in the presence of witnesses from the tribe of Quraysh; also present were Zayd's father and uncle. The adoption entailed two important legal consequences: First, Zayd took the name of his adoptive father, that is to say, he was Zayd b. Muḥammad al-Hāshimī. Second, mutual rights of inheritance were established between father and son. Note well: Zayd was now Muḥammad's son (*ibn*)—his only adult son—and heir (*wārith*).

Following Muḥammad's receipt of the first revelation in 610 C.E., Zayd b. Muḥammad was, according to al-Zuhrī (d. 124/742), the first person to become a believer (according to other authorities, he was the third person and first adult male to become a believer). The Prophet loved Zayd dearly and he was known as "the Beloved of the Messenger of God." In Mecca, Muḥammad arranged for Zayd to marry his former caretaker and surrogate mother, Umm Ayman, who would have been between forty and forty-five years old at the time. By a stroke of good fortune, Umm Ayman became pregnant and, approximately one year later, she gave birth to a son whose birth name—again, note well—would have been Usāma b. Zayd b. Muḥammad al-Hāshimī, even if he is never identified in this manner in any source that I have consulted. Usāma was the Prophet's grandson and arguably the first male born into the new community of believers. The Prophet's love for Usāma is said to have been as great as his love for Zayd, on the one hand, and as great as his love for al-Ḥasan b. ʿAlī, on the other. Usāma was known as "the Beloved Son of the Beloved of the Messenger of God."

Zayd and his family participated in the hijra to Medina in 1/622. Shortly thereafter, Zayd informed his father that he wanted to take a second wife. The woman whom he had identified as a potential marriage partner was Zaynab bt. Jaḥsh al-Asadī, Muḥammad's paternal cross-cousin—both were grandchildren of ʿAbd al-Muṭṭalib. Initially, Muḥammad objected to the marriage on the grounds of social inequality, but Zayd was adamant, and the Prophet soon relented. When Zaynab learned of the marriage proposal, she too objected, on the grounds that she was the most perfect woman in the tribe of Quraysh. God now made the first of a series of interventions by sending down the revelation that would become v. 36 of *Sūrat al-Aḥzāb*: "When God and His messenger have decided a matter, it is not for any believing man or woman to have any choice in the affair. Whoever disobeys God and His Messenger has gone astray in manifest error." As a believing woman, Zaynab had no choice but to obey God and His Messenger. The marriage was consummated. It may come as no surprise, however, that it was unsuccessful, and it was not long before Zayd began to complain to his father about his wife's behavior.

In 5 A.H. Zayd approached Muḥammad and asked him for permission to divorce Zaynab. True to form, Muḥammad had a better idea. Determined to save the marriage, the Prophet paid a visit to the couple with the intention of admonishing Zaynab and teaching her to be a better wife to his son. Upon his arrival, only Zaynab was at home, wearing a thin, light garment. Inadvertently, the Prophet caught a glimpse of his daughter-in-law as she was in the act of rising to her feet and he was immediately transformed by her physical beauty, charm, and grace. "Praise be to God," he is reported to have said, "who can transform a man's heart [in an instant]." When Zayd returned home later the same day, Zaynab regaled her husband with the story of the strange encounter with her father-in-law. Zayd was now more determined than ever to divorce his wife, and the two ceased having sexual relations—a key narrative detail.

Zayd returned to his father and repeated his request for permission to divorce his wife. Although Muḥammad had fallen in love with the woman, he understood that his attraction to Zaynab had brought him to the brink of committing a serious sexual transgression. The Prophet therefore instructed his son *not* to divorce his wife and, fearing criticism from the inhabitants of Medina—believers, Jews, and hypocrites—he kept his feelings for Zaynab a secret.

It was precisely at this moment that God made His second intervention in this episode by delivering the revelation that would become v. 37 of *Sūrat al-Aḥzāb*. The verse opens with God's instruction to His prophet to recall his most recent conversation with "the one on whom God and you yourself have bestowed favor ([*alladhī*] *anʿama allāhu ʿalayhi wa-anʿamta ʿalayhi*)" (emphasis added). Elsewhere in the Qurʾān, the language of "divine favor" or "blessing" (*niʿma*) is used with reference to earlier prophets, e.g., Q. 19:58: "These are those whom God blessed among the prophets of the seed of Adam" (*ulāʾika alladhīna anʿama allāh ʿalayhim min al-nabiyyīn min dhuriyyat Ādam*). In v. 37, the doubly favored man is Muḥammad's son, whose name at the moment on which this revelation was delivered would have been Zayd b. Muḥammad. The subject of the conversation between father and son was the status of Zayd's marriage to his wife, here unnamed, but presumably the beautiful Zaynab bt. Jaḥsh. Although Muḥammad had fallen in love with Zaynab, he initially kept his desire for the woman a secret because he knew that it was a sin for a man to have sexual relations with his daughter-in-law, indeed, even with his former daughter-in-law. Fearing public condemnation if he were to act on his feelings for Zaynab, Muḥammad instructed his son to "keep your wife to yourself and fear God." Remarkably, the Divinity rebuked the Prophet for placing his fear of men ("you feared the people") over his fear of God ("God had a better right to be feared by you") but then introduced a critical distinction between the wife of a biological son and that of an adopted son. Henceforth it would not be a sin for a believer to marry the former wife of his *adopted* son, on the condition that the husband no longer had any sexual interest in his wife—hence the importance of the above-mentioned narrative detail about the cessation of sexual relations between Zayd and Zaynab, which provides support for the specification in v. 37 that Zayd had, in fact, "finished with her." God sanctioned the sexual union between the Prophet and Zaynab by announcing that it was through His divine agency that the marriage had been executed ("We gave her to you in marriage"). By marrying Zaynab, the Prophet had fulfilled a divine command ("God's command was fulfilled").

The Qurʾān has nothing more to say about the events leading up to or following this remarkable episode. This gap is filled by Islamic sources, which teach that Zayd did in fact divorce Zaynab. To insure that she was not carrying his child, Zaynab was required to wait until she had completed three menstrual cycles before she could remarry. This three-month waiting-period created a narrative window in which something truly extraordinary happened. Without any advance warning and for no apparent cause, Muḥammad suddenly terminated the adoptive relationship that had been created more than fifteen years earlier between himself and Zayd. "I am not your father," he said to Zayd. True to form, and without a moment's hesitation, the ever loyal and obedient servant accepted this demotion in his status. "I am Zayd b. Ḥāritha b. Sharāḥīl al-Kalbī," he replied. Thus did Zayd b. Muḥammad, the Beloved of the Messenger of God, the first person (or the first adult male) to become a believer, the man who was favored by both God and His prophet, and the only believer apart from Muḥammad who is identified by name in the Qurʾān, lose his status as the Prophet's son and heir.

At first glance, one might think that Muḥammad repudiated Zayd in order to facilitate his marriage to Zaynab. Examination of the Qurʾān, however, suggests that this could not have been the true cause of the repudiation. Verse 37 of *Sūrat al-Aḥzāb*, it will be recalled, introduces a distinction between biological sons and adopted sons and announces that it would no longer be a sin for a man to marry the former wife of his adopted son. Suppose, for the sake of argument, that Zayd had continued to be Muḥammad's adopted son. Would there have been anything improper about the Prophet's marriage to Zaynab after her divorce from Zayd? In fact, there is nothing in the language of v. 37 to suggest that there would have been any impropriety whatsoever. Thus, there must be some other explanation for Muḥammad's repudiation of Zayd. This explanation is found in yet another divine intervention in this remarkable episode.

No sooner had God introduced the distinction in v. 37 between biological sons and adopted sons than He sent down two revelations that transformed that distinction into the proverbial distinction without a difference. These two revelations would become vv. 4 and 5 of *Sūrat al-Aḥzāb*. Verse 4 states that "God has not put two hearts inside any man," an allusion to the problem of dual loyalty faced by adoptees. Verse 5 adds the instruction, "Call them after their [true] fathers," and it goes on to explain that it is a sin (*junāḥ*) to refer to a man (or woman) as the son (or daughter) of anyone other than his (or her) biological father. It is for this reason, in my view, that Islamic sources studiously avoid referring to Zayd as "the son of Muḥammad" or to Usāma as "the grandson of Muḥammad." These two verses suggest, without explicitly saying so, that the institution of adoption had been abolished. Indeed, the Prophet himself is reported to have said, "There is no adoption in

Islam: the custom of the Age of Ignorance (*jāhiliyya*) has been superseded." The combination of divine revelation and prophetic *sunna* made it clear that Muḥammad had no choice but to repudiate Zayd. Indeed, had he failed to do so, he would have been disobeying God. But Muḥammad's repudiation of Zayd as his son did not change the underlying nature of the relationship between the two men.

Verse 5 also suggests that Zayd was now the Messenger of God's *mawlā*—that is to say, his friend, ward, or protégé—in which capacity he continued to enjoy Muḥammad's confidence. In 6 A.H. the Prophet appointed Zayd as the commander of six military expeditions. In 7 or 8 A.H. he appointed Zayd as the commander of a military expedition that was charged with the task of avenging the treacherous slaying of a Muslim emissary in southern Jordan. Prior to the departure of the expedition, a Jew attempted to deter the Prophet, albeit without success, from sending Zayd to what he suggested would be certain death on the battlefield; the Jew also attempted to deter Zayd, again without success, from participating in what he suggested would be a suicide mission. As the Jew had predicted, Zayd met his death on a battlefield near the village of Muʾtah in Jordan. As a reward for his readiness to sacrifice his life for the sake of God and His prophet, Zayd immediately ascended to Heaven.

The *Sīra*, Revisited

In the Introduction, I attempted to establish what a Muslim living in Baghdad in the middle of the third/ninth century would have known about the man identified as *Zayd* in Q. 33:37 if, contrary to fact, he or she had access *only* to Ibn Hishām's (d. ca. 218/833) redacted version of the *Sīra* of Ibn Isḥāq (d. 150/767).

Our imaginary reader would have known about a man identified as "Zayd b. Ḥāritha" who was "the *mawlā* of the Messenger of God." Zayd joined the community of believers immediately after the Prophet's wife Khadīja and his cousin ʿAlī b. Abī Ṭālib, and just before Abū Bakr. Zayd married and had a son named Usāma. He participated in the hijra to Medina, where he was paired as a "brother" with Ḥamza b. ʿAbd al-Muṭṭalib, who, before he died, entrusted Zayd with his last will and testament. Zayd served as the commander of numerous military expeditions. He was trustworthy and brave but sometimes cruel. In 8 A.H. (according to the *Sīra*), Zayd was martyred while fighting in the village of Muʾtah in southern Jordan. Upon his arrival in Paradise, an attractive slave girl with dark red lips is said to have been waiting for him.[1]

As for Usāma, our imaginary reader would have known that he took care of Muḥammad's daughter Ruqayya before she died in 2 A.H., was appointed by the Prophet as the commander of a military expedition to southern Palestine in 11 A.H., received a blessing from Muḥammad on his deathbed, and, shortly thereafter, helped to prepare the Prophet's body for burial.[2]

The only episode of Zayd's life to which the *Sīra* devotes sustained attention is the Battle of Muʾtah. Otherwise, the portrayal of Zayd in the *Sīra* pales in comparison to his portrayal in historical texts composed over the course of the third century A.H. by Wāqidī (d. 207/823), Ibn Saʿd (d. 230/848), and Balādhurī (d. 279/892). Perhaps the easiest way to document this disparity is to identify what our imaginary reader of the *Sīra* would *not* have known: She or he would not have known that Muḥammad had adopted Zayd as his son circa 605 C.E.; that, as a consequence of the adoption, Zayd was renamed Zayd b. Muḥammad al-Hāshimī and became Muḥammad's heir; that following Muḥammad's emergence as a prophet, Zayd was known as the Beloved of the Messenger of God; and that Zayd had been Muḥammad's adult son and heir for at least fifteen and as many as twenty years, from circa 605 C.E. until 5/626–27.

Our imaginary reader also would not have known about Zayd's marriage to Zaynab bt. Jaḥsh or their subsequent divorce; that the Prophet fell in love with his daughter-in-law after catching a glimpse of her in a state of *dishabille*; that God intervened in history to facilitate the Prophet's marriage to Zaynab by sending down a revelation in which He introduced a distinction between biological sons and adopted sons; that, almost immediately, He intervened in history again to abolish the institution of adoption; and that it was only as a result of this latter intervention that Muḥammad was compelled to relinquish his status as Zayd's father, and that Zayd was compelled to relinquish his status as Muḥammad's son.

As for Usāma, although our imaginary reader would have known that he received a blessing from the Prophet as he lay dying, he or she would not have known that Usāma was the first male born into the community of believers; that he was the Prophet's grandson; that his full name at birth would have been Usāma b. Zayd b. Muḥammad al-Hāshimī; that he was known as the Beloved Son of the Beloved of the Messenger of God; that the

Prophet's love for Usāma was as great as his love for al-Ḥasan b. ʿAlī; that he was solicitous of Usāma's welfare; that bodily fluids were exchanged between the grandfather and his grandson; that the Prophet dressed Usāma in royal garments, adorned him with fine jewelry, and made sure that he rode directly behind him on important occasions; that shortly before he died, the Prophet placed the banner of the community in Usāma's hand; and, finally, that this banner remained in Usāma's possession for more than forty years until his death circa 54/674.

All of these details were pushed from the center to the margins of what would become the standard account of the career of Muḥammad and the emergence of Islam. One wonders why. The process of marginalization appears to have begun in the early ʿAbbasid period. It is certainly understandable that Ibn Hishām would have removed from Ibn Isḥāq's earlier version of the *Sīra* any information relating to the amorous episode involving Muḥammad and Zaynab on the grounds that the episode was offensive to the sensibilities of pious Muslims. But the offensiveness of the episode hardly explains the other omissions.

Let us attempt to account for these omissions by performing a second thought experiment in which we postulate two counterfactuals. Suppose, for the sake of argument, first, that Muḥammad did not repudiate Zayd, and, second, that Zayd outlived the Prophet. The result is as follows: Had Zayd continued to be Muḥammad's son and outlived his father, then (1) the institution of adoption no doubt would have remained in force; and (2) following the Prophet's death in 11/632, Zayd's credentials as the Prophet's son and heir would have made him a strong candidate to succeed Muḥammad as leader of the community.

Let us now modify our experiment by postulating only our first counterfactual. Suppose that Zayd did in fact die in 7 or 8 A.H. but that, at the time of his death, he was still the Prophet's son. If so, then (1) again, the institution of adoption would have remained in force; and (2) following Muḥammad's death in 11 A.H., Usāma's credentials as the Prophet's grandson and heir would have made him a strong candidate to succeed Muḥammad as leader of the community.

Note well: In the standard historical sources, neither Zayd nor Usāma is *ever* mentioned as a candidate for leadership of the community of believers. The two primary contenders for leadership of the community following the death of the Prophet were Abū Bakr b. Abī Quḥāfa and ʿAlī b. Abī Ṭālib. Supporters of each man justified one or the other's right to succeed Muḥammad on the strength of the following criteria: (1) closeness (*qarāba*) to the Prophet through blood and/or marriage; (2) seniority in Islam (*sābiqa*); (3) distinguished service; (4) moral excellence (*faḍl*, pl. *faḍāʾil*); (5) evidence in the Qurʾān; and (6) signs or gestures made by the Prophet shortly before he died. Using these six criteria, let us compare the leadership credentials of Zayd and Usāma, on the one hand, with those of Abū Bakr[3] and ʿAlī,[4] on the other.

CLOSENESS

1. Abū Bakr was the father of Muḥammad's favorite wife, ʿĀʾisha, known as the Beloved of the Beloved of God (*ḥabībat ḥabīb allāh*).[5] He was Muḥammad's friend and advisor (*khalīl*) and the two men reportedly met on a daily basis.

2. ʿAlī b. Abī Ṭālib was Muḥammad's paternal cousin and he grew up in the latter's house after the death of Abū Ṭālib. Immediately following the hijra, Muḥammad created a contract of brotherhood between himself and ʿAlī. In 2/623, Muḥammad arranged for ʿAlī to marry his daughter Fāṭima. ʿAlī was the Prophet's "trustee" (*waṣī*)—indeed, "the seal of trustees"—and one of the persons most loved by Muḥammad.[6] The relationship the two men was like that between Aaron (or Joshua) and Moses.

3. Zayd was Muḥammad's adopted son and heir from circa 605 until 626–27 C.E. The two men were connected by a special bond (*ṣuḥba*). Zayd regarded Muḥammad as having the status of both his father and his mother. He was known as the Beloved of the Messenger of God and was among those most loved by the Prophet.

4. Usāma was Muḥammad's grandson, the Beloved Son of the Beloved of the Messenger of God, one of those most loved by the Prophet, and his *radīf*. Muḥammad played an instrumental role in Usāma's upbringing and there was close physical contact between the two. Shortly before he died, Muḥammad placed one of his hands on Usāma's head and blessed him.

SENIORITY

1. Abū Bakr was the fourth person and the second adult male to become a believer.

2. ʿAlī was the second person and the first male—albeit a minor—to become a believer.

3. Zayd was either the first person to become a believer or the third person and the first adult male to become a believer.

4. Usāma was arguably the first male born into the community of believers.

DISTINGUISHED SERVICE

1. Abū Bakr facilitated the Prophet's escape from would-be assassins in Mecca and the two men hid in a cave outside the city before making their way to Yathrib. He fought at the Battles of Badr, Uḥud, and the Ditch.

2. ʿAlī risked his life by sleeping in the Prophet's bed wrapped in his green mantle on the night before Muḥammad's escape from Mecca. He fought in all major battles—with the exception of Tabuk in 9/630, but only because Muḥammad had put him in charge of Medina (*istakhlafahu ʿalā al-madīna*).[7]

3. Zayd fought in the Battles of Badr, Uḥud, and the Ditch. After becoming the Prophet's *mawlā* in 5 A.H., he was appointed by Muḥammad as the commander of nine military expeditions, including, in 7 or 8 A.H., the ill-fated expedition to Muʾtah, where he was slain as a martyr and is said to have ascended to Heaven.

4. Shortly before he died in 11 A.H., the Prophet placed the standard of the community in Usāma's hands and appointed him as the *amīr* or commander of a military expedition to southern Palestine. The expedition was a success, and not a single believer was killed. The standard remained with Usāma until his death circa 54/674.

MORAL EXCELLENCE

1. Abū Bakr was *al-Ṣiddīq* ("the veracious one") and "the best of mankind."[8]

2. ʿAlī was "the best of mankind."[9]

3. Zayd and Usāma "were among those most beloved to me [viz., the Prophet]" and both were "disposed to goodness."

4. Usāma was, according to Muḥammad, "one of your best."

THE QURʾĀN

1. The Qurʾān contains at least two verses that are said to allude to Abū Bakr. In Q. 9:40, the statement "the second of the two, when the two of them were in the cave" is understood as an allusion to Abū Bakr, who risked his life by hiding in a cave, together with the Prophet, in order to escape detection by would-be assassins. Similarly, in Q. 39:33, "Those who come with the truth and believe it" is understood as an allusion to Abū Bakr, who is known as al-Ṣiddīq (see above).

2. The Shiʿis maintain that ʿAlī was mentioned by name in numerous verses of the Qurʾān, but that these verses were removed by the commission that produced the ʿUthmānic codex. They also maintain that seventy verses of this codex refer to ʿAlī.

3. In Q. 33:37, Zayd is identified by name and characterized as "the one who was favored by God and favored by you [viz., the Prophet]." He is thus the only believer, apart from Muḥammad, who is explicitly mentioned by name in the Qurʾān.

4. There is no mention of Usāma in the Qurʾān or any allusion to him.

PROPHETIC SIGNS AND GESTURES

1. Shortly before he died, Muḥammad instructed Abū Bakr to lead the community in prayer and he is said to have smiled broadly when he saw the Companion carrying out this assignment.[10]

2. Following his performance of his Farewell Pilgrimage in 10 A.H., Muḥammad took ʿAlī by the hand and declared, "Of whomever I am the master (*mawlā*), ʿAlī is his master. May God therefore oppose those who oppose him and defend those who defend him." (Alternatively, this statement was made two or more years earlier as a consequence of a dispute between ʿAlī and Zayd. See Chapter 2, section 2.7).

3. Arguably the last act performed by the Prophet before he died was to appoint Usāma as the commander of a military expedition to southern Palestine. Shortly thereafter Muḥammad became ill and took to his bed. As he lay dying—and unable to speak—he received a visit from Usāma, who kneeled down beside him. The Prophet lifted his hand high in the air and brought it down upon the young man's head and blessed him.

According to every measure, the leadership credentials of Zayd and Usāma are as strong as or stronger than those of Abū Bakr and ʿAlī: (1) Zayd was Prophet's son and heir for at least fifteen and as many as twenty years, whereas Abū Bakr was merely Muḥammad's father-in-law and ʿAlī was his paternal cousin and son-in-law; (2) Zayd was an adult when he joined the community of believers, unlike ʿAlī, who was a minor, and his conversion preceded that of Abū Bakr; (3) whereas Zayd sacrificed his life for the sake of God and His prophet, Abū Bakr and ʿAlī merely risked their lives for Muḥammad; (4) all three men were known for moral excellence; (5) the Qurʾān identifies Zayd by name and characterizes him as having been favored by both God and His prophet; by contrast, neither Abū Bakr nor ʿAlī is mentioned by name in the Qurʾān; and, finally, (6) on his deathbed, the Prophet laid his hand on Usāma's head and blessed him; by comparison, in 10 A.H. the Prophet specified that his *mawlā*s or clients were also ʿAlī's clients, and, in 11 A.H., he appointed Abū Bakr as leader of prayer in his absence.

Muḥammad's sonlessness is taken for granted in Islamic sources. This should come as no surprise as the earliest layers of the Islamic foundation narrative were composed, first, by supporters of the Umayyads and, second, by supporters of the ʿAbbasids. Both dynasties would have had a compelling interest in either downplaying or suppressing any argument based on sonship, which, in combination with the other criteria for leadership, would have trumped the claims of both Abū Bakr and ʿAlī to be the legitimate successor to the Prophet. If there was one thing that united every early political group—supporters of Abū Bakr, ʿUthmān, or ʿAlī, the Umayyads, and the ʿAbbasids—it was that the Prophet must not be remembered as having had a son or grandson, either biological or adopted, who reached the age of maturity and outlived him. It is surely no coincidence that the early Muslim community remembered their prophet as having died without a son and heir, indeed, without any male descendants or ascendants.

Zayd and Usāma posed a political threat to the earliest leaders of the Muslim community, irrespective of the family or faction to which they belonged. If, as I suspect, Ibn Isḥāq's *Sīra* did contain some or all of the narratives about Zayd and Usāma that we have related in Chapters 1, 2, and 4, there would have been a compelling reason for Ibn Hishām to redact the earlier text in such a manner as to downplay the importance of the Prophet's adopted son Zayd and of his grandson Usāma.

The reader may object: The thought experiments that have just been conducted are nothing more than the fantasy of a scholar with an overheated imagination. To this objection I reply: My experiment is merely a variation of thought experiments performed by, or attributed to, prominent Companions of the Prophet and by Muslims living in the first half of the second century A.H. For example, no less an authority than the Prophet's wife ʿĀʾisha (d. 58/678) is reported to have performed a thought experiment in which she postulated only our second counterfactual, to wit, that Zayd did in fact outlive the Prophet. In a tradition related on her authority, ʿĀʾisha is reported to have said: "The Messenger of God never sent Zayd b. Ḥāritha on a military mission without appointing him as the commander. Had [Zayd] outlived [the Prophet], he would have appointed him as his successor."[11] Here, Zayd's credentials as a military commander make him the best candidate to succeed the Prophet after his death. As in our experiment, Zayd poses a political threat to the first four caliphs, the Shiʿis, the Umayyads, and/or the ʿAbbasid family.

The political threat posed by Zayd and Usāma, however, pales in comparison to a *theological* threat, to which we now direct our attention.

The Office of Prophecy in the Qurʾān

The Qurʾān teaches that the biblical prophets were chosen by God from among the Israelites. The first two prophets were Adam and Noah. Subsequently the pool from which prophets were chosen was narrowed to Abraham and his descendants ("the seed of Abraham"). Beginning with Abraham, all of the biblical prophets identified in the Qur'ān are members of this family.

The Qur'ān suggests, without explicitly saying so, that prophecy is the exclusive possession of a single, divinely privileged lineage: Q. 57:26 states that God assigned prophecy and the Book to the progeny (*dhurriyya*) of Noah and Abraham. Q. 4:163 identifies successive generations of prophets within a single family: "We have made revelations to you, as We made them to Noah and the prophets after him, and as We made them to Abraham and Ishmael and Isaac and Jacob and the tribes." According to Q. 29:27, the office of prophecy is reserved for Abraham and his "progeny." In fact, beginning with Abraham, all of the biblical figures identified in the Qur'ān as prophets are members of this family: Lot, Ishmael, Isaac, Jacob, Joseph, Moses, Aaron, David, Solomon, Job, Jonah, Elijah, Elisha, Zechariah, John the Baptist, and Jesus.

In the Qur'ānic worldview, true prophecy is the exclusive possession of a single family and the office of prophecy is transmitted from father to son. One might say that the office of prophecy is hereditary (although the "gene" for prophecy may lie dormant for one or more generations, as happened between Solomon and Jesus). In order to qualify as a prophet, one must be a member of this family. Nowhere in the Qur'ān, however, is Muḥammad identified as a descendant of Abraham. This omission is rectified in the *Sīra*, which opens with a section entitled "Muḥammad's Pure Descent from Adam" in which Muḥammad's genealogy is traced back to Abraham through twenty-nine intervening links, then from Abraham to Noah through ten links, and finally from Noah to Adam through eight links (the upper part of the genealogy, beginning with Nāḥūr, draws on Gen. 5:1–31, 10:21, and 11:10ff.). The list is as follows:

> **Muḥammad**—ʿAbdallāh—ʿAbd al-Muṭṭalib (whose name was Shayba)—Hāshim (whose name was ʿAmr)—ʿAbd Manāf (whose name was al-Mughīra)—Quṣayy (whose name was Zayd)—Kilāb—Murra—Kaʿb—Luʾayy—Ghālib—Fihr—Mālik—al-Naḍr—Kināna—Khuzayma—Mudrika (whose name was ʿĀmir)—Ilyās—Muḍar—Nizār—Maʿadd—ʿAdnān—Udd (or Udad)—Muqawwam—Nāḥūr—Tayrah—Yaʿrub—Yashjub—Nābit—Ismāʿīl—**Ibrāhīm, the friend**

> **of the Compassionate**—Tāriḥ (who is Āzar)—Nāḥūr—Sārūgh—Rāʿū—Fālikh—ʿAybar—Shālikh—Arfakhshadh—Sām—**Nūḥ**—Lamk—Mattūshalakh—Akhnūkh, who is the prophet Idrīs according to what they allege, but God knows best (he was the first of the sons of Adam to whom prophecy and writing with a pen were given)—Yard—Mahlīl—Qaynan—Yānish—Shīth—**Adam**.[12]

By creating a genealogical connection between Muḥammad, on the one hand, and Abraham, Noah, and Adam, on the other, Islamic tradition established that Muḥammad was in fact a member of the family that holds the exclusive right to the office of prophecy. Thus it is proved: Muḥammad was qualified to be *a* prophet.

But Muḥammad was not merely *a* prophet or merely *another* prophet. He was, according to Muslims, the *last* in the series of prophets sent by God to humanity, beginning with Adam and Noah and continuing with Abraham and his descendants, down to Jesus. The Qurʾānic representation of prophecy as a hereditary office that is the exclusive possession of a single family has important consequences for the claim that Muḥammad was the last prophet. The believers who formulated the Islamic foundation narrative would have had to address the following problem: If Muḥammad did have a son who attained physical maturity and outlived his father, the office of prophecy would have passed to that son and/or to his lineal descendants. In that case, however, Muḥammad would not have been the last prophet. Conversely, if Muḥammad was not just another prophet but also the last prophet, he could not be remembered as having had a son who attained physical maturity and outlived him. In other words, the theological doctrine of the finality of prophecy required that the man who brought the office of prophecy to an end must be sonless. One might say that the sonlessness of the last prophet, whoever that person might be, was a theological imperative. This theological imperative demanded a Qurʾānic witness, and this demand, in turn, brings us to v. 40 of *Sūrat al-Aḥzāb.*

Verse 40 of *Sūrat al-Aḥzāb*

The linguistic basis of the theological doctrine of the finality of prophecy is the Arabic phrase *khātam al-nabiyyīn*, literally, "the seal of prophets." The association of a *khātam* or seal with the office of prophecy is found in earlier Jewish, Christian, and Manichean texts in which the metaphor is used to signify the confirmation or fulfillment of prophecy.[13] Thus, in the Qurʾān, the reference to Muḥammad as "the seal of prophets," without any further qualification, is easily understood as signifying that he confirmed or fulfilled the revelations sent previously to Moses and Jesus. How then did the phrase "the seal of prophets" come to signify "the last prophet"?

The phrase *khātam al-nabiyyīn* occurs only once in the Qurʾān, in the revelation that would become v. 40 of *Sūrat al-Aḥzāb*. In fact, v. 40 is the fifth verse in a five-verse pericope located at the center of the *Sūra*. To this point, we have been concerned only with the first two verses in the pericope—v. 36, which reportedly compelled Zaynab's acquiescence to her marriage to Zayd (Chapter 1, section 1.1), and v. 37, which provided divine sanction for her marriage to Muḥammad (Chapter 2, section 2.4). Before turning our attention to vv. 38–40, let us examine the entire pericope:

> 36 When God and His messenger have decided a matter, it is not for any believing man or woman to have any choice in the affair. Whoever disobeys God and His Messenger has gone astray in manifest error.
>
> 37 [Recall] when you said to the one on whom God and you yourself have bestowed favor, "Keep your wife to yourself and fear God," and you hid within yourself what God would reveal, and you feared the people when God had better right to be feared by you. When Zayd had finished with her, We gave her to you in marriage, so that there should be no sin (*ḥaraj*) for the believers concerning the wives of their adopted sons, when they have finished with them. God's command was fulfilled.
>
> 38 There is no sin (*ḥaraj*) for the prophet in that which God has ordained for him: God's practice (*sunnat allāh*) concerning those who passed away previously—God's command is a fixed decree—
>
> 39 Who conveyed God's messages and feared Him and no one else apart from God. God is sufficient as a reckoner.
>
> 40 Muḥammad is not the father of any of your men, but the messenger of God and the seal of Prophets. God is aware of everything.

Although we do not have direct access to the initial understanding of this pericope by its immediate audience, we do have access to its reception by the early Muslim community, as preserved, for example, in the Qurʾān commentary of Muqātil b. Sulaymān, who was a contemporary of Ibn Isḥāq (both men died in 150/767). Let us examine Muqātil's treatment of vv. 38–40.

VERSE 38

Verse 38 opens with the clause, "There is no sin for the prophet in that which God has ordained for him." These words, Muqātil explains, were uttered by unidentified critics of the Prophet who were troubled by the manner in which "God's command" in v. 37 appears to have been designed to satisfy Muḥammad's sexual desires.

The proper response to this charge, the commentator indicates, is found in the continuation of the verse ("God's practice [*sunnat allāh*] concerning those who passed away previously"). The phrase "those who passed away previously," Muqātil explains, refers to earlier prophets. That is to say, it was not only Muḥammad's sexual life that was governed by what the Qurʾān calls *sunnat allāh* but also the sexual lives of earlier prophets.

What is *sunnat allāh* and in what sense did it govern the sexual lives of earlier prophets? Without explicitly asking either of these questions, Muqātil responds to them by comparing the story of Muḥammad's infatuation with, and subsequent marriage to, Zaynab (as just related in his commentary on v. 37),[14] to the biblical account of David's infatuation with, and subsequent marriage to, Bathsheba (II Sam. 11:6–27). Just as the Qurʾān omits the name of the woman (Zaynab) who married first Zayd and then Muḥammad, so too Muqātil omits the name of the woman (Bathsheba) who married first Uriah the Hittite and then David. Just as some rabbis exonerate David on the grounds that the biblical king eventually expressed remorse for his sin, so too Muqātil exonerates David—who, according to the Qurʾān, was a prophet—by correcting what he regarded as a misunderstanding of the biblical narrative. The Muslim commentator explains that the Prophet David did fall in love with the wife of Uriah b. Ḥannān [*sic*]; and that the Prophet Muḥammad did fall in love with Zaynab bt. Jaḥsh, but only because both prophets were being tested by God. And both prophets passed their respective tests. Similarly, Muqātil explains, it was God who united—in the sense of sexual congress—David and the (here unnamed) woman with whom he had fallen in love; and it was God who united—again in the sense of sexual congress—Muḥammad and Zaynab after the Prophet had fallen in love with her.

Muqātil's juxtaposition of the biblical and Qurʾānic episodes serves as a gloss on the meaning of *sunnat allāh*. For the commentator, *sunnat allāh* is the equivalent of what speakers of English call *providential design*, that is to say, God's control over the events of history and His ability to cause those events to unfold according to remarkable patterns that appear with cyclical regularity. Like David's marriage to Bathsheba, Muḥammad's marriage to Zaynab was preordained by a divine playwright who presumably composed the script for His play before creating the world. For this reason, any attempt to resist the instructions of the divine playwright would be sheer folly. As the final clause of v. 38 teaches, "God's command is a fixed decree."

VERSE 39

Muqātil also links v. 39 to the events surrounding Muḥammad's marriage to Zaynab.

The commentator begins by specifying that the general reference in the opening clause to those "who conveyed God's messages and feared Him" refers specifically to the Prophet Muḥammad. Like all earlier prophets, Muḥammad feared God, even if he did experience a momentary lapse during which he placed his fear of men over his fear of God. However, the Prophet overcame this lapse after receiving the revelation that would become v. 37 of *Sūrat al-Aḥzāb*, in which God clarified the terms and conditions of his marriage to the woman who had been his daughter-in-law. One might think that Muḥammad would have wanted to keep the contents of this verse a secret from the community of believers. In fact, precisely this sentiment is attributed, alternatively, to ʿUmar b. al-Khaṭṭāb and to ʿĀʾisha bt. Abī Bakr: "Had the Messenger of God concealed any part of the Qurʾān," each one of these figures is reported to have said, "he would have concealed this [verse, viz., Q. 33:37]."[15] By sharing the contents of v. 37 with the community of believers, Muḥammad demonstrated his fear of God.

The middle clause in v. 39 ("they fear no one apart from God") is also directly related to the Zaynab episode. This clause, Muqātil explains, refers specifically to Muḥammad, who did not fear anyone but God with regard to the contents of v. 37, or, presumably, any other divine revelation. That is to say, the Prophet was not afraid to make public the contents of any revelation that he received, no matter how embarrassing the revelation may have been to him.

Muqātil also connects the formulaic closing of the verse ("God is sufficient as a reckoner") to the Zaynab episode. The commentator explains that after Muḥammad had fallen in love with his daughter-in-law, there was no better witness to the legitimacy of the ensuing marriage than God Himself.

VERSE 40

Verse 40 of *Sūrat al-Aḥzāb* is one of only four verses in the Qur'ān in which Muḥammad is mentioned by name (the other three are Q. 3:144, 47:2, and 48:29). Our concern here is with the function of this verse as the sole textual witness in the Qur'ān to the theological doctrine of the finality of prophecy.

In addition to mentioning the Prophet's name, v. 40 also proclaims his sonlessness and affirms his status as a Messenger of God and as the Seal of Prophets. One might reasonably assume that this verse was revealed about Muḥammad. Not so, according to Muqātil who, in his commentary on v. 40, indicates that the verse was revealed about *Zayd*. The opening clause, "Muḥammad is not the father of any of your men," the commentator explains, refers specifically to Zayd b. Ḥāritha [*sic*]. Muqātil adds that this clause signifies that "Muḥammad is not Zayd's father." Indeed, he continues, the verse indicates that Muḥammad is the Messenger of God and *khātam al-nabiyyīn* or "the seal of prophets." No doubt drawing upon earlier sources and authorities, albeit without attribution, Muqātil explains how the phrase "the seal of prophets" came to be understood as "the last prophet." First, he states that in v. 40 *khātam* ("seal") is used in the sense of *ākhir* ("the last"). If one replaces *khātam* with *ākhir*, the result is *ākhir al-nabiyyīn*, which can only mean that Muḥammad was "the last prophet." To this the commentator adds a second gloss in which he reformulates the idea of finality as follows: "There is no prophet after Muḥammad." These two glosses, in combination, removed any ambiguity that may have been associated with the phrase *khātam al-nabiyyīn*. By the middle of the second century A.H., at the latest, this phrase had come to signify "the last prophet."

Muqātil understood that Muḥammad's status as the last prophet is a theological imperative and that this imperative is directly related to his sonlessness. Like ʿĀ'isha a century earlier, he too performed a thought experiment. Muqātil's experiment unfolds in two stages. He begins by postulating a general counterfactual, to wit, that Muḥammad *did* have a son who lived to the age of maturity. This counterfactual raises the following question: What would the status of this son have been following the Prophet's death? To this, Muqātil responds: "He would have been a prophet [and] a messenger."[16] Building upon this conclusion, the commentator postulates a second, specific counterfactual, to wit, that Muḥammad did *not* repudiate Zayd (the first counterfactual in our second thought experiment above). "If Zayd had been Muḥammad's son," Muqātil states, "he would have been a prophet."[17] The only reason that Zayd did *not* become a prophet, the commentator continues, is because "God is aware of everything," as stated at the end of v. 40. That is to say, God in His supreme wisdom knew that if Zayd had been Muḥammad's son, he would have been a prophet. This is why God once again intervened in history by sending down the revelation that would become v. 40 of *Sūrat al-Aḥzāb*. It was the revelation of this verse, Muqātil concludes, that was the immediate cause of Muḥammad's repudiation of Zayd.[18] After receiving this revelation, he states, Muḥammad approached Zayd and declared, "I am not your father." To this Zayd responded, "O Messenger of God, I am Zayd b. Ḥāritha, and my genealogy is well-known."[19]

Unlike ʿĀʾisha's thought experiment (see above), which suggests that Zayd and Usāma posed a political threat to potential or actual leaders of the early Muslim community, Muqātil's experiment suggests that Zayd—and, by extension, Usāma—posed a theological threat to the doctrine of the finality of prophecy. Attend well to Muqātil's remarkable statement, "Had Zayd been Muḥammad's son, he would have been a prophet." Viewed from the perspective of subsequent history, this statement is literally *unthinkable*. As late as the middle of the second century A.H., however, it was still possible for a scholar such as Muqātil to raise the theoretical possibility that prophecy might have continued after the death of Muḥammad if the Prophet had been survived by a son who had attained manhood. Muqātil understood that just as the office of prophecy was transmitted from Adam to Noah to Abraham to Ishmael, and, after a long gap, to Muḥammad, so too this office would have been transmitted from Muḥammad to Zayd and from Zayd to Usāma. Conversely, Muqātil understood that Zayd's status as Muḥammad's son and Usāma's status as his grandson were incompatible with the theological doctrine that identifies Muḥammad as the Last Prophet. By the middle of the second century A.H., if not before, this doctrine had become an entrenched and unassailable article of faith.

The Finality of Prophecy and the Redaction of the Qur'ān

The finality of prophecy is a key theological doctrine that defines the relationship between Islam, on the one hand, and Judaism and Christianity, on the other. Just as the Jewish doctrine of divine election is linked to domestic relations within the households of Abraham, Isaac, and Jacob, and just as the Christian doctrine of Christology is linked to domestic relations within the household of Joseph and Mary, so too the Islamic doctrine of the finality of prophecy is linked to domestic relations within the household of Muḥammad. In the Islamic case, the episode may be said to have begun with Zayd's marriage to Zaynab shortly after the hijra and to have ended with Muḥammad's marriage to Zaynab in 5/626–27. As in the Jewish and Christian cases, so too in the Islamic case, a key theological doctrine appears to have been a natural outcome of a domestic crisis.

During the course of the Islamic episode, God is said to have intervened in history on four separate occasions: After Zaynab had rejected a marriage proposal from Muḥammad on behalf of his adopted son Zayd, God delivered a revelation to His prophet in which He let it be known that Zaynab had no choice in the matter "after it had been decided by God and His messenger." This revelation would become v. 36 of *Sūrat al-Aḥzāb*. Then, after Muḥammad had fallen in love with his daughter-in-law, God sent down a revelation in which He introduced a distinction between the former wife of a natural son and that of an adopted son. The purpose of this revelation, which would become v. 37 of *Sūrat al-Aḥzāb*, was to facilitate Muḥammad's marriage to Zaynab. Shortly thereafter, God sent down a revelation in which He proclaimed that Muḥammad would die sonless and identified him as *khātam al-nabiyyīn* or "the Seal of Prophets." This revelation would become v. 40 of *Sūrat al-Aḥzāb*, the sole Qur'ānic witness to the doctrine of the finality of prophecy. Finally, God sent down instructions that served as a legal justification for Muḥammad's repudiation of Zayd, to wit, the abolition of the institution of adoption. These instructions would become vv. 4–5 of *Sūrat al-Aḥzāb*.

If we accept the testimony of the Islamic sources, the theological doctrine of the finality of prophecy would have been introduced approximately six years prior to the Prophet's death in 11/632. The traditional account finds support in the fact that in Q. 33:40 the phrase *khātam al-nabiyyīn* or "the seal of prophets" is juxtaposed to Muḥammad's sonlessness ("Muḥammad is not the father of any of your men"). The juxtaposition of these two ideas—Muḥammad's sonlessness and his status as "the seal of prophets"—strongly suggests that, already in the Qur'ān, the phrase *khātam al-nabiyyīn* is best understood as signifying that Muḥammad was the Last Prophet.

The testimony of the Islamic sources may be questioned, however, on several grounds. First, the timing of the revelation of v. 40 is odd. *Sūrat al-Aḥzāb* takes its name from the confederation of enemy forces (*aḥzāb*) that converged upon Medina in 5 A.H. in what came to be known as the Battle of the Trench. The traditional dating of this *Sūra* to the year 5 A.H. is based on allusions to a battle in vv. 9–27 of the *Sūra*. Now the sources report that Muḥammad had many wives and concubines, was sexually active, and was fertile. Indeed, one of his concubines, Māriya the Copt, is said to have given birth to a son, Ibrāhīm, in the year 9 or 10 A.H. Alas, the infant died on 28 Shawwāl 10, less than five months before his father. Had Ibrāhīm lived, it is said, he would have been a prophet (*law ʿāsha la-kāna nabiyy^{an}*)![20] In the year 5 A.H., six years prior to the Prophet's death, only an omniscient deity could have known—indeed, predicted—that Muḥammad would not produce a viable son (and heir). There is something extraordinary—one might say, miraculous—about God's pronouncement in v. 40 that Muḥammad would die without leaving any adult male progeny. The Qur'ānic pronouncement, it will be noted, appears to invert the biblical promise to Abram that his ninety-year-old wife Sarai, hitherto infertile, would give birth to a son who would be his heir (Gen. 17 and 21).

Second, it is difficult to reconcile the bold claim that Muḥammad was the last prophet with the situation in the Hijaz between the years 610 and 632 C.E. In Mecca, Muḥammad's task would have been to persuade pagans and polytheists that there was only one God, that this God communicated with mankind through prophets, and that he was one of those prophets. In Medina, his audience would have expanded to include Jews who are said to have been waiting for the return of true prophecy. With only a handful of exceptions, however, these Jews rejected Muḥammad's claim to be their anticipated prophet. In this context, there would have been little or no force to the claim that Muḥammad was the *last* prophet.

If the doctrine of the finality of prophecy did not originate in Medina in 5 A.H., where, when, and by whom might it have been introduced? In the generation following the death of the Prophet, Muslim armies defeated the Byzantines and Persians and conquered much of the Levant. The rise to power of Muʿāwiya b. Abī Sufyān (r. 41–60/661–80) marked the beginning of the Umayyad dynasty. The legitimacy of the Umayyad caliphs was contested *inter alia* by supporters of ʿAlī, on the one hand, and by members of the family of al-ʿAbbās, on the other. In response to ʿAlid and ʿAbbasid claims, the Umayyads retorted that members of the tribe of Quraysh had been the first to accept Islam (*awwal al-nās islām*[an]); that as direct lineal descendants of ʿAbd Manāf and the most prominent family within this clan they were closer to the Prophet than either the ʿAlids or the ʿAbbasids; and that they were the true *ahl al-bayt* or People of the House.[21] Muʿāwiya called himself "God's deputy" (*khalīfat allāh*),[22] and his agents circulated the claim that "Muʿāwiya almost became a prophet" (*kāda an yakūna Muʿāwiya nabiyy*[an]).[23] However, Muʿāwiya himself did not introduce any major religious reforms during his twenty-year reign, which was devoted largely to military expansion. At the time of his death in 60/680, the Umayyad state stretched from the Maghrib to Khurasan and it included a significant number of Jews, Christians, and Zoroastrians.

It was not until the reign of ʿAbd al-Malik (65–86/685–705) that distinctively Islamic symbols were first introduced on a large scale. The fifth Umayyad caliph sought to legitimize his rule and that of other members of his family through his identification with Islam. It was ʿAbd al-Malik who declared Arabic to be the official language of his administration, minted the first Islamic coins, and commissioned the construction of the Dome of the Rock as a memorial to the Prophet's Night Journey and Ascension to Heaven. At the same time that he was introducing these new Islamic symbols, the caliph was combatting several "false" prophets who are said to have appeared during his reign. These included al-Mukhtār (d. 67/687), whose followers claimed that he received visits from the Angels Gabriel and Michael; al-Ḥārith b. Saʿīd (d. 79/699), who was put to death after claiming to be a prophet; and—perhaps—Abū ʿĪsā al-Iṣfahānī, who claimed to be a prophet (*nabī*) and a Messenger of the Messiah (*rasūl al-masīḥ*) sent by God to deliver the Children of Israel from their oppressors.[24] Claims about Muḥammad's sonlessness and his status as "the seal of prophets" arguably make much better sense in Umayyad Damascus or Jerusalem in the last half of the seventh century C.E. than they do in Mecca or Medina in the first third of that century.

Islamic sources report that the early community of believers experimented with the formulation of the "seal" metaphor and its placement in the so-called ʿUthmānic codex ("so-called" because the text itself is no longer extant). As noted, the sole Qurʾānic witness to Muḥammad's status as "the seal of prophets" in the "ʿUthmānic" codex is found in v. 40 of *Sūrat al-Aḥzāb*. There is reason to believe, however, that this was not always the case.

It is reported that in the codex of the Companion Ubayy b. Kaʿb (d. between 19/640 and 35/656), the revelation that would become v. 6 of *Sūrat al-Ṣaff* ("The Battle Array") read as follows: "And [recall] when Jesus, the son of Mary said, 'O Children of Israel, I am God's messenger to you, bringing you an announcement of a prophet whose community will be the last one among the communities (*ākhir al-umam*), and by means of whom God seals the messengers and the prophets (*yakhtum allāh bihi al-anbiyāʾ wa'l-rusul*).'"[25] Here Jesus explains to the Israelites that he was sent to them as a messenger and also announces the future appearance of an unidentified prophet whose unidentified community would be the last community—presumably, the last community to receive a divine revelation. By means of this prophet, God would "seal the messengers and the prophets."

The Arabic phrase *yakhtum allāh bihi al-anbiyāʾ wa'l-rusul* bears a striking resemblance to the Hebrew phrase *laḥtôm ḥazôn ve-navī* ("to seal prophetic vision," literally "to seal vision and prophecy") in Daniel 9:24. In its biblical context, the Hebrew phrase refers to the confirmation of a prophetic vision that was received seventy "weeks" earlier. In late antiquity, the Church Fathers cited the book of Daniel in support of the claim that Rome was the last worldly empire and that God had chosen its emperors to prepare the way for the second coming of Christ and the Kingdom of God. This claim was an integral part of a widespread belief that the eschaton or endtime was about to commence. The linguistic and semantic connections between Ubayy's formulation (*yakhtum allāh bihi al-anbiyāʾ wa'l-rusul)*, on the one hand, and that of Daniel 9:24 (*laḥtôm ḥazôn ve-navî*), on the other, suggest that the first believers may have regarded themselves as the religious community that had been specially chosen by God to usher in the eschaton. A new prophet—Muḥammad—would be sent to a people—the Arabs—who would establish a new religious community—Islam. Paradoxically, this new religious community would be the last religious community, that is to say, the rise of Islam signaled the beginning of the end time. The arrival of the eschaton would seal (*yakhtum*), that is to say, confirm or fulfill the earlier prediction of the unidentified "messenger" whose words are quoted in this very verse. In the formulation of Q. 61:6 attributed to Ubayy, it will be noted, there is no reference to either Muḥammad or his sonlessness.[26]

Let us perform a third and final thought experiment in which we make two assumptions: first, that Ubayy's version of what would become v. 6 of *Sūrat al-Ṣaff* was the earliest formulation of the theological doctrine that would come to be known as the finality of prophecy; and, second, that this formulation was at one time the sole Qurʾānic witness to this theological doctrine. If so, we would still have a doctrine of finality, in the sense of the eschaton or endtime, but there would be no reason to think that Muḥammad was sonless. Had Ubayy's version of Q. 61:6 prevailed, any claim to leadership based on sonship would have posed a continuing threat to any leader of the Muslim community who was not a direct lineal descendant of the Prophet.

In fact, however, the eschaton failed to materialize and the prediction contained in Ubayy's version of Q. 61:6 proved false. This may explain why Ubayy's version of Q. 61:6 was *not* included in what would become the standard text of the Qurʾān, where we find the following: "And [recall] when Jesus, the son of Mary said, 'O Children of Israel, I am God's messenger to you, confirming the Torah that was [revealed] before me, and giving you good tidings of a messenger who will come after me, whose name will be more praiseworthy *(aḥmad)*.' And when he brought them clear proofs, they said, 'This is clear magic.'"

Here, the earlier unidentified messenger of God has become Jesus son of Mary, and the messenger's unidentified audience ("you") has become the Children of Israel. In addition, the content of the announcement has changed: Rather than announcing the arrival of a future prophet whose community will be the last community, Jesus confirms the validity of the Torah and predicts the appearance of a future messenger whose name will be even more praiseworthy (*aḥmad*) than his—no doubt a reference to Muḥammad. Note well: In the standard version of Q. 61:6, there is no reference to the messenger by means of whom "God seals the messengers and prophets" and no reference to the notion of finality. In place of eschatology and a prediction of the endtime, we find a reference to the confirmation or fulfillment of the Torah.

The reformulation of Q. 61:6 would have created a need for another Qurʾānic witness to the doctrine of the finality of prophecy. One wonders if this need may not explain the "revelation" of vv. 36–40 of *Sūrat al-Aḥzāb*. As noted in the Introduction, it is reported on the authority of three Companions that this *Sūra* originally contained either 129, 200, or 286 verses. If so, then between 56 and 213 verses were removed, leaving the 73 verses currently found in the standard text of the Qurʾān.[27] Although the sources preserve the memory of a large-scale editorial project, they are silent about the contents of the verses that were removed from the *sūrah*, with the exception of *āyat al-rajm* or "the stoning verse." It stands to reason that if fifty or more verses could be removed from *Sūrat al-Aḥzāb*, five or more verses could have been added. Where, when, and by whom would these changes have been made? And whose interest would have been served?

At the time of Muḥammad's death in 11/632, the revelations that he received are said to have been memorized by his Companions and also inscribed on palm branches, animal bones, stones, and other writing surfaces. There was as yet no codex or book. Over the course of the next generation, these materials were collected, placed in sequential order, divided into chapters, edited, and redacted. As is well known, a first collection is said to have been commissioned by Abū Bakr and a second by ʿUthmān. Less well known is the editorial project undertaken by ʿAbd al-Malik, who had not only an interest in a revised text of the Qurʾān but also the resources to carry out such a project. The sources report that the caliph instructed his advisor, al-Ḥajjāj b. Yūsuf (d. 95/714), to revise the text of the Qurʾān by changing the consonantal skeleton of certain words, establishing the canonical order of verses and chapters, introducing vowels and diacritical marks for the first time, and removing several verses in an effort to resolve certain unspecified disagreements. Copies of the newly revised text—what might be called the Umayyad codex—were sent to Egypt, Syria, Medina, Mecca, Kufa, and Basra. The sources also report that any codex whose consonantal skeleton was not identical to that of the Umayyad codex was recalled and destroyed. This would explain why little or no manuscript evidence has survived that would make it possible to verify the nature of any change or changes introduced at that time.[28]

Chase Robinson has recently argued that "the task of producing, distributing, and enforcing a uniform Qurʾānic text fits . . . neatly into ʿAbd al-Malik's reign."[29] In my view, the editorial project authorized by ʿAbd al-Malik provides a plausible historical context in which a five-verse pericope that stretches from v. 36 to v. 40 of *Sūrat al-Aḥzāb* might have been formulated and inserted into the text of the Qurʾān. The caliph's primary objectives would have been to disarm attacks on Umayyad legitimacy by eliminating the argument for leadership based on sonship, to silence "false" prophets, and to promote Islam and its prophet as the culmination of sacred history. These goals would have been accomplished by formulating the "revelation" that would become v. 40 of *Sūrat al-Aḥzāb*, in which Muḥammad's sonlessness is juxtaposed to his status as "the seal of prophets," a combination that clearly signifies finality. This new theological doctrine was then fitted out with a Qurʾānic *sabab* or occasion of revelation (vv. 36–37), a theological justification for the actions attributed to the Prophet in the Zaynab episode (vv. 38–39), and, finally, a legal justification for Muḥammad's repudiation of Zayd (vv. 4–5).

Just as God sent Joseph to Egypt to facilitate the salvation of the Israelites in "an extraordinary deliverance" (Gen. 45:5), so too He sent Zayd to Arabia to facilitate the process whereby Muḥammad became the Last Prophet. The rest is history.

Notes

Introduction

1. Ibn Ḥanbal, *Musnad*, nos. 21525–26; Suyūṭī, *al-Itqān*, 2:33.19–26; see also Burton, *Collection of the Qur'ān*, 80–84; *EQ*, s.v. Collection of the Qur'ān (J. Burton).

2. See *EQ*, s.v. Sīra and Qur'ān (Wim Raven).

3. On the term *mawlā*, see Badawi and Haleem, *Arabic-English Dictionary of Qur'anic Usage*, s.v. *w-l-y*; and Dakake, *The Charismatic Community*, chap. 1. Over the course of the first two centuries A.H., the term *mawlā* came to be used as a technical legal term referring to a person who converted to Islam by attaching himself or herself to an Arab-Muslim tribesman as a "client." In this technical, legal sense, *mawlā* may refer to either side of the relationship, i.e., to either the patron or the client. See *EI*², s.v. Mawlā (P. Crone).

4. *Life of Muhammad*, trans. Guillaume, 114–15.

5. Ibid., 186.

6. Ibid., 308.

7. Shortly before the hijra, Abū Salama ʿAbdallāh b. ʿAbd al-Asad is said to have migrated to Yathrib in order to escape mistreatment by the Quraysh. Ibid., 213.

8. Ibid., 213–18.

9. Ibid., 221–22.

10. Ibid., 222–23.

11. Ibid., 223–24.

12. Ibid., 224–27. The earliest extant version of these two episodes is found in the *Sīra* of Wahb b. Munabbih. This text has been edited by R. G. Khoury and analyzed by M. J. Kister, "On the Papyrus of Wahb b. Munabbih."

13. *The Life of Muhammad*, trans. Guillaume, 218, 227.

14. Ibid., 234.

15. Ibid., 293; cf. p. 327, where one finds a list of the Muslims who were present at Badr. The first four names on the list are Muḥammad, Ḥamza, ʿAlī, and Zayd. Note that Zayd is identified here as Zayd b. Ḥāritha b. Shuraḥbīl b. Kaʿb b. ʿAbd al-ʿUzzā b. Imru 'l-Qays al-Kalbī.

16. Ibid., 308, 364–65.
17. Ibid., 314.
18. Ibid., 234.
19. Ibid., 385, 387.
20. Ibid., 364.
21. Ibid., 662–64.
22. Ibid., 664.
23. Ibid., 791. This narrative is related on the authority of a great-grandson of ʿAlī b. Abī Ṭālib.
24. Ibid., 533.
25. Ibid., 539.
26. Ibid., 534.
27. Ibid.
28. Ibid., 531–40.
29. Ibid., 652, 678 (where the short notice is repeated). In fact, two of the first Emigrants were exempted from the expedition: Abū Bakr and ʿUmar b. al-Khaṭṭāb. See Chapter 4.
30. Ibid., 679.
31. Ibid.
32. Ibid., 680.
33. Ibid., 687.
34. In his notes, Ibn Hishām does provide some additional information about Zayd: His full name, the circumstances of his capture, the despair of his father Ḥāritha, his manumission and adoption by Muḥammad, his conversion to Islam, and his reversion to his birth name following the revelation of Q. 33:5. See ibid., 714–15*n*151. I will have more to say about all of these matters in Chapters 1–4.

Chapter 1. Zayd

1. *EI*², s.v. Kalb b. Wabara (J. W. Fück).
2. The detail of the sidelock (Ar.: *dhū dhuʾāba*) suggests that Zayd may have been Jewish. On early Jewish converts to Islam, see M. Lecker, "Zayd b. Thābit, 'A Jew with Two Sidelocks': Judaism and Literacy in Pre-Islamic Medina (Yathrib)"; idem, "Ḥudhayfa b. al-Yamān and ʿAmmār b. Yāsir, Jewish Converts to Islam."
3. Ibn Abī Shayba, *al-Kitāb al-muṣannaf fī al-aḥādīth wa'l-āthār*, 14:321, no. 18,453.
4. Qurṭubī, *Jāmiʿ*, 14:118; cf. Ibn ʿAsākir, *Taʾrīkh madīnat Dimashq*, 19:346.11–23.
5. Ibn ʿAsākir, *Taʾrīkh madīnat Dimashq*, 10:137.
6. Ibn Saʿd, *Kitāb al-ṭabaqāt al-kabīr,* III/i, 27–32; the narrative is related on the authority of Hishām b. Muḥammad b. al-Sāʾib al-Kalbī (d. 204–6/819–21), on the authority of his father (d. 146/763), who was an exegete and proto-Shiʿi; and on the authority of Jamīl b. Marthad al-Ṭāʾī (d. ?) and (unidentified) others. Cf. Balādhurī, *Ansāb al-ashrāf*, 1:467–69; *The History of al-Ṭabarī*, trans. Landau-Tasseron, 39:6–9; Qurṭubī, *Jāmiʿ*, 14:118 (*ad* Q. 33:4), 14:193 (*ad* Q. 33:37).
7. Ibn Saʿd, *Kitāb al-ṭabaqāt al-kabīr,* III/i, 27.9–23; cf. Ibn Qutayba, *al-Maʿārif*, 144.9–13.

8. For the full text of the poem in Arabic, see Ibn Saʿd, *Kitāb al-ṭabaqāt al-kabīr,* III/i, 27–28; Balādhurī, *Ansāb al-ashrāf,* 1:467 (bottom)–468.7. For an English translation, see *The History of al-Ṭabarī,* trans. Landau-Tasseron, 39:7.

9. Ibn Saʿd, *Kitāb al-ṭabaqāt al-kabīr,* III/i, 28.6–8; cf. Balādhurī, *Ansāb,* 1:468.12.

10. Ibn Saʿd, *Kitāb al-ṭabaqāt al-kabīr,* III/i, 28.9–11; *The History of al-Ṭabarī,* trans. Landau-Tasseron, 39:7. The second line of the poem attributed to Zayd ("Let go of the grief that has overtaken you; // don't send camels running all over the land") responds to the sixth line of the poem attributed to Ḥāritha ("I shall hasten all my reddish-white camels all over the earth, toiling // Neither I nor the camels will be weary of wandering"). The literary connection between the two poems points to the activity of storytellers and poets, after the fact.

11. Ibn Saʿd, *Kitāb al-ṭabaqāt al-kabīr,* III/i, 28.12–13.

12. Qurṭubī, *Jāmiʿ,* 14:193.9–14.

13. Ibn Saʿd, *Kitāb al-ṭabaqāt al-kabīr,* III/i, 28.13–17; cf. Balādhurī, *Ansāb,* 1:468.15–17; Ibn ʿAsākir, *Taʾrīkh madīnat Dimashq,* 19:347–48.

14. Ibn Saʿd, *Kitāb al-ṭabaqāt al-kabīr,* III/i, 28.17–20; cf. Ibn ʿAsākir, *Taʾrīkh madīnat Dimashq,* 19:348.

15. Ibn Saʿd, *Kitāb al-ṭabaqāt al-kabīr,* III/i, 28.20–22.

16. Indeed, one might think that this episode would have been the occasion for the revelation of Q. 33:4. To the best of my knowledge, however, no Qurʾān commentator has ever made this connection. See the report cited in Ṭabarī, *Jāmiʿ,* 21:119 (top), on the authority of al-Zuhrī (d. 124/742): "I have been informed that this [verse, that is to say, Q. 33:4, was revealed] about Zayd b. Ḥāritha, about whom God coined a simile, which means: the son of another man is not your son." In this account, the simile at the beginning of Q. 33:4 refers to Zayd, following his adoption by Muḥammad (see Chapter 1, section 1.5). Here al-Zuhrī does connect the revelation of Q. 33:4 to Zayd, even if he does not refer to the narrative moment in which Zayd is forced to choose between his biological father and his slave master.

17. Qurṭubī, *Jāmiʿ,* 14:193.14–17.

18. The separation of a disciple from his biological parents and attachment to a father-figure is a topos in biblical literature. See, for example, 1 Kings 19:19–21, where Elisha asks Elijah for permission to kiss his father and mother goodbye before following the prophet and becoming his attendant. Cf. Matt. 10:37, where Jesus says, "Whoever loves father and mother more than me is not worthy of me." When a disciple became a member of the new movement, Jesus became his or her spiritual or surrogate father, just as Muḥammad became Zayd's surrogate father, and, subsequently the surrogate father of all those who joined the new community of believers. Note, however, the third epithet at the beginning of this chapter, a statement attributed to ʿUmar: "Do not forsake your fathers for it is [an act of] infidelity on your part." According to al-Zuhrī, ʿUmar regarded this statement as having once had the status of revelation ("We used to recite"). See al-Zuhrī, *al-Maghāzī al-Nabawiyya,* 140; cf. al-Hindī, *Kanz al-ʿUmmāl,* 2:596 (no. 4818), 6:208 (no. 5371); El-Hibri, *Parable and Politics,* 355*n*62.

19. Ibn Saʿd, *Kitāb al-ṭabaqāt al-kabīr,* III/i, 28.22–26; Ibn ʿAsākir, *Taʾrīkh madīnat Dimashq,* 19:348. This type of prognostication is a common topos in the *Sīra.*

20. Ibn Saʿd, *Kitāb al-ṭabaqāt al-kabīr,* III/i, 28.26–27.

21. Ibid. Text: *arithuhu wa-yarithunī.* Cf. Balādhurī, *Ansāb al-ashrāf,* 1:469.3.

22. Text: *annī al-wārith wa'l-mawrūth*. Qurṭubī, *Jāmiʿ*, 14:193.

23. Ibn Saʿd, *Kitāb al-ṭabaqāt al-kabīr,* III/i, 28.27–28; Ibn Qutayba, *al-Maʿārif,* 144.15–17.

24. Ibn Saʿd, *Kitāb al-ṭabaqāt al-kabīr,* III/i, 28.28.

25. See Westermann, *Genesis 12–36: A Commentary*, 220.

26. Ibn Ḥajar al-ʿAsqalānī, *al-Iṣāba* (Cairo, 1328 A.H.), 1:563, no. 2890, cited in Maghen, "Intertwined Triangles," 74*n*161.

27. Joseph weeps in private after hearing his brothers admit their guilt and express regret for their mistreatment of him (Gen. 42:24) and again after seeing his brother Benjamin (Gen. 43:30). He weeps in public after revealing himself to his brothers (Gen. 45:14) and again at Goshen, when he is reunited with his father Jacob (Gen. 46:29).

Chapter 2. Zaynab

1. The citation is from a letter said to have been written by ʿAlī to Muʿāwiya just prior to the battle of Ṣiffīn (37/657). See Madelung, *The Succession to Muḥammad*, 212–13.

2. *Life of Muhammad*, trans. Guillaume, 111–15; cf. Ibn Qutayba, *al-Maʿārif,* 168.15–18.

3. Ibn Saʿd, *Kitāb al-Ṭabaqāt al-kabīr,* III/i, 30.1–10; idem, *al-Ṭabaqāt al-kubrā,* 4:61.15; Balādhurī, *Ansāb*, 1:470.17–18, 471.1–5; Ibn ʿAsākir, *Taʾrīkh madīnat Dimashq,* 19:353–54; al-Nābulusī, *Ghāyat al-maṭlūb fī maḥabbat al-maḥbūb*, 114. See also Kister, "*Al-Taḥannuth*: An Inquiry into the Meaning of a Term," 225, end of note 13 (on the authority of al-Zuhrī). Zayd's status as the first Muslim was contested by ʿAbd al-Razzāq, who observed, "I don't know of anyone who mentioned this [viz., Zayd's being the first Muslim] except for al-Zuhrī" (al-Nābulusī, *Ghāyat al-maṭlūb,* 114).

4. Ibn Saʿd, *Kitāb al-ṭabaqāt al-kabīr,* III/i, 30.1–10; idem, *al-Ṭabaqāt al-kubrā,* 4:61.15; Balādhurī, *Ansāb*, 1:470.17–18, 471.1–5; Ibn ʿAsākir, *Taʾrīkh madīnat Dimashq,* 19:353–54; Kister, "*Al-Taḥannuth*: An Inquiry into the Meaning of a Term," 225, end of note 13 (on the authority of al-Zuhrī).

5. Balādhurī, *Ansāb*, 1:467; Ibn ʿAsākir, *Taʾrīkh madīnat Dimashq*, 19:343, 351; al-Nābulusī, *Ghāyat al-maṭlūb*, 110ff.

6. A heavenly voice identifies Jesus as "the beloved son" in Matt. 3:17, 12:18, and 17:5; and an unidentified disciple of Jesus is called "the disciple whom Jesus loved" or "the beloved disciple" in John 13:22–25, 19:26–27, 20:1–10, and 21:1–25. The epithet "beloved," referring to Jesus, is also prominent in the so-called Judaeo-Christian writings of late antiquity. See, for example, the *Ascension of Isaiah*, *Odes of Solomon*, and the *Pseudo-Clementine Writings*.

7. Al-Nābulusī, *Ghāyat al-maṭlūb*, 114–15, 117.

8. Balādhurī, *Ansāb*, 1:470.6–8.

9. Ibid., 1:470.9–15.

10. Alternatively, it is reported that Muḥammad inherited Baraka from his father ʿAbdallāh or that he inherited her status as a client (*walāʾ*) from his father. All of these possibilities are rehearsed in Balādhurī, *Ansāb*, 1:476.6–9.

11. Ayman reportedly became a Muslim and was martyred at the Battle of Ḥunayn in 8/630. See Balādhurī, *Ansāb*, 1:471.19; *The History of al-Ṭabarī,* trans. Landau-Tasseron, 39:192.

12. On Umm Ayman, see Balādhurī, *Ansāb*, 1:472; Ibn Qutayba, *al-Maʿārif*, 144.7–13, 150.9, 164.4–5; *The History of al-Ṭabarī,* trans. Landau-Tasseron, 39:191–92, 199, 287.

13. On Usāma, see Ibn Saʿd, *al-Ṭabaqāt al-kubrā*, 4:61–72; Balādhurī, *Ansāb*, 1:473–76; *The History of al-Ṭabarī*, trans. Landau-Tasseron, 39:65, 99, 289; *EI*², s.v. Usāma b. Zayd (V. Vacca).

14. Muqātil b. Sulaymān, *Tafsīr*, 3:47.2–5.

15. Ibid., 3:46–47; cf. al-Ṭabarī, *Jāmiʿ* (1954–68), 22:11, *ad* Q. 33:36, where there is no mention of Muḥammad's opposition to the marriage and he simply orders Zaynab to marry Zayd.

16. On Jaḥsh b. Riʾāb al-Asadī, see *The History of al-Ṭabarī,* trans. Landau-Tasseron, 39:9*n*30, 168, 180*n*806. See also Ibn Ḥajar al-ʿAsqalānī, *al-Iṣāba fī tamyīz al-ṣaḥāba*, 1:466, no. 1109, where al-Dāraquṭnī is quoted as saying that his birth name was Barra until the Prophet changed it to Jaḥsh ("a young ass").

17. On ʿAbdallāh b. Jaḥsh, see *The History of al-Ṭabarī,* vol. 7, trans. McDonald, index, s.v. ʿAA b. Jaḥsh.

18. Muqātil b. Sulaymān, *Tafsīr*, 3:46–47. The idea of social equality between marriage partners (*kafāʾā*) would have been a subject of great interest to an ʿAbbasid audience in the second half of the second century A.H.

19. Zayd is also said to have married Umm Kulthūm bt. ʿUqba—the sister of al-Walīd, who was later governor of Kufa under ʿUthmān. Following Zayd's death at Muʾtah, Umm Kulthūm married al-Zubayr b. al-ʿAwwām, with whom she had a daughter; after she was divorced by al-Zubayr she married ʿAbd al-Raḥmān b. ʿAwf, with whom she had a son named Ḥumayd. Note well the circumstances of Umm Kulthūm's marriage to Zayd: When the Prophet instructed Umm Kulthūm to marry Zayd, she found the idea repugnant. God intervened in history by sending down the revelation that would become Q. 33:6 ("When God and His messenger have decided a matter, it is not for any believing man or woman to have any choice in the affair. Whoever disobeys God and His Messenger has gone astray in manifest error"). Thus, Umm Kulthūm had no choice but to marry Zayd. She bore him no children. See Wāqidī, *Maghāzī*, 3:1126–27; Ibn Ḥazm, *Jamharat ansāb al-ʿarab*, 115. Clearly, we are dealing here with a doublet: The *sabab* or occasion for the revelation of Q. 33:36 was either Zaynab's reluctance to marry Zayd or Umm Kulthūm's reluctance to marry Zayd. The duplication, which is a sign of early uncertainty, merits attention.

20. Muqātil b. Sulaymān, *Tafsīr*, 3:47.11–14; cf. 3:47.20–21, where Muqātil preserves another version of the negotiations in which there is no mention of ʿAlī's role as an intermediary. Here, ʿAbdallāh b. Jaḥsh transfers his authority over Zaynab to Muḥammad, whereupon Zaynab says to the Prophet, "Authority over me has been placed in your hands, O Messenger of God." Once Muḥammad had acquired this authority, he was legally empowered to marry Zaynab to his son Zayd. And he did.

21. Ibid., 3:47.14–18.

22. Ibid., 3:47.20–23.

23. Ṭabarī, *Jāmiʿ al-bayān* (1954–68), 22:13.9–12.

24. Qurṭubī, *al-Jāmiʿ*, 14:190.5–6, cited on the authority of a source that the commentator chose not to mention. Cf. Ṭabarsī, *Majmaʿ al-bayān*, 8:178.10–19.

25. Ṭabarī, *Jāmiʿ* (1954–68), 22:13.9–12; Qurṭubī, *al-Jāmiʿ*, 14:189.10–11.

26. Muqātil b. Sulaymān, *Tafsīr*, 3:47–48.

27. See Ṭabarsī, *Majmaʿ al-bayān*, 8:181 (bottom).

28. Muqātil b. Sulaymān, *Tafsīr*, 3:48.8–9.

29. Another function of the Zaynab episode was to provide support for the right of a woman to remarry after divorce. See Powers, *Muḥammad Is Not the Father of Any of Your Men*, 29–30.

30. On adoption in the ancient Near East, see R. Westbrook (ed.), *A History of Ancient Near Eastern Law*, 1:50–54.

31. Muqātil b. Sulaymān, *Tafsīr*, 3:49.

32. Ibid., 3:35.1. A longer genealogy is recorded in *The History of al-Ṭabarī*, trans. Poonawala, 9:6.

33. See Ṭabarsī, *Majmaʿ al-bayān*, 8:182.3; Ibn Kathīr, *Tafsīr al-qurʾān al-ʿaẓīm* (3rd ed., 1373/1954), 3:466.

34. Qurṭubī, *Jāmiʿ*, 14:192.3–6.

35. Ibid., 14:192.7–13; cf. Muslim, *Ṣaḥīḥ*, Nikāḥ, bāb 15, no. 3575.

36. Qurṭubī, *Jāmiʿ*, 14:192.17–18. Text: *wa-hādhā imtiḥān*[un] *li-Zayd wa'khtibār*[un] *lahu ḥattā yuẓhira ṣabrahu wa'nqiyādahu wa-ṭawʿahu.*

37. Al-Iskāfī, *al-Miʿyār wa'l-muwāzana*, 210ff.; al-Sharīf al-Murtaḍā, *Talkhīṣ al-Shāfī*, 200ff.; Ibn Shahrāshūb, *Manāqib Āl Abī Ṭālib*, 3:34ff.; Afsaruddin, *Excellence and Precedence*, 159ff. Cf. *The Life of Muhammad*, trans. Guillaume, 285, where Ibn Isḥāq specifies that Muḥammad "spoke the well-known words to ʿAlī"—without specifying the contents of the Prophet's statement—during the raid on al-ʿUshayra, which took place shortly before the Battle of Badr.

38. For references, see previous note.

39. One wonders about the reason for this stipulation. Did Sarah fear that if Abraham were to dismount he might be persuaded to reverse his decision to make Isaac his heir; or that if the patriarch were to dismount, he might have sexual relations with Ishmael's wife, that is to say, with his daughter-in-law? Cf. Gen. 24:61–67, where Rebecca arrives in Canaan riding a camel and dismounts just before Isaac takes her as his wife.

40. Summary based on Bakhos, *Ishmael on the Border*, 107.

41. Bethuel plays no part in Genesis 24. In rabbinic *midrash*, Bethuel is said to have been the king of Aram Naharaim, a murderer, thief, and rapist. He would have committed incest with his virgin daughter Rebecca but for the fact that he himself was poisoned by food that he had prepared for a guest. See L. I. Rabinowitz, "The Study of a Midrash," 143–61. The assumption that Bethuel was dead is made explicit in Josephus's retelling of Genesis 24, where Rebecca says, "My father was Bethuel, but he is dead; and Laban is my brother and, together with my mother, takes care of all our family affairs, and is the guardian of my virginity." See *Jewish Antiquities*, chapter 16, 248. According to some modern scholars, Bethuel's name was added to Gen. 24:15, 24, and 44 in anticipation of the genealogy in Gen. 25:20 and 28:2, 5. See Westermann, *Genesis 12–36: A Commentary*, 86 (*ad* Gen. 24:15–16), 387 (*ad* 24:23–25), 387–88 (*ad* 24:28–32), 388–89 (*ad* 24:42–48); *Anchor Bible Commentary: Genesis* (trans. Speiser), 180–81*nn*28, 50.

42. Muqātil b. Sulaymān, *Tafsīr*, 3:48. See the Conclusion.

Chapter 3. Muʾtah

1. Madelung, *The Succession to Muḥammad*, 212–13.

2. *The History of al-Ṭabarī*, trans. Landau-Tasseron, 39:10; Ibn Kathīr, *al-Bidāya wa'l-nihāya*, 4:254–55.

3. *EI*[2], s.v. Boṣrā (A. Abel).

4. Wāqidī, *Maghāzī*, 2:756.6–9; cf. *The Life of Muhammad*, trans. Guillaume, 531–32; Ibn Saʿd, *al-Ṭabaqāt al-kubrā*, 2:128; Ibn Qutayba, *al-Maʿārif*, 163.1–5; *The History of al-Ṭabarī*, trans. Fishbein, 8:152; Ibn Kathīr, *al-Bidāya wa'l-nihāya*, 4:241.15–18 (citing Wāqidī); ʿAlī b. Burhān al-Dīn, *al-Sīra al-ḥalabiyya*, 2:787.1–2 (where the story, cited without attribution, is clearly dependent on Wāqidī).

5. ʿAwn and Muḥammad died at Karbalāʾ fighting alongside al-Ḥusayn b. ʿAlī. As for ʿAbdallāh, he abandoned all political ambitions after the murder of ʿAlī in 40/661, at which time he made common cause with Muʿāwiya, who rewarded him with an annual stipend of one million dirhams. See Madelung, *The Succession to Muḥammad*, 329.

6. On Jaʿfar, see Balādhurī, *Ansāb al-ashrāf*, 1:198; Ibn Qutayba, *al-Maʿārif*, 120.15–20; 161.16–17, 203–4, 205.12–14; Ibn Kathīr, *al-Bidāya wa'l-nihāya*, 4:255–57; *EI*[2], s.v. Djaʿfar b. Abī Ṭālib (L. Veccia Vaglieri); Madelung, "The Hāshimiyyāt of al-Kumayt and Hāshimī Shiʿism," 5–26.

7. Blankinship, "Imārah, Khilāfah, and Imāmah," 34.

8. Fifty verses attributed to ʿAbdallāh b. Rawāḥa have survived, many of them in the *Sīra*. On this figure, see Balādhurī, *Ansāb al-ashrāf*, 1:244, 252, 340, 378, 380; Ibn al-Jawzī, *Kitāb al-quṣṣāṣ wa'l-mudhakkirīn* (trans. Swartz), 102, 107, 223*n*2; Ibn Kathīr, *al-Bidāya wa'l-nihāya*, 4:257–59; Watt, *Muhammad at Medina*, index, s.v.; *EI*[2], s.v. ʿAbd Allāh b. Rawāḥa (A. Schaade).

9. Wāqidī, *Maghāzī*, 2:756.9–12; cf. ʿAlī b. Burhān al-Dīn, *al-Sīra al-ḥalabiyya*, 2:787.4–6; Ibn Kathīr, *al-Bidāya wa'l-nihāya*, 4:241.18–20.

10. On *dābār*, see I. Rabinowitz, *Witness Forever*, chapter 1.

11. Wāqidī, *Maghāzī*, 2:756.12–14; cf. Alī b. Burhān al-Dīn, *al-Sīra al-ḥalabiyya*, 2:787.7–9.

12. In one early source, the revelation of Q. 3:92 is said to have been followed by a verbal exchange between Muḥammad and Zayd in which Zayd dedicates his horse, Sabal, to the path of God (*fī sabīl allāh*)—a play on words, after which the Prophet instructs Usāma to take the horse. See al-Fazārī, *Kitāb al-siyar*, 134, no. 87.

13. Wāqidī, *Kitāb al-maghāzī*, 2:757–58. These instructions belong to the genre known as *siyar* or the Islamic law of nations. See Abū Yūsuf, *Kitāb al-kharāj*, trans. Ben Shemesh as *Taxation in Islam*, 79–93; Muslim, *Ṣaḥīḥ*, no. 4292; *The Islamic Law of Nations: Shaybānī's* Siyar, trans. Majid Khadduri; R. Peters, *Jihad in Classical and Modern Islam*, 10–12.

14. On the etiological function of the Thaniyya ("Heights") toponym, see Noth, *The Early Arabic Historical Tradition*, 191.

15. It is reported that when Muḥammad bade farewell to ʿAbdallāh b. Rawāḥa, the Companion asked that he assign him a special task. The Prophet responded by telling ʿAbdallāh that upon arriving at his destination, he should pray frequently. Not satisfied, ʿAbdallāh asked the Prophet to assign him another special task. The Prophet responded by instructing him to "remember God, for He will help you to obtain your objective." As ʿAbdallāh stood up to depart, he took one step but then turned back, intending to solicit yet another special task from the Prophet. Before he could say anything, the Prophet cut him off, advising him that if he were to perform only one good deed it would compensate for ten evil deeds that he had committed. Apparently satisfied, ʿAbdallāh now promised not to ask the Prophet for anything else. Wāqidī, *Kitāb al-maghāzī*, 2:758.

16. Ibid. Cf. *The Life of Muhammad*, trans. Guillaume, 532; Ibn Saʿd, *al-Ṭabaqāt al-*

kubrā, 2:128; *The History of al-Ṭabarī*, trans. Fishbein, 8:152–53; Ibn Kathīr, *al-Bidāya wa'l-nihāya*, 4:241–42.

17. On the image of Heraclius in Islamic sources, see Conrad, "Heraclius in Early Islamic Kerygma."

18. Wāqidī, *Kitāb al-maghāzī*, 2:760; cf. *The Life of Muhammad*, trans. Guillaume, 532–33; Ibn Saʿd, *al-Ṭabaqāt al-kubrā*, 2:128–29; *The History of al-Ṭabarī*, trans. Fishbein, 8:153–55; Ibn Kathīr, *al-Bidāya wa'l-nihāya*, 4:242–43.

19. Wāqidī, *Kitāb al-maghāzī*, 2:760. On two good outcomes (*al-ḥusnayayn*), see Q. 9:52: "Say: 'Are you waiting for anything but one of two fairest things to befall us?'" The word *al-ḥusnayayn* in this verse is glossed by Ibn ʿAbbās and Mujāhid as "victory or martyrdom." See Ṭabarī, *Tafsīr* (ed. Shākir), 9:291–93, no. 16796. (Traditional Muslim sources identify Q. 9 as the 113th *Sūra* revealed to Muḥammad; if so, then ʿAbdallāh b. Rawāḥa's speech anticipated the revelation of Q. 9:52.) On God's "promise," see Q. 8:7 ("God promised that one of the two parties should be yours") and Q. 9:111 ("Who fulfills His covenant more fully than God?").

20. The number seventy-two brings to mind the number of names attributed to God by Jewish kabbalists, six times the number of Jesus' disciples, the number of men who translated the Septuagint, the number of people who were martyred with Ḥusayn at Karbala, and the number of sects into which the Muslim community would be divided. On numerical symbolism, see Conrad, "Seven and the *Tasbīʿ*: On the Implications of Numerical Symbolism for the Study of Medieval Islamic History."

21. Wāqidī, *Kitāb al-maghāzī*, 2:761; cf. *The Life of Muhammad*, trans. Guillaume, 534–35; Ibn Saʿd, *al-Ṭabaqāt al-kubrā*, 2:129; Ibn Qutayba, *al-Maʿārif*, 205.8–11; *The History of al-Ṭabarī*, trans. Fishbein, 8:156; Ibn Kathīr, *al-Bidāya wa'l-nihāya*, 4:244.

22. The Arabic verb *istashhada* means *to bear witness*; the passive form *ustushhida* means *to be slain as a martyr* (shahīd) *in the cause of God's religion* (Lane, *Arabic-English Lexicon*, s.v. sh-h-d); cf. Greek *martys*, "witness in law"; Syriac *sāhdā*, "witness" or "martyr."

23. Wāqidī, *Kitāb al-maghāzī*, 2:761.16–762.4.

24. Ibid., 2:762.4–8.

25. Ibid., 2:762.9–12; cf. Ibn Saʿd, *al-Ṭabaqāt al-kubrā*, 2:130; Yaʿqūbī, *Ta'rīkh*, 2:54; *The History of al-Ṭabarī*, trans. Fishbein, 8:158; Ibn Kathīr, *al-Bidāya wa'l-nihāya*, 4:246.17–18.

26. Wāqidī, *Kitāb al-maghāzī*, 2:761–62; cf. *The Life of Muhammad*, trans. Guillaume, 535, 537–40; Ibn Saʿd, *al-Ṭabaqāt al-kubrā*, 2:129–30; *The History of al-Ṭabarī*, trans. Fishbein, 8:158; Ibn ʿAsākir, *Ta'rīkh madīnat Dimashq*, 19:368–69; Ibn Kathīr, *al-Bidāya wa'l-nihāya*, 4:245–47. In Wāqidī's account, Zayd b. Ḥāritha enters the Garden *before* Jaʿfar b. Abī Ṭālib, but Jaʿfar, by virtue of his wings, is *above* Zayd. The spatial relationship between the two men in the Garden became a matter of dispute between what might be called the Party of Zayd and the Party of Jaʿfar. Who was closer to the Prophet and who was the more important figure? In a variant of the Prophet's vision, Muḥammad is made to say, "I saw Jaʿfar transformed into an angel who flies in the Garden, with his two forearms bleeding. And I saw Zayd below him." The spatial relationship between the two men surprised the Prophet, who now adds: "I didn't think that Zayd would be below Jaʿfar." This tension—or anxiety—was resolved by means of a miraculous intervention. The Prophet concludes his narration: "The angel Gabriel came and said, 'Zayd is not below Jaʿfar, but we have given preference to Jaʿfar because of his kinship (*qarāba*) with respect to you.'" That is to say, even if, in terms of spatial relationship, Jaʿfar—who was a close

blood relative of the Prophet—was above Zayd, the Beloved of the Messenger of God, it nevertheless remained the case that Zayd—who had been Muḥammad's son—entered the Garden before Jaʿfar and was above (lit. "not below") him. Wāqidī, *Kitāb al-maghāzī*, 2:762; cf. Ibn Saʿd, *al-Ṭabaqāt al-kubrā*, 2:130; Yaʿqūbī, *Taʾrīkh*, 2:54; *The History of al-Ṭabarī*, trans. Fishbein, 8:158; Ibn Kathīr, *al-Bidāya wa'l-nihāya*, 4:246.17–18.

27. On Khālid, see Balādhurī, *Ansāb al-ashrāf*, 5:271–72; Conrad, "Al-Azdī's History of the Arab Conquests in Bilād al-Shām," 39–42; Klier, *Ḫālid und ʿUmar: Quellenkritische Untersuchung zur Historiographie der früislamischen Zeit*; *EI*[2], s.v. Khālid b. al-Walīd (P. Crone).

28. Wāqidī, *Kitāb al-maghāzī*, 2:763; cf. Ibn Kathīr, *al-Bidāya wa'l-nihāya*, 4:245.

29. Wāqidī, *Kitāb al-maghāzī*, 2:764–65.

30. Ibid., 2:763; cf. *The Life of Muhammad*, trans. Guillaume, 535; Ibn Saʿd, *al-Ṭabaqāt al-kubrā*, 2:129–30; *The History of al-Ṭabarī*, trans. Fishbein, 8:158.

31. Wāqidī, *Kitāb al-maghāzī*, 2:763; cf. *The Life of Muhammad*, trans. Guillaume, 535; Ibn Saʿd, *al-Ṭabaqāt al-kubrā*, 2:130; Ibn Kathīr, *al-Bidāya wa'l-nihāya*, 4:248.

32. See Conrad, "Heraclius in Early Islamic Kerygma," 113–56; Wansbrough, *The Sectarian Milieu*, 1–49.

33. Ibn Kathīr, *al-Bidāya wa'l-nihāya*, 4:250 (top, citing Bayhaqī).

34. On Khālid as Sayf Allāh, see *The History of al-Ṭabarī*, trans. Fishbein, 8:158; Balādhurī, *Ansāb al-ashrāf*, 5:272; Conrad, "Al-Azdī's History of the Arab Conquests in Bilād al-Shām," and the sources mentioned there.

35. *The Life of Muhammad*, trans. Guillaume, 772*n*791 (on the authority of al-Zuhrī).

36. Ibn Kathīr, *al-Bidāya wa'l-nihāya*, 4:259.1–15.

37. Wāqidī, *Kitāb al-maghāzī*, 2:769; cf. *The Life of Muhammad*, trans. Guillaume, 540.

38. Wāqidī, *Kitāb al-maghāzī*, 2:764–65; cf. Ibn Kathīr, *al-Bidāya wa'l-nihāya*, 4:248.8–13, 253.17–18.

39. *The History of al-Ṭabarī*, trans. Fishbein, 8:159; Ibn Kathīr, *al-Bidāya wa'l-nihāya*, 4:249.4–7.

40. Wāqidī, *Kitāb al-maghāzī*, 2:765; cf. *The History of al-Ṭabarī*, trans. Fishbein, 8:159; Ibn Kathīr, *al-Bidāya wa'l-nihāya*, 4:249.4–7.

41. Wāqidī, *Kitāb al-maghāzī*, 2:765.

42. Ibn Saʿd, *Kitāb al-ṭabaqāt al-kabīr*, III/I, 32; cf. Balādhurī, *Ansāb*, 1:473.4–12; Ibn ʿAsākir, *Taʾrīkh madīnat Dimashq*, 19:370–71.

43. On the speed of communication in late antiquity, see Silverstein, *Postal Systems in the Pre-Modern Islamic World*.

44. Wāqidī, *Kitāb al-maghāzī*, 2:766.

45. *EI*[2], s.v. al-ʿAbbās b. ʿAbd al-Muṭṭalib (W. Montgomery Watt).

46. Wāqidī, *Kitāb al-maghāzī*, 2:766–67; cf. *The Life of Muhammad*, trans. Guillaume, 535–36; *The History of al-Ṭabarī*, trans. Fishbein, 8:158; Ibn Kathīr, *al-Bidāya wa'l-nihāya*, 4:251–53 (see ibid., 252.8–9, where Muḥammad says that ʿAbdallāh b. Jaʿfar looks like him and acts like him).

47. Wāqidī, *Kitāb al-maghāzī*, 2:766.

48. See, for example, *Pesikta de-Rab Kahana*, 613–14.

49. *Pirkei de Rabbi Eliezer*, chap. 31; cf. Spiegel, *The Last Trial*, 30–31.

50. According to *Pseudo-Jonathan*, angels transported Isaac to the "school of Shem the great," where he remained for three years.

Chapter 4. Usāma

1. Ibn Saʿd, *al-Ṭabaqāt al-kubrā*, 4:61.12; Balādhurī, *Ansāb*, 1:472.19; Ṭabarī, *History*, trans. Landau-Tasseron, 39:289; Ibn ʿAsākir, *Taʾrīkh Madīnat Dimashq*, 19:351.8; al-Nābulusī, *Ghāyat al-maṭlūb*, 114 (bottom).

2. Ibn Saʿd, *al-Ṭabaqāt al-kubrā*, 4:61.18 ("*wa-kāna rasūl allāh yuḥibbuhu ḥubb*^{an} *shadīd*^{an}").

3. Ibid., 4:65.22, 66.6, 66.20–21; cf. al-Nābulusī, *Ghāyat al-maṭlūb*, 123–24, 129.

4. Al-Nābulusī, *Ghāyat al-maṭlūb*, 124.

5. Ibid., 131. This is no doubt anti-Shiʿi polemic. Compare Muhammad's instruction to love the people of his house, that is to say, ʿAlī, Fāṭima and their children. See Ibn Ṭāʾūs, *al-Ṭarāʾif*, 159–60.

6. Ibn Saʿd, *al-Ṭabaqāt al-kubrā*, 4:62.16–20.

7. Ibid., 4:62.10–15; Ibn Ḥanbal, *Musnad*, nos. 22130, 22172. Again, this is anti-Shiʿi polemic. Cf. Ibn Shahrāshūb, *Manāqib Āl Abī Ṭālib*, 432–34, where Muḥammad expresses his love for al-Ḥasan and al-Ḥusayn—with no mention of Usāma.

8. Wāqidī, *Maghāzī*, 3:1125–26.

9. Ibn Saʿd, *al-Ṭabaqāt al-kubrā*, 4:61–62; cf. Balādhurī, *Ansāb*, 1:475–76, where Sharīk b. ʿAbdallāh (d. 177/793) specifies that the Prophet did not allow the blood to enter his throat. The consumption of blood is prohibited in Q. 2:173.

10. On the exchange of fluids in connection with the transfer of authority, see al-Khawārazmī, *Manāqib*, 223–24, where the Prophet tells Anas b. Mālik that the first person to walk through the door will be the Commander of the Believers and the Seal of the Trustees. Although Anas secretly expressed the wish that a Helper would be the first to walk through the door, it was in fact ʿAlī who did so, whereupon Muḥammad rose to his feet and embraced him. After wiping the sweat off of first his own face and then ʿAlī's, the Prophet rubbed the liquid mixture onto his face. This mixing of bodily fluids has been explained by Afsaruddin as a symbol of the Prophet's anointment of ʿAlī as his successor. See Afsaruddin, *Excellence and Precedence*, 227.

11. Ibn Saʿd, *al-Ṭabaqāt al-kubrā*, 4:63.19 (*afṭas aswad*).

12. Ibid., 4:63.5–17; Wāqidī, *Maghāzī*, 3:1126.10–13; Ibn ʿAsākir, *Taʾrīkh madīnat Dimashq*, 19:351; cf. Bukhārī, *Ṣaḥīḥ*, bāb 24, Manāqib, no. 3595; bāb 31, Farāʾiḍ, nos. 6856–57; Muslim, *Ṣaḥīḥ*, bāb 11, Riḍāʿ, no. 3691; Abū Dāʾūd, *Sunan*, 31, Ṭalāq, no. 2269; Nasāʾī, *Sunan*, 51, Ṭalāq, no. 3507; Ibn Māja, *Sunan*, 21, Aḥkām, no. 2439.

13. Wāqidī, *Maghāzī*, 3:1125.6–10 (fifteen years old); Ibn Saʿd, *al-Ṭabaqāt al-kubrā*, 4:72.6–13 (fourteen years old).

14. Ibn Saʿd, *al-Ṭabaqāt al-kubrā*, 4:69; Balādhurī, *Ansāb*, 1:474.18–23 (specifies 7 A.H.).

15. Ibn Saʿd, *al-Ṭabaqāt al-kubrā*, 4:65.7–14. The structure of this narrative is similar to that of the narratives in which Ḥakīm b. Ḥizām purchases Zayd on behalf of Khadīja, who gifts the slave to her husband Muḥammad (see Chapter 1).

16. Ibn Saʿd, *al-Ṭabaqāt al-kubrā*, 4:64.20–65.6; cf. Ibn Ḥanbal, *Musnad*, nos. 22129, 22131.

17. On clothes and authority, see further *Sunan Abī Dāʾūd*, book 32, nos. 4023 ff. Note especially no. 4036, in which the Prophet receives as a gift from the king of Byzantium a fur garment with silk brocade and then gives it to Jaʿfar b. Abī Ṭālib. Jaʿfar wore the garment but was then instructed by the Prophet to send it to the Negus in Ethiopia.

18. Ibn Saʿd, *al-Ṭabaqāt al-kubrā*, 4:62.5–9; cf. 4:62.3–4. In a variant reported by Wāqidī, it is not Usāma but his dark-skinned son about whom the Prophet says, "If God wills, [she (*sic*) will be decked with] two silver bracelets and two earrings." Wāqidī, *Maghāzī*, 3:1125.12–16. Cf. Balādhurī, *Ansāb*, 1:476.2.

19. Balādhurī, *Ansāb*, 1:469.17–22; Lane, *An Arabic-English Lexicon*, s.v. r-d-f. On Zayd as the Prophet's *radīf*, see *The Life of Muhammad*, trans. Guillaume, 279.

20. Ibn Saʿd, *al-Ṭabaqāt al-kubrā*, 4:64.14–16. Together with the Prophet and Bilāl, Usāma was one of the first three members of the community of believers to enter the Kaʿba. Muḥammad assigned to Usāma the task—or privilege—of erasing the icons on the inside wall of the Kaʿba, using a cloth dampened with water drawn from the well of Zamzam. See Balādhurī, *Ansāb*, 1:475.13–15.

21. Ibn Saʿd, *al-Ṭabaqāt al-kubrā*, 4:64.1–2.

22. Ibid., 4:64.1–5; cf. Balādhurī, *Ansāb*, 1:470.1–5; Ibn Ḥanbal, *Musnad*, nos. 22092, 22099, 22103, 22104, 22126, 22133, 22136, 22146, 22156, 22165.

23. Ibn Saʿd, *al-Ṭabaqāt al-kubrā*, 4:63.17–23.

24. Ibn Qutayba, *al-Maʿārif*, 651.1–7.

25. Ibn Manẓūr, *Lisān*, IX, 117, s.v. *radīf*: *ardāf al-mulūk hum alladhīna yakhlifūnahum fi'l-qiyām bi-amr al-mamlaka—bi-manzilat al-wuzarāʾ fi'l-islām.*

26. *The History of al-Ṭabarī*, trans. Friedmann, 12:3.

27. Ibid. Text: *baʿda raʾīsihim*. See El-Hibri, *Parable and Politics*, 278, 427*n*39.

28. Wāqidī, *Maghāzī*, 3:1117.1–12; *The History of al-Ṭabarī*, trans. Poonawala, 9:163–64; cf. Ibn Saʿd, *al-Ṭabaqāt al-kubrā*, 4:66.9–14; Ibn Ḥanbal, *Musnad*, nos. 22128, 22168.

29. Gil, *A History of Palestine, 634–1099*, 32, 821; *Encyclopedia Biblica*, s.v. Yavneel (Mazar, Tur-Sinai, and Yeivin). Note, however, that Balādhurī identifies the target of the expedition as Muʾtah (*Ansāb*, 1:474.3).

30. Wāqidī, *Maghāzī*, 3:1117.12–1118.2.

31. Ibid., 3:1118.9–11. On the significance of the banner, see El-Hibri, *Parable and Politics*, 94*n*50, 229, and 412*n*56, and the sources mentioned there. Shiʿi sources report that prior to the expedition to Dhāt al-Salāsil in Jumāda II 8 A.H., the Prophet summoned ʿAlī and handed the banner to him—after Abū Bakr, ʿUmar, and Khālid b. al-Walīd had all declined to serve as commander of the expedition and had returned the banner to the Prophet. See Kister, "On the Papyrus of Wahb b. Munabbih," 560.

32. *The Life of Muhammad*, trans. Guillaume, 652, 678 ("all of the first emigrants went with Usāma"); Wāqidī, *Maghāzī*, 3:1118.14–15 ("not one of the first emigrants remained but that he answered the summons to the raid"); cf. Balādhurī, *Ansāb*, 1:474.1–4.

33. Wāqidī, *Maghāzī*, 3:1118.17–19 (*ghulām*); cf. Ibn Saʿd, *al-Ṭabaqāt al-kubrā*, 4:66.22–24 (eighteen years old); Balādhurī, *Ansāb*, 1:475.12–13 (twenty-one years old—or a few months short of twenty-one).

34. Wāqidī, *Maghāzī*, 3:1118.20–1119.9; cf. Ibn Saʿd, *al-Ṭabaqāt al-kubrā*, 4:65.15–66.8, 66.15–21, 67.4–9, and 68.14–19; Balādhurī, *Ansāb*, 1:474.4–6; *The History of al-Ṭabarī*, trans. Poonawala, 9:164, 166.

35. See al-Nābulusī, *Ghāyat al-Maṭlūb*, 123.

36. Balādhurī, *Ansāb*, 1:560–61.

37. In Ibn Isḥāq's version of this speech by the Prophet, Muḥammad does *not* mention that Zayd and Usāma were among those most beloved to him (*min aḥabb al-nās ilayya*). See *Life of Muhammad*, trans. Guillaume, 679.

38. Ibid., 682.

39. Wāqidī, *Maghāzī*, 3:1119.9–12; cf. Ibn Saʿd, *al-Ṭabaqāt al-kubrā*, 4:67.10 (where the command to "carry out Usāma's mission" is repeated twice).

40. Cf. 1 Kings 1, where Bathsheba intercedes with King David on his deathbed in an effort to secure the succession for their son, Solomon.

41. Wāqidī, *Maghāzī*, 3:1119.12–15.

42. Ibid., 3:1119.16–1120.3; cf. Ibn Saʿd, *al-Ṭabaqāt al-kubrā*, 4:68.20–24; Ibn Ḥanbal, *Musnad*, no. 22098. The laying on of hands was associated with the ordination of rabbis in the first century C.E., and, in the New Testament, with the ordination of clergy. See Acts 13:3, where the laying on of hands signifies that Barnabas and Paul have been commissioned for the task to which the Holy Spirit has called them; and Luke 24:50: "Then he [viz., Jesus] led them [viz., the apostles] out as far as Bethany, and, lifting up his hands, he blessed them." *Anchor Bible Dictionary*, s.v. "Hands, Laying On of: New Testament" (R. F. O'Toole).

43. Ibid., 3:1120.8–14; cf. Ibn Saʿd, *al-Ṭabaqāt al-kubrā*, 4:68.10–13, where it is Usāma's wife, Fāṭima bt. Qays, not his mother Umm Ayman, who sends him a message about the Prophet's imminent demise.

44. *The Life of Muhammad*, trans. Guillaume, 687; Ibn Qutayba, *al-Maʿārif*, 166.9. The other men who are said to have prepared the Prophet's body for burial were al-ʿAbbās and his sons al-Faḍl and Qutham, and ʿAlī b. Abī Ṭālib—all Hāshimīs.

45. Wāqidī, *Maghāzī*, 3:1120.4–8. Cf. Q. 9:86, which criticizes "men of wealth" who ask for permission "to be among those who sit at home" while others are striving in the path of God.

46. Wāqidī, *Maghāzī*, 3:1120.19–1121.1; cf. Balādhurī, *Ansāb*, 1:475.15–16.

47. Wāqidī, *Maghāzī*, 3:1121.1–5; cf. Ibn Saʿd, *al-Ṭabaqāt al-kubrā*, 4:66.9–14. On the wars of *ridda* or "apostasy," see *EI*², s.v. al-Ridda (M. Lecker).

48. Wāqidī, *Maghāzī*, 3:1121.5–12; cf. Ibn Saʿd, *al-Ṭabaqāt al-kubrā*, 4:67.13–17; *The History of al-Ṭabarī*, trans. Donner, 10:14.

49. Wāqidī, *Maghāzī*, 3:1121.12–19; cf. Ibn Saʿd, *al-Ṭabaqāt al-kubrā*, 4:67.17–19; Balādhurī, *Ansāb*, 1:475.17–21; *The History of al-Ṭabarī*, trans. Donner, 10:14–15.

50. Cf. Ibn Kathīr, *al-Bidāya wa'l-nihāya*, 5:37.11, where Abū Bakr is the commander (*amīr*) and ʿAlī is the one commanded (*maʾmūr*).

51. Wāqidī, *Maghāzī*, 3:1121.19–1122.4; cf. Balādhurī, *Ansāb*, 1:474.8–11; *The History of al-Ṭabarī*, trans. Donner, 10:11, 16–17.

52. Wāqidī, *Maghāzī*, 3:1122.4–6; cf. Balādhurī, *Ansāb*, 1:475.20–21.

53. Ibid., 3:1122.7–12; cf. *The History of al-Ṭabarī*, trans. Donner, 10:15–16; Ibn Ḥanbal, *Musnad*, no. 22168.

54. In the Hebrew Bible, the verb *tsivah* ("to command") is used to signify the transfer of authority from Moses to Joshua. See Deut. 31:14, 23; Josh. 1:9; Deut. 2:21–28.

55. Wāqidī, *Maghāzī*, 3:1122.12–18.

56. Ibn Saʿd, *al-Ṭabaqāt al-kubrā*, 4:68.1–2, 6; cf. Balādhurī, *Ansāb*, 1:474.10–11.

57. Wāqidī, *Maghāzī*, 3:1122.19–1123.4. The understanding of hijra or emigration manifested in this text is inconsistent with what would become the standard view, according to which the obligation to emigrate ceased with the conquest of Mecca in 8/630. See further P. Crone, "The First-Century Concept of *Hiǧra*."

58. Wāqidī, *Maghāzī*, 3:1123.4–7; cf. Ibn Ḥanbal, *Musnad*, no. 22168. Note the use

of the terms *waṣiyya* and *ʿahd*—both associated with a last will and testament and final instructions to a community.

59. Ibid., 3:1123.7–8.

60. Ibid., 3:1123.9–11; cf. Ibn Saʿd, *al-Ṭabaqāt al-kubrā*, 4:67.20–24, where Usāma instructs his men to inflict severe wounds on the people of Ubna so as to terrorize them.

61. Wāqidī, *Maghāzī*, 3:1123.11–17.

62. Ibid., 3:1123.17–1124.1.

63. Ibid., 3:1124.1.

64. In 7 or 8 A.H., men from the village of Kathkath are said to have confronted Zayd b. Ḥāritha on his way to Muʾtah and captured several of his best men. Three or four years later, as the Muslim forces were leaving Ubna, they were again attacked by Kathkathī fighters. Usāma and his men responded by burning their settlement and driving off their sheep and goats. Two of the Kathkathīs were taken as prisoners and brought to Medina, where they were beheaded. Ibid., 3:1124.11–14.

65. Ibid., 3:1124.2–5; cf. Ibn Saʿd, *al-Ṭabaqāt al-kubrā*, 4:68; Balādhurī, *Ansāb*, 1:475.15–16.

66. Balādhurī, *Ansāb*, 1:473.22–3 ("forty nights or two months"); *The History of al-Ṭabarī*, trans. Donner, 10:17 ("within forty days"), 10:40 ("forty days").

67. *The History of al-Ṭabarī*, trans. Donner, 10:17.

68. Wāqidī, *Maghāzī*, 3:1125.3–5. A brief summary of the episode is found in Balādhurī, *Ansāb*, 1:384.16–21 and 473.19–23.

69. Ibn Saʿd, *al-Ṭabaqāt al-kubrā*, 4:71.12–13; 4:72.17.

70. Ibid., 4:72.17–18.

71. See, for example, al-Iskāfī, *al-Miʿyār wa'l-muwāzana*, 21, 34–35.

72. Ibn Saʿd, *al-Ṭabaqāt al-kubrā*, 4:71.17–22.

73. Ibid., 4:71.10–16; cf. Ibn Ḥanbal, *Musnad*, nos. 22087, 22096, 22124, 22134, 22160.

74. Wāqidī, *Maghāzī*, 4:71.5–9. The statement attributed to Maymūna is a polemical reference to the corrupting influence of worldly luxury. Cf. Abū Bakr's advice (*waṣiyya*) to ʿUmar: "Beware a coterie of the [C]ompanions of the Messenger of God who have grown fat, become ambitious, and each of them seeks only his own personal welfare" (Abū Yūsuf, *Kitāb al-Kharāj*, Beirut, 1979, cited in El-Hibri, *Parable and Politics*, 359–60*n*100).

75. Ibn Saʿd, *al-Ṭabaqāt al-kubrā*, 4:71 (bottom)–72.5.

76. Balādhurī, *Ansāb*, 1:472 (bottom). The recycling of the names of key members of the Prophet's family merits further attention.

77. Ibn Saʿd, *al-Ṭabaqāt al-kubrā*, 4:70.18–23.

78. Ibid., 4:70 (bottom)–71.1–4.

79. Ibid., 4:72.14–20.

80. On *ḥerem*, see Monroe, *Josiah's Reform and the Dynamics of Ritual Defilement*, 9, 43, 46, 71.

Conclusion

1. *The Life of Muhammad*, trans. Guillaume, 114–15, 186, 213 ff., 218, 227, 234, 293, 308, 314, 327, 364, 531–40, 662–63, 664, 791.

2. Ibid., 308, 364–65, 652, 678–80, 687.

3. On Abū Bakr's merits and qualifications for leadership, see Afsaruddin, *Excellence and Precedence*, 59–60, 65–66, 69–70, 87, 100–101, 152–54, 157, 166–67, 181, 184, 190, 256, 272. See also *EI*[2], s.v.; *EQ*, s.v.

4. On ʿAlī's merits and qualifications for leadership, see Afsaruddin, *Excellence and Precedence*, 53–57, 94–95, 109, 155–58, 161, 168, 172–75, 181–82, 187, 194–95, 209, 215, 217, 219, 226–27, 230, 233–34, 239, 242, 251, 258, 274, 276. See also *EI*[2], s.v.; *EQ*, s.v.; Madelung, *The Succession to Muḥammad*, index, s.v.

5. On ʿĀʾisha, see Ibn Saʿd, *Ṭabaqāt*, 8:64–66.

6. Ibn Ḥanbal, *Faḍāʾil al-ṣaḥāba*. 2:615, no. 1052.

7. Ibn Saʿd, *Ṭabaqāt*, 3:17.

8. Ibn Abī Shayba, *Muṣannaf*, 6:349, no. 31930.

9. Al-Jāḥiẓ, *al-ʿUthmāniyya*, 135–36; Ibn Ṭāwūs, *Ṭarāʾif*, 77, 89.

10. Balādhurī, *Ansāb*, 1:560–61.

11. Text: *wa-law baqiya baʿdahu istakhlafahu*. See also Ibn Saʿd, *Kitāb al-ṭabaqāt al-kabīr*, III/i, 31.9–13; Ibn ʿAsākir, *Taʾrīkh madīnat Dimashq*, 19:366.6–18. Cf. Balādhurī, *Ansāb*, 1:476 (bottom), where the text has been amended to read: *wa-in baqiya baʿdahu istakhlafahu ʿalā al-madīna*, i.e., he would have put him in charge of Medina.

12. *The Life of Muhammad*, trans. Guillaume, 3; cf. Ibn Qutayba, *al-Maʿārif*, 117.

13. See, for example, Hag. 2:23, Dan. 9:24, I Cor. 9:2. See also Colpe, *Das Siegel der Propheten*; G. Stroumsa, "'Seal of the Prophets': The Nature of a Manichean Metaphor"; Simon, "Mānī and Muḥammad."

14. Muqātil b. Sulaymān, *Tafsīr*, 3:46–48.

15. Ibid., 3:48.4–6, *ad* Q. 33:37 (ʿUmar); Tirmidhī, *Sunan*, bāb *tafsīr Sūrat al-Aḥzāb* (ʿĀʾisha). The attribution of this statement to both ʿUmar and ʿĀʾisha suggests that these two figures played a key role—or were remembered as having played a key role—in the production of what might be called *l'affaire de Zaynab*. This connection merits further attention.

16. Muqātil b. Sulaymān, *Tafsīr*, 3:49. Text: *wa-law anna li-Muḥammad*[in] *walad*[an] *la-kāna nabiyy*[an] *rasūl*[an].

17. Ibid. Text: *law kāna Zayd*[un] *ibn*[a] *Muḥammad la-kāna nabiyy*[an].

18. Ibid.

19. Ibid.

20. See Friedmann, *Prophecy Continuous*, 60 (and the sources cited there); *EI*[2], s.v. Māriyah (F. Buhl).

21. Sharon, "The Development of the Debate Around the Legitimacy of Authority in Early Islam," 126–27, 136; Crone, "*Mawālī* and the Prophet's Family," 172.

22. Crone and Hinds, *God's Caliph*, 6–7.

23. Sharon, "The Development of the Debate Around the Legitimacy of Authority in Early Islam," citing al-Suyūṭī, *Laʾālī* (Cairo, 1933?), 1:419. Cf. Muqātil's statement that if Zayd had outlived Muḥammad, he would have been a prophet.

24. See *EI*[2], s.v.v. Abū ʿĪsā al-Iṣfahānī (S. M. Stern), al-ʿĪsāwiyya (S. Pines), and al-Mukhtār b. Abī ʿUbayd (G. R. Hawting); Dunlop, "Al-Ḥārith b. Saʿīd al-Kadhdhāb," 12–18; Wasserstein, "The ʿĪsāwiyya Revisited"; Ess, *Anfänge muslimischer Theologie*, 228–30; Friedmann, *Prophecy Continuous*, 65–70.

25. Jeffery, *Materials*, 170.

26. On eschatology in the Qurʾān, see Shoemaker, *The Death of a Prophet*, chapter 4

and idem, "'The Reign of God Has Come': Eschatology and Empire in Late Antiquity and Early Islam," *Arabica* 61 (2014).

27. Ibn Ḥanbal, *Musnad*, nos. 21525–26; Suyūṭī, *al-Itqān*, 2:33.19–26; Burton, *Collection of the Qur'ān*, 80–84; *EQ*, s.v. Collection of the Qur'ān (J. Burton).

28. See Ibn Abī Dā'ūd, *Kitāb al-Maṣāḥif*, 49–50, 117–18; Balādhurī, *Ansāb al-Ashrāf*, 4:2, 586; de Prémare, "'Abd al-Malik b. Marwān," 202–3; Hoyland, *Seeing Islam as Others Saw It*, 501; Déroche, *La transmission manuscrite du Coran aux débuts de l'islam: Le codex Parisino-petropolitanus*.

29. C. Robinson, *'Abd al-Malik*, 103–4.

Bibliography

Primary Sources

ʿAbd al-Razzāq al-Ṣanʿānī. *al-Muṣannaf.* Ed. Ḥabīb al-Raḥmān al-Aʿẓamī. 11 vols. Beirut: al-Maktab al-islāmī, 1970–72; 2nd ed. 1983.

———. *Tafsīr*. 3 vols. Beirut: Dār al-Kutub al-ʿIlmiyya, 1419/1999.

Abū Dāʾūd. See al-ʿAẓīmābādī.

Abū Yūsuf, *Kitāb al-kharāj*. Beirut, 1979. Trans. A. Ben Shemesh as *Taxation in Islam*, vol. 3. Leiden: Brill, 1969.

ʿAlī b. Burhān al-Dīn. *al-Sīra al-ḥalabiyya fī sīrat al-amīn al-maʾmūn: insān al-ʿuyūn*. 3 vols. Beirut: Dār al-Maʿrifa li'l-Ṭibāʿa wa'l-Nashr, 1980.

The Anchor Bible Commentary: Genesis. Trans. E. A. Speiser. Garden City, N.Y.: Doubleday 1964.

al-ʿAẓīmābādī. *ʿAwn al-maʿbūd: sharḥ sunan Abī Dāʾūd*. 14 vols. Medina: al-Maktaba al-Salafiyya, 1968–.

The Babylonian Talmud. Trans. with notes, glossary, and indices under the editorship of I. Epstein. 18 vols. London: Soncino Press, 1978. [*BT*]

al-Balādhurī, *Ansāb al-ashrāf.* Vol. 1, ed. Muḥammad Ḥamīd Allāh. Cairo: Dār al-Maʿārif, 1987. Vol. 4:2, ed. ʿAbd al-ʿAzīz ad-Dūrī and ʿIṣām ʿUqla. Bibliotheca Islamica 28e. Beirut: Das Arabische Buch, 2001. Vol. 5, ed. Iḥsān ʿAbbās. Bibliotheca Islamica 28g. Beirut: Franz Steiner, 1996.

The Book of Jubilees or the Little Genesis. Trans. R. H. Charles. London: A. and C. Black, 1902; Jerusalem: Makor, 1972.

Al-Bukhārī, Muḥammad b. Ismāʿīl. *Ṣaḥīḥ*. Ed. M. Ludolf Krehl and Th. W. Juynboll. 4 vols. Leiden: Brill, 1862–98.

The Chronicle of Theophanes Confessor: Byzantine and Near Eastern History AD 284–813. Trans. Cyril Mango and Roger Scott. Oxford: Clarendon Press, 1997.

al-Fazārī, Abū Isḥāq. *Kitāb al-siyar*. Ed. Fārūq Ḥamāda. Beirut: Muʾassasat al-Risāla, 1408/1987.

Genesis Rabbah, The Judaic Commentary to the Book of Genesis, A New American Translation. Trans. Jacob Neusner. 3 vols. Atlanta: Scholars Press, 1985.

al-Hindī, ʿAlāʾ al-Dīn al-Muttaqī. *Kanz al-ʿummāl fī sunan al-aqwāl wa'l-afʿāl*. Ed. Ṣafwat al-Saqqā and Bakrī al-Ḥayyānī. 5th ed. 16 vols. Beirut: Muʾassasat al-Risāla, 1985.

The History of al-Ṭabarī. Vol. 7, *The Foundation of the Community*. Trans. M. V. McDonald and W. Montgomery Watt. Albany: State University of New York Press, 1987.

The History of al-Ṭabarī. Vol. 8, *The Victory of Islam*. Trans. Michael Fishbein. Albany: State University of New York Press, 1997.

The History of al-Ṭabarī. Vol. 9, *The Last Years of the Prophet*. Trans. Ismail K. Poonawala. Albany: State University of New York Press, 1990.

The History of al-Ṭabarī. Vol. 10, *The Conquest of Arabia*. Trans. Fred M. Donner. Albany: State University of New York Press, 1993.

The History of al-Ṭabarī. Vol. 39, *Biographies of the Prophet's Companions and Their Successors*. Trans. Ella Landau-Tasseron. Albany: State University of New York Press, 1998.

Ibn ʿAbd al-Barr. *al-Istīʿāb fī maʿrifat al-aṣḥāb*, On the margins of Ibn Ḥajar al-ʿAsqalānī, *al-Iṣāba fī tamyīz al-ṣaḥāba*. 4 vols. Cairo: Matbaʿat al-Saʿāda, 1328.

Ibn Abī Dāʾūd al-Sijistānī, Abū Bakr. *Kitāb al-maṣāḥif*. Ed. Arthur Jeffery. Cairo: al-Maṭbaʿa al-Raḥmāniyya, 1355/1936.

Ibn Abī Shayba. *al-Kitāb al-muṣannaf fī al-aḥādīth wa'l-āthār*. Ed. Mukhtār Aḥmad al-Nadwī. 15 vols. Bombay: al-Dār al-Salafiyya, 1403/1983.

Ibn ʿAsākir. *Taʾrīkh madīnat Dimashq*. Ed. ʿUmar b. Gharāma al-ʿAmrawī. 80 vols. Beirut: Dār al-Fikr, 1415/1995–2000.

Ibn Ḥajar al-ʿAsqalānī. *al-Iṣāba fī tamyīz al-ṣaḥāba*. Ed. ʿAlī Muḥammad al-Bajāwī. 8 vols. Cairo: Dār Nahdat Miṣr li'l-Ṭabʿ wa'l-Nashr, 1970–.

———. *Tahdhīb al-tahdhīb*. 12 vols. Hayderabad: Dāʾirat al-Maʿārif al-ʿUthmāniyya, 1325–27/1907–9; repr. Beirut: Dār Ṣādir, 1968.

Ibn Ḥanbal, Aḥmad. *Faḍāʾil al-ṣaḥāba*. Ed. Waṣī Allāh Muḥammad ʿAbbās. 2 vols. Mecca: Jāmiʿat Umm al-Qurā, Markaz al-Baḥth al-ʿIlmī wa-Iḥyāʾ at-Turāth al-Islāmī, 1403/1983.

———. *al-Musnad*. Riyāḍ: Bayt al-Afkār al-Duwaliyya li'l-Nashr wa'l-Tawzīʿ, 1419/1998.

Ibn Ḥazm, ʿAlī b. Aḥmad b. Saʿīd al-Andalusī. *Jamharat ansāb al-ʿarab*. Ed. ʿAbd al-Salām Muḥammad Hārūn. Cairo: Dār al-Maʿārif bi-Miṣr, 1382/1962.

Ibn Hishām, ʿAbd al-Malik. *Kitāb Sīrat Rasūl Allāh*. Ed. F. Wüstenfeld. 2 vols. in 3. Göttingen: Dieterichsche Universitäts-Buchhandlung, 1858–60. See also *The Life of Muhammad*.

Ibn al-Jawzī's Kitāb al-quṣṣāṣ wa'l-mudhakkirīn. Including a critical edition, annotated translation, and introduction by Merlin L. Swartz. Beyrouth: Dar El-Machreq Éditeurs, 1986.

Ibn Kathīr. *al-Bidāya wa'l-nihāya*. 14 vols. in 7. 1st ed. Beirut: Maktab al-Maʿārif and al-Riyāḍ: Maktab al-Naṣr, 1966.

———. *Tafsīr al-qurʾān al-ʿaẓīm*. 4 vols. 3rd ed. Cairo: Maṭbaʿat al-Istiqāma, 1373/1954.

———. *Tafsīr al-qurʾān al-ʿaẓīm*. Ed. Sāmī b. Muḥammad al-Salāma. 8 vols. Riyāḍ: Dār Ṭība li'l-Nashr wa'l-Tawzīʿ, 1418/1997.

Ibn Manẓūr. *Lisān al-ʿarab*. 6 vols. Cairo: Dār al-Maʿārif, 1981.

Ibn Qutayba, ʿAbdallāh b. Muslim. *al-Maʿārif*. Ed. Tharwat ʿUkāsha. Cairo: Dār al-Maʿārif, 1969.

Ibn Saʿd. *Kitāb al-ṭabaqāt al-kabīr*. 8 vols. plus index. Ed. E. Sachau et al. Leiden: Brill, 1904–40.

———. *al-Ṭabaqāt al-kubrā*. 9 vols. Beirut: Dār Ṣādir, 1957–68.

Ibn Shahrāshūb, Abū Jaʿfar b. Muḥammad. *Manāqib Āl Abī Ṭālib*. Ed. Yūsuf al-Biqāʿī. 5 vols. Qumm: Intishārāt Dhū al-Qurbā, 1980.

Ibn Ṭāwūs, Raḍī al-Dīn Abū al-Qāsim ʿAlī b. Mūsā. *al-Ṭarāʾif fī maʿrifat madhāhib al-ṭawāʾif*. Qum: Matbaʿat al-Khayyām, 1400/1979.

Iskāfī, Abū Jaʿfar Muḥammad b. ʿAbdallāh al-Muʿtazilī. *Al-Miʿyār wa'l-Muwāzana fī faḍāʾil al-Imām Amīr al-Muʾminīn ʿAlī b. Abī Ṭālib*. Ed. Muḥammad Bāqir al-Maḥmūdī. 1402/1981.

The Islamic Law of Nations: Shaybānī's Siyar. Trans. Majid Khadduri. Baltimore: Johns Hopkins Press, 1966.

al-Jāḥiẓ, ʿAmr b. Baḥr. *al-ʿUthmāniyya*. Ed. ʿAbd al-Salām Hārūn. Cairo: n.p., 1474/1955.

Josephus, Flavius. *Jewish Antiquities*. Trans. William Whiston. Wordsworth Classics of World Literature. London: Wordsworth Editions, 2006.

Khalīfa b. Khayyāt. *Kitāb al-ṭabaqāt*, part 1. Ed. Suhayl Zakkār. Damascus: Maṭābiʿ Wizārat al-Thaqāfa, 1966.

al-Khawārizmī, Muwaffaq b. Aḥmad al-Makkī. *Al-Manāqib*. Najaf, 1385/1965.

The Life of Muhammad: A Translation of Ibn Ishaq's Sirat Rasul Allah. Trans. Alfred Guillaume. Oxford: Oxford University Press, 1955. *See also* Ibn Hishām.

Midrash ha-Gadol. Ed. Mordechai Margaliot et al. 5 vols. Jerusalem: Rav Kook, 1947–72.

Midrash Rabbah. Trans. H. Freedman and Maurice Simon. 10 vols. London: Soncino Press, 1939.

al-Mizzī, Jamāl al-Dīn. *Tahdhīb al-kamāl fī asmāʾ al-rijāl*. Ed. Bashshār ʿAwwād Maʿrūf. 35 vols. Beirut: Muʾassasat al-Risāla, 1400/1980.

Muqātil b. Sulaymān. *Tafsīr*. Ed. Aḥmad Farīd. 3 vols. Beirut: Dār al-Kutub al-ʿIlmiyya, 1424/2003.

Muslim b. Ḥajjāj. *Ṣaḥīḥ*. 5 vols. Cairo: Dār Iḥyāʾ al-Kutub al-ʿArabiyya, 1375/1955.

al-Nābulusī, ʿAbd al-Ghanī. *Ghāyat al-maṭlūb fī maḥabbat al-maḥbūb*. Ed. Bakrī ʿAlāʾ al-Dīn and Shīrīn Maḥmūd Daqūrī. Damascus: Dār Shahrazād al-Shām, 2007.

Pĕsiḳta dĕ-Rab Kahăna: R. Kahana's Compilation of Discourses for Sabbaths and Festal Days. Trans. William G. (Gershon Zev) Braude and Israel J. Kapstein. Philadelphia: Jewish Publication Society of America, 2002.

Pirḳe de-Rabbi Eliezer . . . im beʿûr *ha-Bayit ha-gadôl* me-et Avraham Aharôn ben ha-Rav Shalom. Bene Beraq, 2005.

The Qurʾān. Trans. Alan Jones. Exeter: Gibb Memorial Trust, 2007.

al-Qurṭubī. *al-Jāmiʿ li-aḥkām al-qurʾān*. Ed. ʿAbd al-Munʿim ʿAbd al-Maqṣūd. 20 vols. Cairo: Dār al-Kutub al-Miṣriyya, 1387/1967.

Die Schriften des Johannes von Damaskos. Ed. Bonifatius Kotter. Byzantisches Institut der Abtei Scheyern, Patristische Texte und Studien, Berlin: de Gruyter, 1969–.

al-Shaybānī. See *Islamic Law of Nations*.

Sifre: A Tannaitic Commentary on the Book of Deuteronomy. Trans. Reuven Hammer. New Haven, Conn.: Yale University Press, 1986.

al-Suyūṭī, Jalāl al-Dīn ʿAbd al-Raḥmān. *al-Durr al-manthūr fī al-tafsīr al-maʾthūr*. 6 vols. Beirut: Dār al-Kutub al-ʿIlmiyya, 1411/1990.

———. *al-Itqān fī ʿulūm al-qurʾān*. 2 vols. in 1. Bombay: Abnāʾ Mawlawī Muḥammad b. Ghulām Rasūl al-Sūratī, 1978.

———. *Lubāb al-nuqūl fī asbāb al-nuzūl*. On the margin of al-Maḥallī, *Tafsīr*. Cairo: Dār al-Qalam, 1966.

al-Ṭabarī, Muḥammad b. Jarīr. *Jāmiʿ al-bayān ʿan taʾwīl āy al-qurʾān*. 30 vols. in 12. 3rd ed. Cairo: Muṣṭafā al-Bābī al-Ḥalabī, 1954–68.

———. *Tafsīr al-Ṭabarī: Jāmiʿ al-bayān ʿan taʾwīl āy al-qurʾān*. Ed. M. M. Shākir and Aḥmad Muḥammad Shākir. 16 vols. Cairo: Dār al-Maʿārif, 1969.

———. *Taʾrīkh al-rusul waʾl-mulūk*. Ed. M. Abū al-Faḍl Ibrāhīm. 11 vols. Cairo: Dār al-Maʿārif, 1960–77. See also *The History of al-Ṭabarī*.

al-Ṭabarsī. *Majmaʿ al-bayān li-ʿulūm al-qurʾān*. 9 vols. Cairo: Dār al-Taqrīb bayna al-Madhāhib al-Islāmiyya, 1395/1975.

Tanakh, The Holy Scriptures: The New JPS Translation According to the Traditional Hebrew Text. Philadelphia: Jewish Publication Society, 1985.

al-Wāqidī, Muḥammad b. ʿUmar. *Kitāb al-maghāzī*. Ed. Marsden Jones. 3 vols. London: Oxford University Press, 1966.

Yalkut Shimʿoni: Midrash ʿal Torah, Neviʾim u-Khetuvim. 5 vols. Jerusalem: Hotsaʾat Yerid ha-sefarim, 2006.

al-Yaʿqūbī. *Taʾrīkh*. Ed. Muḥammad Ṣādiq Baḥr al-ʿUlūm. 3 vols. Najaf: al-Maktaba al-Ḥaydariyya, 1384/1964.

al-Zuhrī, Muḥammad b. Muslim b. ʿUbaydallāh b. Shihāb. *al-Maghāzī al-Nabawiyya*. Ed. Suhayl Zakkār. Damascus: Dār al-Fikr, 1980.

Secondary Sources

Ackerman, Susan. "'And the Women Knead Dough': The Worship of the Queen of Heaven in Sixth-Century Judah." In *Gender and Difference*, ed. Peggy Day. Minneapolis: Fortress Press, 1989, 109–24.

Afsaruddin, Asma. *Excellence and Precedence: Medieval Islam's Discourse on Legitimate Leadership*. Leiden: Brill, 2002.

The Anchor Bible Dictionary. Ed. David Noel Freedman. 6 vols. New York: Doubleday, 1992.

Andrae, Tor. *Mohammed, The Man and His Faith*. 1936; repr. New York: Harper and Row, 1955.

Arazi, Albert. "Les enfants adultérins [*daʿīs*] dans la société arabe ancienne: L'aspect littéraire." *Jerusalem Studies in Arabic and Islam* 16 (1993): 1–34.

ʿAthāmina, Khalil. "*al-Qasas*: Its Emergence, Religious Origin and Its Socio-Political Impact on Early Muslim Society." *Studia Islamica* 76 (1992): 53–74.

Auerbach, Erich. *Mimesis: The Representation of Reality in Western Literature*. Trans. Willard Trask. Garden City, N.Y.: Doubleday, 1957.

Bakhos, Carol. *Ishmael on the Border: Rabbinic Portrayals of the First Arab*. Albany: State University of New York Press, 2006.

Bashear, Suliman. "Riding Beasts on Divine Missions: An Examination of the Ass and Camel Traditions." *Journal of Semitic Studies* 37, 1 (1991): 37–71.

Berg, Herbert. "ʿAbbasid Historians' Portrayals of al-ʿAbbās b. ʿAbd al-Muṭṭalib." In *ʿAbbasid Studies II*. Occasional Papers of the School of ʿAbbasid Studies Leuven, 28 June – 1 July 2004. Leiden: Uitgeverij Peeters en Departement Oosterse Studies, 2010, 13–38.

Bewer, Julius A. "Eliezer of Damascus." *Journal of Biblical Literature* 27, 2 (1908): 160–62.

Biddle, Mark E. "Ancestral Motifs in I Samuel 25: Intertextuality and Characterization." *Journal of Biblical Literature* 121, 4 (2002): 617–38.

Bijlefeld, W. A. "A Prophet and More Than a Prophet? Some Observations on the Qurʾanic Use of the Terms 'Prophet' and 'Apostle'." *Muslim World* 59 (1969): 1–28. Repr. in *Koran: Critical Concepts in Islamic Studies*, ed. Colin Turner. 4 vols. London: RoutledgeCurzon, 2004, 2: 295–322.

Blankinship, Khalid Yahya. "Imārah, Khilāfah, and Imāmah: The Origin of the Succession to the Prophet Muhammad." In *Shiʿite Heritage: Essays on Classical and Modern Traditions*, ed. Lynda Clarke. Binghamton, N.Y.: Global Publications, 2001, 19–44.

Bowersock, G. W. *Martyrdom and Rome*. Cambridge: Cambridge University Press, 1995.

Boyarin, Daniel. *Border Lines: The Partition of Judaeo-Christianity*. Philadelphia: University of Pennsylvania Press, 2004.

———. *Dying for God: Martyrdom and the Making of Christianity and Juda-*

ism. Stanford, Calif.: Stanford University Press, 1999.

———. *Intertextuality and the Reading of Midrash*. Bloomington: Indiana University Press, 1990.

Bravmann, M. M. "Equality of Birth of Husband and Wife (*kafāʾah*), an Early Arab Principle." In idem, *The Spiritual Background of Early Islam: Studies in Ancient Arab Concepts*. Leiden: Brill, 1972, 301–10.

———. "The Origin of the Principle of *ʿIṣmah*: Muḥammad's Immunity from Sin." *Le Muséon* 88 (1975): 221–25.

Brock, Sebastian. "Genesis 22 in Syriac Tradition." In *Mélanges Dominique Barthélemy*, ed. Pierre Casetti, Othmar Keel, and Adrian Schenker. Göttingen: Vandenhoeck & Ruprecht, 1981, 2–30.

Burton, John. *The Collection of the Qurʾān*. Cambridge: Cambridge University Press, 1977.

Caetani, Leone. *Annali dell'Islām*. 10 vols. in 12. Milano: U. Hoepli, 1905–26.

Collins, John J. "The Zeal of Phineas: The Bible and the Legitimation of Violence." *Journal of Biblical Literature* 122, 1 (2003): 3–21.

Colpe, Carsten. *Das Siegel der Propheten: Historische Beziehungen zwischen Judentum, Judenchristentum, Heidentum und frühem Islam*. Berlin: Institut Kirche und Judentum, 1989.

Conrad, Lawrence I. "Al-Azdī's History of the Arab Conquests in Bilād al-Shām: Some Historiographical Observations." In *Proceedings of the Second Symposium on the History of Bilād al-Shām During the Early Islamic Period Up to 40 A.H./640 A.D.*, vol. 1, ed. Adnan Bakhit. Amman: University of Jordan, 1987, 28–61.

———. "Heraclius in Early Islamic Kerygma." In *The Reign of Heraclius (610–641): Crisis and Confrontation*, ed. Gerrit J. Reinink and Bernard H. Stolte. Leuven: Peeters, 2002, 113–56.

———. "Seven and the *Tasbīʿ*: On the Implications of Numerical Symbolism for the Study of Medieval Islamic History." *Journal of the Economic and Social History of the Orient* 31 (1988): 42–73.

Crone, Patricia. "In Defence of Ali." *Times Literary Supplement*. 7 February 1997, 28.

———. "The First-Century Concept of *Hiǧra*." *Arabica* 41, 3 (1994): 352–87.

———. "*Mawālī* and the Prophet's Family: An Early Shīʿite View." In *Patronate and Patronage in Early and Classical Islam*. Ed. Monique Bernards and John Nawas. Leiden: Brill, 2005, 167–93.

———. "A Note on Muqātil b. Ḥayyān and Muqātil b. Sulaymān." *Der Islam* 74 (1997): 238–49.

———. "What Do We Actually Know About Mohammed?" www.openDemocracy.net, 31 August 2006, 1–5.

Crone, Patricia, and Martin Hinds. *God's Caliph: Religious Authority in the First Centuries of Islam.* Cambridge: Cambridge University Press, 1986.

Dähne, Stephan. "Context Equivalence: A Hitherto Insufficiently Studied Use of the Quran in Political Speeches from the Early Period of Islam." In *Ideas, Images, and Methods of Portrayal: Insights into Classical Arabic Literature and Islam*, ed. Sebastian Günther. Leiden: Brill, 2005, 1–16.

Dakake, Maria Massi. *The Charismatic Community: Shiʿite Identity in Early Islam.* Albany: State University of New York Press, 2007.

Déroche, François. *La transmission manuscrite du Coran aux débuts de l'islam: Le codex Parisino-petropolitanus.* Leiden: Brill, 2009.

Donner, Fred McGraw. *The Early Islamic Conquests.* Princeton, N.J.: Princeton University Press, 1982.

———. *Muhammad and the Believers: At the Origins of Islam.* Cambridge, Mass.: Belknap Press, 2010.

———. *Narratives of Islamic Origins: The Beginnings of Islamic Historical Writing.* Princeton, N.J.: Darwin Press, 1998.

Donner, Herbert. "Adoption oder Legitimation? Erwägungen zur Adoption im Alten Testament auf dem Hintergrund der altorientalischen Rechte." *Oriens Antiquus* 8 (1969): 87–119.

Duri, ʿAbd al-ʿAziz. *The Rise of Historical Writing Among the Arabs*. Ed. and trans. Lawrence I. Conrad. Princeton, N.J.: Princeton University Press, 1983.

Ehrman, Bart D. *Lost Christianities: The Battle for Scripture and the Faiths We Never Knew.* Oxford: Oxford University Press, 2003.

El-Hibri, Tayeb. *Parable and Politics in Early Islamic History: The Rashidun Caliphs.* New York: Columbia University Press, 2010.

Encyclopaedia Biblica, A Critical Dictionary of the Literary, Political and Religious History, the Archaeology, Geography, and Natural History of the Bible. Ed. T. K. Cheyne and J. Sutherland. New York: Macmillan, 1899–1903.

Encyclopaedia of Islam. 2nd ed. 11 vols. Leiden: Brill, 1954–2002. [*EI*²]

Encyclopaedia of Islam. 3rd ed. Leiden: Brill (in progress). [*EI*³]

Encyclopaedia of the Qur'ān. Ed. Jane Dammen McAuliffe. 5 vols. plus index. Leiden: Brill, 2001–6. [*EQ*]

Ess, Josef Van. *Anfänge muslimischer Theologie: zwei antiqadaritische Traktate aus dem ersten Jahrhundert der Hiğra*. Beirut: Orient-Institut; Wiesbaden: F. Steiner, 1977.

———. *The Flowering of Muslim Theology*. Cambridge, Mass.: Harvard University Press, 2006.

———. *Theologie und Gesellschaft im 2. und 3. Jahrhundert Hidschra: eine Geschichte des religiösen Denkens im frühen Islam*. 6 vols. Berlin: Walter de Gruyter, 1991–97.

Firestone, Reuven. "Abraham's Journey to Mecca in Islamic Exegesis: A Form-Critical Study of a Tradition." *Studia Islamica* 76 (1992): 5–24.

———. *Journeys in Holy Lands: The Evolution of the Abraham-Ishmael Legends in Islamic Exegesis*. Albany: State University of New York Press, 1990.

———. "Merit, Mimesis, and Martyrdom: Aspects of Shiʿite Meta-Historical Exegesis on Abraham's Sacrifice in Light of Jewish, Christian, and Sunni Muslim Tradition." *Journal of the American Academy of Religion* 66, 1 (1998): 93–116.

Friedmann, Yohanan. "Finality of Prophethood in Sunnī Islam." *Jerusalem Studies in Arabic and Islam* 7 (1986): 177–215.

———. *Prophecy Continuous: Aspects of Aḥmadī Religious Thought and Its Medieval Background*. Berkeley: University of California Press, 1989.

Gil, Moshe. *A History of Palestine, 634–1099*. Cambridge: Cambridge University Press, 1983.

Gilliot, Claude. "The Beginnings of Qur'ānic Exegesis." *Revue du Monde Musulman et de la Méditerranée* 58 (1990): 82–100. Reprinted in *The Koran: Critical Concepts in Islamic Studies*, ed. Colin Turner. 4 vols. London: RoutledgeCurzon, 2004, 4:248–70.

———. "Creation of a Fixed Text." In *The Cambridge Companion to the Qur'ān*, ed. Jane Dammen McAuliffe. Cambridge: Cambridge University Press, 2006, 41–58.

———. "Muqātil, grand exégète, traditionniste et théologien maudit." *Journal Asiatique* 279 (1991): 39–92.

Ginsberg, H. L. "Abram's 'Damascene' Steward." *Bulletin of the American Schools of Oriental Research* 200 (1970): 31–33.

Ginzberg, Louis. *The Legends of the Jews*. 7 vols. Philadelphia: Jewish Publication Society of America, 1906–38.

Goldfeld, Isaiah. "Muqātil Ibn Sulaymān." *Arabic and Islamic Studies* 2 (1978): 1–18.

Goldziher, Ignaz. *Muslim Studies*. Ed. S. M. Stern. 2 vols. Chicago: Aldine, 1971.

Gwynne, Rosalind Ward. *Logic, Rhetoric, and Legal Reasoning in the Qur'ān: God's Arguments*. London: RoutledgeCurzon, 2004.

Hakim, Avraham. "The Death of an Ideal Leader: Predictions and Premonitions." *Journal of the American Oriental Society* 126, 1 (2006): 1–16.

———. "ʿUmar b. al-Ḫaṭṭāb, calife par la grâce de Dieu." *Arabica* 54 (2007): 317–61.

Hasan, Ahmad. "The Concept of Infallibility in Islam." *Islamic Studies* 11 (1972): 1–11.

Hayward, Robert. "The Present State of Research into the Targumic Account of the Sacrifice of Isaac." *Journal of Jewish Studies* 32 (1981): 127–50.

Hirschfeld, Hartwig. *New Researches into the Composition and Exegesis of the Qoran*. Asiatic Monographs 3. London: Royal Asiatic Society, 1902.

Horovitz, Josef. *The Earliest Biographies of the Prophet and Their Authors*. Studies in Late Antiquity and Early Islam, 11, ed. Lawrence I. Conrad. Princeton, N.J.: Darwin Press, 2002.

Hoyland, Robert G. *Seeing Islam as Others Saw It*. Studies in Late Antiquity and Early Islam 13. Princeton, N.J.: Darwin Press, 1997.

Jeffery, Arthur. "Ghevond's Text of the Correspondence Between ʿUmar II and Leo III." In *The Early Christian-Muslim Dialogue: A Collection of Documents from the First Three Islamic Centuries (632–900 A.D.): Translations with Commentary*, ed. N. A. Newman. Hatfield, Pa.: Interdisciplinary Biblical Research Institute, 1993.

_____. *Materials for the History of the Qur'ān*. Leiden: Brill, 1937. *See also* Ibn Abī Dāʾūd.

———. *The Qur'ān as Scripture*. New York: Russell F. Moore Company, 1952.

Juynboll, G. H. A. *Encyclopedia of Canonical Ḥadīth*. Leiden: Brill, 2007.

Kaegi, Walter. *Byzantium and the Early Islamic Conquests*. Cambridge: Cambridge University Press, 1992.

Kermode, Frank. *The Genesis of Secrecy: On the Interpretation of Narrative*. Cambridge, Mass.: Harvard University Press, 1979.

Khoury, R. G. *Wahb b. Munabbih: Der Heidelberger Papyrus PSR Heid. Arab. 23*. Wiesbaden: O. Harrassowitz, 1972.

Kister, M. J. "*Ḥaddithū ʿan banī isrāʾīla wa-lā ḥaraja*: A Study of an Early Tradition." *Israel Oriental Society* 2 (1972): 215–39.

———. "On the Papyrus of Wahb b. Munabbih." *Bulletin of the School of Oriental and African Studies* 37, 3 (1974), 545–71.

———. "*Al-Taḥannuth*: An Inquiry into the Meaning of a Term." *Bulletin of the School of Oriental and African Studies* 31:2 (1968): 223–36.

Klemm, Verena. "Image Formation of an Islamic Legend: Fāṭima, the Daughter of the Prophet Muḥammad." In *Ideas, Images, and Methods of Portrayal: Insights into Classical Arabic Literature and Islam*, ed. Sebastian Günther. Leiden: Brill, 2005, 181–208.

Klier, Klaus. *Ḫālid und ʿUmar: Quellenkritische Untersuchung zur Historiographie der frühislamischen Zeit*. Berlin: Klaus Schwarz Verlag, 1998.

Kristeva, Julia. *Desire in Language: A Semiotic Approach to Literature and Art*. Ed. Leon S. Roudiez. Trans. Thomas Gora, Alice Jardine, and Leon S. Roudiez. New York: Columbia University Press, 1980.

———. *Sēmeiōtikē: Recherches pour une sémnalyse*. Paris: Éditions du Seuil, 1969.

Lammens, Henri. *Fatima et les filles de Mahomet: Notes critiques pour l'étude de la Sira*. Rome: sumptibus Ponificii instituti biblici, 1912.

Landau-Tasseron, Ella. "Adoption, Acknowledgement of Paternity and False Genealogical Claims in Arabian and Islamic Societies." *Bulletin of the School of Oriental and African Studies* 66, 2 (2003): 169–92.

Lane, Edward William. *Arabic-English Lexicon*. London: Williams and Norgate, 1863. Repr. Cambridge: Islamic Texts Society, 1984.

Lecker, Michael. "Ḥudhayfa b. al-Yamān and ʿAmmār b. Yāsir, Jewish Converts to Islam." *Quaderni di Studi Arabi* 11 (1993): 149–62.

———. "King Ibn Ubayy and the *Quṣṣāṣ*." In *Method and Theory in the Study of Islamic Origins*, ed. Herbert Berg. Leiden: Brill, 2003, 29–72.

———. "Zayd b. Thābit, 'A Jew with Two Sidelocks': Judaism and Literacy in Pre-Islamic Medina (Yathrib)." *Journal of Near Eastern Studies* 56, 4 (1997): 259–73.

Leemhuis, Fred. "Origins and Early Development of the *Tafsīr* Tradition." In *Approaches to the History of the Interpretation of the Qurʾān*, ed. Andrew Rippin. Oxford: Clarendon Press, 1988, 13–30.

Levenson, Jon D. *The Death and Resurrection of the Beloved Son: The Transformation of Child Sacrifice in Judaism and Christianity*. New Haven, Conn.: Yale University Press, 1993.

Lévi, Israel. "Le Sacrifice d'Isaac et la mort de Jésus." *Revue des Etudes Juives* 64 (1912): 161–84.

Lewinstein, Keith. "The Revaluation of Martyrdom in Early Islam." In *Sacrificing the Self: Perspectives on Martyrdom and Religion*, ed. Margaret Cormack. Oxford: Oxford University Press, 2001, 78–91.

Lowin, Shari I. *The Making of a Forefather: Abraham in Islamic and Jewish Exegetical Narratives*. Leiden: Brill, 2006.

Madelung, Wilfred. "The Hāshimiyyāt of al-Kumayt and Hāshimī Shiʿism." *Studia Islamica* 70 (1989): 5–26.

———. *The Succession to Muḥammad: A Study of the early Caliphate*. Cambridge: Cambridge University Press, 1997.

Maghen, Ze'ev. "Davidic Motifs in the Biography of Muḥammad." *Jerusalem Studies in Arabic and Islam* 34 (2008): 91–140.

———. "Intertwined Triangles: Remarks on the Relationship Between Two Prophetic Scandals." *Jerusalem Studies in Arabic and Islam* 33 (2007): 17–92.

Mann, Jacob. *The Bible as Read and Preached in the Old Synagogue*. 2 vols. Cincinnati: Union of American Hebrew Congregations, 1940.

Mitter, Ulrike. "Unconditional Manumission of Slaves in Early Islamic Law: A *ḥadīth* Analysis." *Der Islam* 78 (2001): 35–72.

Monroe, Lauren A. S. *Josiah's Reform and the Dynamics of Ritual Defilement: Israelite Rites of Violence and the Making of a Biblical Text*. New York: Oxford University Press, 2011.

Motzki, Harald. "The Collection of the Qurʾān: A Reconsideration of Western Views in Light of Recent Methodological Developments." *Der Islam* 78 (2001): 1–34.

Nagel, Tilman. *Mohammed: Leben und Legende*. Munich: Oldenbourg, 2008.

Nöldeke, Theodor. *Geschichte des Qorāns*. Ed. Friedrich Schwally. 3 vols. Leipzig, 1909. Repr. Hildesheim: Georg Olms, 1961.

Noth, Albrecht. *The Early Arabic Historical Tradition: A Source-Critical Study*. 2nd ed. Trans. Michael Bonner. Princeton, N.J.: Darwin Press, 1994.

Oeste, Gordon. "The Shaping of a Prophet: Joshua in Deuteronomic History." In *Prophets, Prophecy, and Ancient Israelite Historiography*, ed. Mark J. Boda and Lissa M. Wray Beal. Winona Lake, Ind.: Eisenbrauns, 2013, 23–42.

Pagels, Elaine. "The Social History of Satan, the 'Intimate Enemy': A Preliminary Sketch." *Harvard Theological Review* 84, 2 (1991): 105–28.

Perry, Menakhem. "Counter-Stories in the Bible: Rebekah and Her Bridegroom, Abraham's Servant." *Prooftexts* 27 (2007): 275–23.

Peters, F. E. *Muhammad and the Origins of Islam*. Albany: State University of New York Press, 1994.

Pines, Shlomo. "'Israel, My Firstborn' and the Sonship of Jesus: A Theme of Moslem Anti-Christian Polemics." In *Studies in the History of Religions*, ed. Guy G. Stroumsa. Jerusalem: Magnes Press, 1996, 116–31.

Pollack, Daniel, Moshe Bleich, Charles J. Reid, Jr., and Mohammad H. Fadel. "Classical Religious Perspectives of Adoption Law." *Notre Dame Law Review* 79 (2003–4): 693–753.

Powers, David S. *Muḥammad Is Not the Father of Any of Your Men: The Making of the Last Prophet*. Philadelphia: University of Pennsylvania Press, 2009.

Prémare, Alfred-Louis de. "ʿAbd al-Malik b. Marwān et le processus de constitution du Coran." In *Die dunklen Anfänge: Neue Forschungen zur Entstehung und frühen Geschichte des Islam*, ed. Karl-Heinz Ohlig and Gerd-R. Puin. Berlin: Hans Schiler, 2005, 179–212.

———. *Les Fondations de l'Islam: Entre écriture et histoire*. Paris: Seuil, 2002.

al-Qāḍī, Wadād. "The Term 'Khalīfa' in Early Exegetical Literature." *Die Welt des Islams* 28 (1988): 392–411.

Rabinowitz, Isaac. *A Witness Forever: Ancient Israel's Perception of Literature and the Resultant Hebrew Bible*. Bethesda, Md.: CDL Press, 1993.

Rabinowitz, L. I. "The Study of a Midrash." *Jewish Quarterly Review* n.s. 58:2 (1967): 143–61.

Reeves, John C., ed. *Bible and Qur'ān: Essays in Scriptural Intertextuality*. Atlanta: Society of Biblical Literature, 2003.

Renan, Ernest. "Muhammad and the Origins of Islam." In *The Quest for the Historical Muhammad*, ed. and trans. Ibn Warraq. New York: Prometheus Books, 2000, 127–68.

———. *Qu'est-ce que'une nation?* Paris: Presses Pocket, 1992.

Roberts, Robert. *The Social Laws of the Qorân: Considered, and Compared with Those of the Hebrew and Other Ancient Codes*. London: Curzon Press, 1925.

Robinson, Chase F. *Islamic Historiography*. Cambridge: Cambridge University Press, 2003.

Rubin, Uri. *Between Bible and Qur'ān: The Children of Israel and the Islamic*

Self-Image. Princeton, N.J.: Darwin Press, 1999.

———. *The Eye of the Beholder: The Life of Muhammad as Viewed by the Early Muslims*. Princeton, N.J.: Darwin Press, 1995.

———. "Prophets and Caliphs: The Biblical Foundations of the Umayyad Authority." In *Method and Theory in the Study of Islamic Origins*, ed. Herbert Berg. Leiden: Brill, 2003, 73–99.

Sachedina, Abdulaziz. "Early Muslim Traditionists and Their Familiarity with Jewish Sources." In *Studies in Islamic and Judaic Traditions: Papers Presented at the Institute for Islamic-Judaic Studies, Center for Judaic Studies, University of Denver*, vol. 2, ed. William M. Brinner and Stephen D. Ricks. Atlanta: Scholars Press, 49–59.

Sahas, Daniel J. *John of Damascus on Islam: The "Heresy of the Ishmaelites."* Leiden: Brill, 1972.

Sanders, E. P. *The Historical Figure of Jesus*. London: Penguin, 1993.

Savant, Sarah Bowen. "Isaac as the Persians' Ishmael: Pride and the Pre-Islamic Past in Ninth and Tenth-Century Islam." *Comparative Islamic Studies* 2, 1 (2006): 5–25.

Schoeler, Gregor. "Foundations for a New Biography of Muḥammad: The Production and Evaluation of the Corpus of Traditions from ʿUrwah b. al-Zubayr." In *Method and Theory in the Study of Islamic Origins*, ed. Herbert Berg. Leiden: Brill, 2003, 21–28.

Schoeler, Gregor, and Andreas Görke. *Die Ältesten Berichte über das Leben Muḥammads: Das Korpus ʿUrwa Ibn Az-Zubair*. Princeton, N.J.: Darwin Press, 2008.

Schoeps, H. J. "The Sacrifice of Isaac in Paul's Theology." *Journal of Biblical Literature* 65 (1946): 385–92.

Scott, James M. *Adoption as Sons of God: An Exegetical Investigation into the Background of ΥΙΟΘΕΣΙΑ in the Pauline Corpus*. Wissenschaftliche Untersuchungen zum Neuen Testament 2, Reihe 48. Tübingen: J. C. B. Mohr (Paul Siebeck), 1992.

Seters, John Van. "Jacob's Marriages and Ancient Near East Customs: A Re-examination." *Harvard Theological Review* 62, 4 (1969): 377–95.

Sezgin, Fuat. *Geschichte des arabischen Schrifttums*. 13 vols. Leiden: Brill, 1967–2007.

Sharon, Moshe. "*Ahl al-bayt*: People of the House." *Jerusalem Studies in Arabic and Islam* 8 (1986): 169–84.

Shoemaker, Stephen J. *The Death of a Prophet: The End of Muhammad's Life and the Beginnings of Islam*. Philadelphia: University of Pennsylvania Press, 2012.

———. "'The Reign of God Has Come': Eschatology and Empire in Late Antiquity and Early Islam." *Arabica* 61 (2014).

Silva, David A. *4 Maccabees*. Sheffield: Sheffield Academic Press, 1998.

Silverstein, Adam J. "Haman's Transition from the *Jāhiliyya* to Islam." *Jerusalem Studies in Arabic and Islam* 34 (2008), 285–308.

———. *Postal Systems in the Pre-Modern Islamic World*. Cambridge Studies in Islamic Civilization. Cambridge: Cambridge University Press, 2007.

Simon, Róbert. "Mānī and Muḥammad." *Jerusalem Studies in Arabic and Islam* 21 (1997): 118–41.

Sizgorich, Thomas. "'Do Prophets Come with a Sword?' Conquests, Empire, and Historical Narrative in the Early Islamic World." *American Historical Review* 112, 4 (2007): 993–1015.

———. "Narrative and Community in Islamic Late Antiquity." *Past & Present* 185 (2004): 9–42.

Sonbol, Amira al-Azhary. "Adoption in Islamic Society: A Historical Survey." In *Children in the Middle East*, ed. Elizabeth Warnock Fernea. Austin: University of Texas Press, 1995, 45–67.

Spellberg, D. A. *Politics, Gender, and the Islamic Past: The Legacy of ʿĀ'isha bint Abi Bakr*. New York: Columbia University Press, 1994

Speyer, Heinrich. *Die Biblischen Erzählungen im Qoran*. Hildesheim: Georg Olms, 1931. Repr. 1961.

Spiegel, Shalom. *The Last Trial, on the Legends and Lore of the Command to Abraham to Offer Isaac as a Sacrifice: The Akedah*. Trans. Judah Goldin. New York: Schocken Books, 1969.

Stowasser, Barbara Freyer. *Women in the Qur'an, Traditions, and Interpretation*. New York: Oxford University Press, 1994.

Strauss, Leo. *Persecution and the Art of Writing*. Glencoe, Ill.: Free Press, 1952.

Stroumsa, Guy. "'Seal of the Prophets': The Nature of a Manichaean Metaphor." *Jerusalem Studies in Arabic and Islam* 7 (1986): 61–74.

Swetnam, James. *Jesus and Isaac: A Study of the Epistle to the Hebrews in Light of the Aqedah*. Rome: Biblical Institute Press, 1981.

Unger, Merrill F. "Some Comments on the Text of Genesis 15 2, 3." *Journal of Biblical Literature* 72, 1 (1953): 49–50.

Van Ess, Josef. *See* Ess, Josef Van.

Van Seters, John. *See* Seters, John Van.

VanderKam, James C. *The Book of Jubilees*. Sheffield: Sheffield Academic Press, 2001.

Vermes, Geza. "New Light on the Sacrifice of Isaac from 4Q225." *Journal of Jewish Studies* 32 (1981): 140–45.

———. *Scripture and Tradition*. Leiden: Brill, 1961.

Voorhis, John W. "John of Damascus on the Muslim Heresy." In *The Early Christian-Muslim Dialogue: A Collection of Documents from the First Three Islamic Centuries (632–900 A.D.), Translations with Commentary*, ed. N. A. Newman. Hatfield, Pa.: Interdisciplinary Biblical Research Institute, 1993, 133–62.

Wansbrough, John. *Quranic Studies: Sources and Methods of Scriptural Interpretation*. Oxford: Oxford University Press, 1977.

———. *The Sectarian Milieu: Content and Composition of Islamic Salvation History*. Oxford: Oxford University Press, 1978.

Wasserstrom, Steven M. "The ʿĪsāwiyya Revisited." *Studia Islamica* 75 (1992): 57–80.

Watt, W. Montgomery. *Muhammad at Medina*. Oxford: Clarendon Press, 1956.

Westbrook, Raymond, ed. *A History of Ancient Near Eastern Law*, 2 vols. Leiden: Brill, 2003.

Westermann, Claus. *Genesis 12–36: A Commentary*. Trans. John J. Scullion, S.J. Minneapolis: Augsburg, 1981.

White, Hayden. *The Content of the Form: Narrative Discourse and Historical Representation*. Baltimore: John Hopkins University Press, 1987.

Citation Index

Subject Index

ʿArafāt, 73
Aram Naharaim, 41, 130*n*41. *See also* Iraq; Mesopotamia
Aramaens, 65–68. *See also* Ammonites; Amorites; Midianites
Asad (tribe), 32, 99, 129*n*16
ascension, 64, 67; of Dammesek Eliezer, 48; of Isaac, 64, 67; of Zayd, 67. *See also* topos
Ascension (*Miʿrāj*), 5–6, 56, 119
Asenath, daughter of Poti-phera (OT), 26. *See also* Joseph
Ashkelon, 73
Asmāʾ bt. Abī Bakr, 8
Asmāʾ bt. ʿUmays, 51, 61–62. *See also* Jaʿfar b. Abī Ṭālib
al-ʿAwātiq, 84
ʿAwn b. Jaʿfar b. Abī Ṭālib, 51, 131*n*5
āyat al-rajm: removed from *Sūrat al-Aḥzāb*, 122
Ayman, 31, 128*n*11
ʿAyyāsh b. Abī Rabīʿa, 6, 76
Azd (tribe), 50, 54

Badr, Battle of (2/624), 8–9, 49, 51, 55, 58, 86, 106, 125*n*15, 130*n*37
Baghdad: imaginary reader in, 5, 14–15
Bahrāʾ (tribe), 55
Bakr (tribe), 55
Balādhurī (historian, d. 279/892), 103
Balī (tribe), 55
Balqāʾ, 13, 55
banner, 73, 79, 84, 104, 135*n*31. *See also* standard; standard-bearer
Banū ʿAbd Wadd (clan), 37
Banū ʿAdī b. Kaʿb (clan), 59
Banū ʿĀmir b. Luwayy (clan), 59
Banū Fazāra (clan), 11
Banū al-Ḥārith b. al-Khazraj (clan), 59
Banū Hāshim (clan), 13, 17, 20, 23, 49, 59, 69, 136*n*44. *See also* Muʾtah, Battle of
Banū al-Ḥibb ("sons of the Beloved"), 86. *See also* Usāma b. Zayd
Banū al-Maʿn (clan), 18
Banū Māzin (clan), 59
Banū al-Najjār (clan), 59
Banū al-Qayn b. Jasr (clan), 18
Banū ʿUdhra (tribe), 82
Baraka. *See* Umm Ayman
Barnabas (NT), 136*n*42. *See also* hands, laying on of
Barra: birth name of Jaḥsh b. Riʾāb al-Asadī, 129*n*16
Barza bt. al-Ribʿī: wife of Usāma b. Zayd, 85–86
Basra, 85, 122
al-Baṭḥāʾ, 17
Bathsheba (OT), 36, 42–43, 46–47, 113–14, 136*n*40. *See also* David; Solomon; Uriah the Hittite
battle cry, 83
battle instructions, 52, 82–83, 93
Bedouin, 53–54, 73, 80
Beloved of the Messenger of God. *See* Zayd b. Muḥammad
Beloved Son of the Beloved of the Messenger of God. *See* Usāma b. Zayd
Benjamin (OT), 24–25, 128*n*27
best of creation/mankind, 69, 76–77, 107
Bethany (NT), 136*n*42
Bethuel ben Milcah (OT), 42, 45, 130*n*41. *See also* Laban; Rebecca
Bible, Hebrew, 27, 36, 48, 90, 136*n*54. *See also* Torah
biblical narrative, 27–28, 43–45, 47, 67–68, 91, 93, 113
Bilāl (Companion): enters the Kaʿba, 135*n*20
Bint Abī Ḥamdān al-Sahmī: wife of Usāma b. Zayd, 85
biographical dictionaries, 4
blood, 37–38, 54, 70, 105, 133*n*26, 134*n*9; consumption of, 134*n*9. See also *faḍl*; *qarāba*; *sābiqa*
blood money, 7
bodily fluids: mixing or transfer of, 70, 72, 104, 134*n*10. *See also* blood; clothing; jewelry
Book of God. *See* Qurʾān
booty, 10, 53, 72, 83–84, 90, 93–94
brotherhood contracts (*muʾākhāt*), 8, 14, 102, 105
Burayda b. al-Ḥuṣayb al-Aslamī, 75, 79–80, 82–84. *See also* standard; standard-bearer
Buṣrā/Bostra, 50
Byzantines/Byzantium, 10, 12, 16, 54, 67–68, 80, 119
Byzantium, king of: sends royal garment to Muḥammad, 134*n*17

Caleb ben Jephunneh (OT), 88, 91
camel, 18–19, 42, 44, 47, 73, 127*n*10, 130*n*39; as instrument of torture, 11; purchased by Abū Bakr, for hijra to Yathrib, 7–8; as reward for capture of Muḥammad, 8; ridden by Abraham, 44, 47, 130*n*39; ridden by Muḥammad, 7, 73; ridden by Rebecca (OT),

31–32, 98, 128*n*10; one of the women of Paradise, 32; and Zayd, 31, 69, 98. *See also* Usāma b. Zayd
Umm Ḥabīb bt. Jaḥsh: and hijra to Yathrib, 6
Umm al-Ḥakam bt. ʿUtba b. Abī Waqqāṣ: wife of Usāma b. Zayd, 85
Umm Kulthūm bt. ʿUqba: marriage to Zayd, 129*n*19
Umm Qirfa: tortured by Zayd, 11
Umm Salama: wife of the Prophet, 60
Uriah b. Ḥannān, 113. *See also* Uriah the Hittite
Uriah the Hittite, 36, 41–43, 46–47, 63, 66, 95–96, 113; compared to Zayd, 46–47, 95–96. *See also* Bathsheba; David
Usāma b. Zayd b. Muḥammad (after 5 A.H., Usāma b. Zayd b. Ḥāritha, Companion, d. 54/674), ix-x, 6, 9, 13–14, 31–32, 60, 69, 71–86, 90–96, 98, 102–9, 131*n*12, 134*n*7, 135*n*18, 135*n*20, 135*n*37, 136*n*39, 136*n*43, 137*n*60, 137*n*64; and ʿĀʾisha, 70, 73; and ʿAlī b. Abī Ṭālib, 85; Beloved Son of the Beloved of the Messenger of God, 69, 70–71, 78, 98, 103, 105; best of creation, one of the, 77, 107; birth of, 32, 69, 98; children of, 85–86; death of, 79, 86; *dhū baṭan*, 85; "disposed to goodness," 107; first male born into community of believers, 98, 103, 106; and al-Ḥasan b. ʿAlī b. Abī Ṭālib, 70, 85, 98, 104, 134*n*7; a Hāshimī, 69, 71, 98, 103; and Ibn ʿUmar, 86; and jewelry, 73, 90, 96, 104, 135*n*18; and the Kaʿba, 135*n*20; and Kathkath, 137*n*64; leadership credentials of, 13, 104, 106–8; military experience, 71, 91–92; and Muḥammad, 14, 32, 69, 70–71, 73, 76, 78–79, 92, 98, 103–5, 107–9, 116; name, changes, to Usāma b. Zayd b. Ḥāritha al-Kalbī, 71; and Nuhayk b. Mirdās, 72; opposition to his appointment as commander, 76, 81; paternity of, contested, 71, 77; and piety, 85; potential prophet, 116; *al-radīf*, 73, 90, 106; and Ruqayya bt. Muḥammad, 8, 14, 103; skin color, 70, 73, 77; sons of, 85–86; and Ubna, 13–14, 73, 81–84, 91, 103, 106, 108, 137*n*60; and ʿUmar b. al-Khaṭṭāb, 76–77, 80–81, 86; vows not to slay a believer, 72; wives of, 71, 85; and Zayd b. Ḥāritha/Muḥammad, x, 6, 9, 13–14, 32–33, 60, 69–71, 73–74, 76–77, 82–84, 86, 94–95, 98, 102, 107–9, 116, 131*n*12; and Zaynab bt. Ḥanzala, 71, 85
al-ʿUshayra: raid on, 130*n*37
ʿUthmān b. ʿAffān (caliph, r. 23–35/644–56), 73, 80, 86, 109, 122, 129*n*19; codex of, 120; and collection of the Qurʾān, 1–2, 122; *radīf* of ʿUmar, 73; and Ruqayya bt. Muḥammad, 8

vengeance, 10, 87; divine, 88. *See also* revenge; war/warfare
vision, prophetic, 56–57, 61, 67, 120, 133*n*26. See also *khātam*
vision, supernatural: 25, 56–57, 61, 67. *See also* topos

Wadi Arnon (OT), 89
Wādī al-Qurā, 10–11, 54, 82, 84–85
Wādī Sirhan, 16
Wadi Zered (OT), 89
Wahb b. Munabbih: *Sīra* of, 125*n*12
Wahb b. Saʿd b. Abī Sarḥ al-Qurashī (Companion): slain at Muʾtah, 59
Waḥshī (slave): kills Ḥamza, 10. *See also* Jubayr b. Muṭʿim
Wāʾil (tribe), 55
waiting period: before remarriage (*ʿidda*), 46–47, 100
walāʾ. See *mawlā*
al-Walīd b. al-Mughīra, 58
al-Walīd b. ʿUqba, 129*n*19
Wāqidī (historian, d. 207/823), 59, 103
war/warfare/warrior, 53, 59, 61, 90, 136*n*47; and *casus belli*, 66; and rules of military engagement, 50, 53. *See also* banner; standard; revenge; vengeance
Waraqa b. Nawfal: acquires Zayd, acting on behalf of Khadīja, 17. *See also* Ḥakīm b. Ḥizām b. Khuwaylid
waṣī ("executor of last will and testament"), 105
waṣiyya ("last will and testament"), 137*n*58; of Abū Bakr, 137*n*74; of Ḥamza b. Abī Ṭālib, 10, 14, 52, 102; of Muḥammad, 81, 83

al-Yaʾjaj (toponym), 9
yakhtum, 121. See also *khātam*
Yathrib, 6–8, 76, 106, 125*n*7. *See also* Mecca; Medina
Yavneh. *See* Ubna
Yazīd b. Kaʿb b. Sharāḥīl, 18
Yemen/Yemenis, 72–73
Yosef. *See* Joseph (OT)

Zadok the priest (OT), 87
Zamzam, well of, 135*n*20

Acknowledgments

The idea to write this book, and its title, were both suggested to me by my friend and colleague Brink Messick in March 2008. The book began as a "play" but became a biography thanks to the intervention of Ze'ev Maghen. Its final shape is a combined product of a suggestion made by my daughter Katherine Powers during the course of a lovely bike ride in October 2012 and an eleventh-hour intervention by Jerry Singerman in August 2013. I thank my colleagues Richard Gauvain, Tayeb El-Hibri, Pavel Pavlovitch, Adam Silverstein, and Munther Younes, all of whom read drafts of the manuscript and provided me with important suggestions for improvement; Samuela Pagani for bringing to my attention a treatise by ʿAbd al-Ghanī al-Nābulusī in which the Prophet's relationship with the Beloved of the Messenger of God serves as a model for a loving relationship between masters and their disciples; Stephen Shoemaker for sharing with me a prepublication version of his essay on eschatology in late antiquity; and all of my students at Cornell who read and discussed with me many of the Arabic sources used in this project. I also thank the two readers of the manuscript, Tayeb El-Hibri (again) and John C. Reeves, for helpful observations and suggestions; and Patricia Crone for saving me from an embarrassing error.